Scotland and Tourism

T0298380

Tourism has long been important to Scotland. It has become all the more significant as the financial sector has faltered and other mainstays are in apparent long-term decline. Yet there is no assessment of this industry and its place over the long run, no one account of what it has meant to previous generations and continues to mean to the present one, of what led to growth or what indeed has led people of late to look elsewhere.

This book brings together work from many periods and perspectives. It draws on a wide range of source material, academic and non-academic, from local studies and general analyses, visitors' accounts, hotel records, newspaper and journal commentaries, photographs and even cartoons. It reviews arguments over the cultural and economic impact of tourism, and retrieves the experience of the visited, of the host communities as well as the visitors. It questions some of the orthodoxies – that Scott made Scott-land, or that it was charter air flights that pulled the rug from under the mass market – and sheds light on what in the Scottish package appealed, and what did not, and to whom; how provision changed, or failed to change; and what marketing strategies may have achieved. It charts changes in accommodation, from inn to hotel, holiday camp, caravanning and timeshare. The role of transport is a central feature: that of the steamship and the railway in opening up Scotland, and later of motor transport in reshaping patterns of holidaymaking. Throughout there is an emphasis on the comparative: asking what was distinctive about the forms and nature of tourism in Scotland as against competing destinations elsewhere in the UK and Europe. It concludes by reflecting on whether Scotland's past can inform the making and shaping of tourism policy and what cautions history might offer for the future.

This prolific long-term analysis of tourism in Scotland is a must-read for all those interested in tourism history.

Alastair J. Durie is an honorary lecturer at Stirling University, UK, and has had a long academic career in teaching, research and administration as lecturer and senior lecturer at various Scottish universities and in North America. His early research was on eighteenth-century Scotland, with books on linen and banking, but over the past twenty years he has made the study of the history of tourism very much his speciality, assisted by awards from the Wellcome Trust and other funding bodies.

Routledge Advances in Tourism

Edited by Stephen Page
School for Tourism, Bournemouth University

For a full list of titles in this series, please visit www.routledge.com/series/SE0258

Scotland and Tourism
The Long View, 1700–2015

Alastair J. Durie

Routledge
Taylor & Francis Group

LONDON AND NEW YORK

First published 2017 by Routledge

2 Park Square, Milton Park, Abingdon, Oxon OX14 4RN
605 Third Avenue, New York, NY 10017

Routledge is an imprint of the Taylor & Francis Group, an informa business

First issued in paperback 2022

Publisher's Note

The publisher has gone to great lengths to ensure the quality of this reprint but points out that some imperfections in the original copies may be apparent.

British Library Cataloguing in Publication Data
A catalogue record for this book is available from the British Library

Library of Congress Cataloging in Publication Data
A catalog record for this book has been requested

ISBN: 978-1-138-85460-4 (hbk)
ISBN: 978-1-03-233973-3 (pbk)
DOI: 10.4324/9781315721002

Typeset in Times New Roman
by Taylor & Francis Books

Contents

Illustrations

Figures

Table

Preface

The writing of books is not always an enjoyable process, but this has been. The history of tourism is a subject that it has been a pleasure to teach, speak and write about. Students seem to have enjoyed it, as have local history and heritage societies as well as academic gatherings. And they in their turn have fed back comments and questions, ideas and anecdotes. It was someone in an audience who told me about 'sleeping the Rothesay way'; that when she and her family went to Rothesay during the height of the summer season when accommodation was at a premium, the children were told to sleep across the bed, not up and down, to fit all six of them in. In that engagement lies much of the appeal of tourism. It is an experience which all have participated in, as children or adults, and of which all have first-hand memories, mostly pleasant but not necessarily so. For some their memories are of returning year after year to the same resort, for others, particularly those younger, there has been the increasing discovery of foreign parts, where the sun always shines, unlike Scotland. For most, holidays mean the seaside – paddling, ice creams and sandcastles – but for others it means golf or culture, or niche experiences – scuba diving or pampering at a spa. For all there are the questions of how to travel, what the budget is, which clothing to take – and what you have forgotten.

It may be helpful, or just self-indulgent, to sketch my own history. I am a part of that generation of post-war boomers who came to take a holiday for granted. The question as a middle-class Edinburgh family was not whether we would holiday, but where. Both parents had travelled abroad before the war; my father to Denmark and my mother throughout Europe. She was a keen skier, and had wintered in Switzerland with the Public Schools Alpine Club. Our post-war holidays began modestly; a week in the Highlands, and then with a house exchange with a family in London. My only memory of that is how the marks of the blitz were still everywhere – burnt-out streets and willowherb growing on bomb sites. We forayed further afield in the 1950s, to Devon; Dawlish Warren was where I learnt to swim. The best things were the steam trains and the beach huts with their distinctive smell of sand, saltwater and wet swimming costume; the worst was the very long drive in the pre-motorway age, with lengthy traffic jams at places like Carlisle and Exeter. We first went abroad as a family in 1957, to Portugal, by boat from Tilbury, with the car loaded in the hold, for the drive back through Spain and France. The following year it was Denmark. And then back once more to the South West, to Falmouth, where my brother and I went racing in the hotel boat. Our holidays were always activity packed – golf for all, except my sister who was too bad-tempered. But air travel was not part of the experience; that was to come in the 1960s, by which time we were holidaying separately. Then of course, with marriage and children, the cycle restarted. Where would we go, and what the budget would allow were now questions for us as parents.

Every family has its own narrative and memories, which is why tourism is such a good subject, interesting to people of all backgrounds. This may, of course, be why the academic community was so slow to take tourism seriously as an industry and an activity. A few pioneers aside, such as Eric Simpson, the study of tourism in Scotland was a blank page until the 1980s. There were accounts of travellers, big names such as Johnson and Boswell, and some interest in resorts from geographers, but the history of tourism was taught nowhere at university level. That has now changed. Academics such as John Walton have won academic respectability for the study of tourism history and a new generation of scholars are carrying the torch on. Whereas twenty years ago, the publications on the history of tourism would have fitted onto a short shelf, now there is a profusion. Even during the writing of this book important new work has appeared, filling gaps, raising fresh issues and new insights. Indeed, knowing that I was writing about tourism, people have approached me with family diaries and journals which have long lain unappreciated but of which I have been delighted to make use. In today's post has arrived a newspaper clipping about the chance rediscovery of a visitors' book for a hotel at Pitlochry from the 1890s, complete with the signature of William Gladstone.

This study owes much to those who encouraged my original entry into the field, especially George Dixon, Neil Tranter and George Peden, and of course Jack Simmons, the doyen of British railway historians. I have been much helped by others such as Kate Durie and Jacqueline Young, who have read sections; they have tried to correct my grammar and tighten my thinking. I am grateful to Stephen Page, and my editor Philippa Mullins, whose patience has been very gracious, and to the many archivists, local studies librarians and others on whose help I have drawn. A particular thanks to the long suffering staff of Stirling Central Library, who have been helpfulness itself. Some of the research has been supported by grants from the Railway History foundation and the Wellcome Trust, whose assistance is gratefully acknowledged.

Stirling July 2016

1 Introduction

Tourism is now a worldwide industry of major importance to many countries. Amongst these is Scotland, where it has been a staple for a long time and indeed has both outlived and outperformed many of the traditional pillars of the Scottish economy such as shipbuilding or coal. It is a continuing success story, creating and sustaining employment, attracting interest in heritage, generating spend and shaping culture. And one which developed, as this study will show, from a very small base with virtually no government support or even interest. Not until after the Second World War did government start to get increasingly involved in the promotion and development of tourism in Britain.

Where tourism differs from other industries and indeed other leisure activities is that, whereas not many people have worked in coal mining or steel making, nor are sport or music or theatre the enthusiasms of all, virtually everyone has first-hand experience of holidaymaking. Every household has its albums or snaps, cine or video, knick-knacks and souvenirs; every individual their memories, good and bad, of travelling away from home. The destinations may be much more far-flung, and it is remarkable how once remote locations have become commonplace, yet there is a commonality of experience with travellers a century ago; we worry over the same things as them: getting there, the quality of accommodation, what to do and to see.

One of the key problems is to define just what tourism is. When is a traveller a tourist? Are all forms of travel other than that for business some form or another of tourism, whether for pilgrimage or for wine tasting or golf, to visit the seaside or the hills? If the accepted definition nowadays is travel[1] involving at least one night's stay away from home, does that exclude the day tripper, or the Sunday School or works outing? Usage has changed, and blurred. The term 'tourism' used to be confined to those who were on a tour – scenic, literary or cultural – respecting a schedule already defined by cultural fashion, a pre-set agenda as to where to go and what to see. It broadened to include those who were travelling for the sake of their health – les hivernants overwintering on the Riviera at Cannes or Mentone, and sportsmen on the hunt for some quarry to kill – grouse in Scotland, chamois in the Alps or even tigers in India. Many of the traditional types of tourism still flourish, but there are now so many more forms which are either niche or general, for example, dark tourism, even death tourism. Here we will be using a broad-brush definition: tourism is any form of travel for pleasure, but excluded is business tourism.

If tourism is a slippery concept to define, so also are the reasons why people chose to go where. Some of course had no choice in the matter: the destination was chosen for them. Children went with their parents, servants and nannies accompanied their employers, ladies took companions and so on. It is much easier to be clear on the general reasons why tourists came to Scotland. Some arrived with very specific objectives in mind: scientists and botanists to explore the Scottish countryside, sportsmen for deer or grouse. Oxbridge students came north for reading parties.[2] In his travels Lord Cockburn noticed several such parties, including a group of twenty, with two tutors, spending the summer of 1840 at Inveraray, and others at Oban and Callander.[3] Some came for their health, to a spa or hydro hotel, or for a spell at the seaside; others were attracted by scenery or literature. What drew people was often a variety of motives, which overlapped. A spell on the golf course was both sociable and good exercise, if not, depending on how one was playing, always pleasurable. Some were persuaded by advertising or word of mouth, or advised by their doctor. Others were just following in the steps of either people that they knew, or big names: the purchase of Balmoral and the Royal presence there every summer firmly put Deeside on the map. The degree of choice as to where to go and what to do depended on income and free time, but also reflected other variables such as class, age and physical fitness. Of course, some travelled regardless, as was true of Samuel Johnson – sixty-four years old and with a variety of physical problems. Some of the appeal was long-standing, such as the fascination with Walter Scott and those places he had captured in poetry and prose; some pursuits once established had a permanent popularity, as is the case still with grouse-shooting and deer-stalking. But some enthusiasms have been overtaken by time. Few now visit the many Covenanting memorials. The Scottish spas, never very popular, were to fade in the later nineteenth century and others were short-lived or ephemeral, as with the craze for collecting ferns. Places enjoyed a brief popularity, thanks to some literary or other association: there is (or used to be) a weather-beaten sign beside a rickle of stones beside the road at Tweedsmuir, claiming that this was the site of Tilliedlum, a castle to which Scott had referred. But with the decline in Scott's popularity, who now cares? There was the short-term appeal of exhibitions and ceremonies, of which George IV's visit to Edinburgh in 1822 was the trailblazer. But as we shall see, part of Scotland's strength as a tourist destination was the number of strings which it had to its bow, and the ability to continuously add to its portfolio, not all of which are handed down from the Victorian period, such as the Loch Ness monster or the Hogwarts express at Glenfinnan.

What is clear is that tourism, which started as an elite experience, became one shared – with varying degrees of participation – by all levels of society and in every part of Scotland. By the end of the nineteenth century no part of

Scotland was untouched. Some places were destinations to which tourists went, others places from which holidaymakers came, and some both source and destination with a crossover: as the visitors arrived so the locals departed, as was true of Edinburgh. Early visitors in Scotland had favoured such destinations as Callander and the Trossachs, Dunkeld and Iona, and these retained their appeal and popularity, but others, thanks to better transport, were later additions to the tourist map. Even the remotest parts saw visitors. Trips to St Kilda at the turn of the twentieth century were advertised with the slogan 'come and see Britain's modern primitives'. Locals would turn a profit by selling eggs and tweeds, as would the local post office from the sale of postcards, letters and stamps. Scots were partakers in tourism as visitors and holidaymakers and some were providers of tourist facilities. Least likely to be holiday takers were farmers and farm workers, yet even they might put up visitors and reap some benefit from tourism. Resorts and localities rose, but over time their popularity might falter. Glasgow was in the later eighteenth century an attractive city and worth visiting but became by the twentieth century one only from which to leave. Yet that has changed again.

If the definition of tourism is a problem, even more difficult is to profile it in terms of who went where, and for how long, those basic measures of activity. Government kept no statistics, and no count was ever kept of tourists entering Scotland. Moreover, while local authorities might undertake an occasional count of summer visitors in residence, as at Moffat 1866–1869 and 1872–1878[4] and North Berwick in August 1918,[5] there was no way of keeping tabs on the number of day trippers. On the Continent things were different, which gave their resorts more of a profile, but while the Scots were not generally backward in the collection of statistics, tourism was ignored. It was a weakness, or so Thomas Boyd, the editor of the *Oban Visitors' Register,* thought in 1891, when he wrote: 'It is a pity some sort of visitors' census was not taken annually so as to enable one to form an opinion exactly how matters stand.'[6] The decennial census might have been helpful, had it been taken in midsummer, as was the case in 1841, but after 1851, with the solitary exception of 1921, it was taken on the last weekend in March or the first in April, when the tourist season had hardly got under way. A few visitors 'for the sake of their health' show up at the spas,[7] but not in any number at the seaside, although the census enumerator for the parish of Dunoon, where the population had risen from 2,416 in March 1831 to 4,211 in June 1841, considered that this was 'attributable to the influx of about 1,000 persons for the benefit of sea bathing'.[8] Exceptionally, the 1921 census was taken at the end of June, and showed some striking contrasts with the previous pre-war census in that, for example, Millport's population had apparently trebled since 1911. But the increase was entirely due to the timing, which took in the arrival of the first summer visitors. While the census is not of much service in establishing levels of tourism, the enumerators' books do contain a wealth of information about those who served the summer visitors, hotel proprietors and their staff, lodging house owners and the numbers of houses shut up, awaiting the summer arrivals.

Statistics are few and it is very hard to build up a picture of who went where and for how long. Transport agencies, railway and bus companies can help with figures for tickets sold, or receipts for landings at pier heads. But unfortunately such figures tend to be aggregates for all travellers without separately distinguishing tourists and holidaymakers. One can infer, however, that the increase in summer traffic reflects tourism. Newspapers carried estimates of holiday traffic, often generated by calling at the local railway station. But not till post the Second World War did counting become more than guesswork or occasional. There are, however, some indicators of where Victorian and Edwardian tourists were calling or staying. Hotels kept registers and all tourist attractions kept books or albums for visitors to sign; the date of the visit, their name and address were what was required, but sometimes a column for comments was provided, which further spices up their value for present day analysis, as well as being a source of amusement for contemporaries. Reading through the book or books whiled away many an evening before radio or TV. Most have been lost or have disappeared, including, for example, the album of visitors to Iona and Staffa kept at the Sound of Ulva Inn, which is known to have had poetry by Scott. But where they survive, they can be used to build a picture of visitor numbers, where they were from, and indeed why they were on tour. Mr and Mrs Robertson, who signed in at the Atholl Hotel in Dunkeld on 7 June 1836, announced proudly that they were on a 'honeymoon tour'. The earliest surviving run in Scotland is for New Lanark for the years 1795–1799 with a second series for 1821–1832; the longest is for Abbotsford House from 1832 to the present day. Those for Tibbie Shiels, a fishing inn at St Mary's Loch, cover with some gaps the period 1866–1922.[9] Other surviving runs include books for Doune Castle, Heriot's School and the Glasgow Necropolis, the last a popular attraction of the 1830s – now a form of tourism very much back in vogue – with its own tourist handbook.[10] Sadly not a single register has survived for any of the Scottish hydros, though each and every one will have had them; they served not just to record who was in the hotel, but where left or lost property or mail could be sent. And of course, there was the Sunday register required of hotels and inns for the bona fide traveller. By law, the Forbes Mackenzie Act, drink could be sold on the Sunday only to those who were genuine travellers, on a trip of four miles or more, and the register had to ask therefore not just where a person was from, but where they were travelling to. Every hotel and inn will have had its Sunday register, and yet, as far as is known, that for the Tormaukin Hotel in Glendevon in the late 1930s is a unique survivor of the many thousands that there once were. Its Sunday visitors came from round and about, for a Sunday drive – and a drink. The Tormaukin Hotel register also has a column for time of arrival, mostly ignored, but one party from Dunfermline in June 1938 had no qualms about signing themselves in at 11.45 a.m.

Hotel registers are still part of present day life, and for B & Bs, and to be found open in many churches and great houses, though the turnstile has taken over at most attractions. There was another nineteenth-century source of information about where people were staying, the lists of visitors which were published in the local press, a genre which faded away after the First World War. The practice seems to have originated at spa resorts in England, such as Harrogate, as a kind of social register. The first that we have for Scotland are for Peterhead in the late 1770s, Peterhead at that time being a fashionable cure centre. These lists became a staple of the local newspaper in the nineteenth century, published on a weekly basis, sometimes as a freestanding supplement, as at Oban. Lists can found for Elie, Gullane, North Berwick, Pitlochry and Peebles, and indeed wherever there was a community of summer residenters staying in local villas, cottages and lodgings. These lists, however, took no account of day trippers and weekenders. Nor were hotels always willing to participate by supplying lists of their guests, but some did, and a few went beyond the basics of who from where. The Union Hotel at Inverness supplied the local paper with a list of arrivals and what their agenda was, whether making a tour, on their way north or south, on a fishing or botanical excursion, or en route to shooting quarters.[11] But the lists of visitors, when systematically analysed, do show the scale of this constituency of steady respectable summer visitors. The *Badenoch Herald*'s Strathspey Supplement for 18 July 1891 carried details of all the families staying in and around Grantown-on Spey, but also of those in the area at Advie, Aviemore, Dulnairn and Boat of Garten; the last had seven families, all from central Scotland And they also show how families came back year after year to the same locality. They played a considerable part in the summer life of such areas, playing sport, supporting the local bazaars, and attending church.

Other sources of information about holidaymaking, tourism and visitor experience are many. One of the greatest resources that the Scottish historian enjoys, as against his counterparts elsewhere in the UK, are the Statistical Accounts of Scotland. This is a parish-by-parish survey, each account being generally written by the local minister, with the First or Old Statistical Account published in the 1790s. The organising editor and driving force behind this scheme, Sir John Sinclair, had sent out in May 1790 a template as to what topics could be covered. It included no explicit question on tourism, although there was one on whether spa waters were present. Those compilers who did refer to tourism did so somewhat guiltily as they seem to have felt that they were straying from the task set them. The Rev. Fraser did draw attention to the recent increase in the number of travellers who had viewed the pleasure ground at Inveraray Castle: 'This perhaps may not be considered as strictly analogous to the statistical account of the parish: at the same time, it would have been unpardonable to have passed over in silence, a place which is so deservedly an object of curiosity to travellers of all ranks'.[12] As we shall see, there are gleanings from this source to be had on the rise of visitors to particular localities, the arrival of sea bathing and spa regimes. This remarkable enterprise was run again for Scotland in the 1830s in the Second or New Statistical Account, in which tourism featured quite prominently. That the coming of the steamboat had opened up coastal tourism around the Firth of

Clyde was a point made by many of the contributors. The writer of the account for Rothesay,[13] the Rev. Craig, drew attention to how Rothesay had 'now become a fashionable watering place'; and his counterpart at Dunkeld waxed lyrical about the landscape there and its alpine scenery. Between 1815 and 1842 on average over 2,000 visitors a year, or some 60,000 in all, had visited the Duke of Atholl's pleasure ground,[14] persons 'of all ranks'. He had obviously studied the registers of visitors and he further stated that nearly 4,000 of whom were 'foreigners', which in contemporary usage meant either Continental or American, but not from England. The mantle of such local assessment was carried on by the Ordnance Gazetteer of Scotland, which first appeared in the 1860s and went through several editions, providing a wealth of topographical information and detail: when a local golf course had been opened, a hotel renovated or other tourist amenities provided. After a long interval a Third Statistical Account began to appear in the 1950s, by which time tourism and holidaymaking had qualified for separate and distinct treatment. Recently (2003–9) a Fourth Statistical Account for East Lothian has been published.

There are also town council records, regulations as to who bathed where, for example, enquiries into road and rail provision, reports by the railway companies to their shareholders, local newspapers with their reports of outings from or to their locality, whether the Sunday school treat or the works outings. Tourism even surfaces in the police regulations. By general order no 12 the Chief Constable of the Argyleshire force in 1892 instructed members of his police force to be very careful not to get involved in disputes between hotel-keepers and visitors over alleged overcharges. Hotels and hoteliers feature frequently in bankruptcy proceedings, as in the case of William Macdonald of the Atholl Palace Hydro (see Chapter 7), or even just in arguments over the level of rates that their business should be paying. Andrew Philp of the Glenburn Hydro in Rothesay appealed in 1887 against what he regarded as the overvaluation of his premises. Led in evidence was detail as to accommodation, clientele and the level of occupancy and the level of rent paid at Glenburn, as against other local hotels and hydros elsewhere in Scotland.[15] Philp secured a sizeable reduction. It is hard to find any sources which draw a complete blank, though the record of the takings at the Carnoustie beach urinals is better noted than interpreted. Indeed in many ways, a key problem in the study of tourism is the profusion of information, micro rather than macro, which makes the identification of trends and changes much more of a challenge. It is too easy to let the detail swamp.

There is no shortage of material as to visitor experience. Visitor accounts of their holidays are ten a penny. Most, perhaps all, visitors will have kept a written record of their holidays, often illustrated by sketches and drawings. Some were individual; others a group exercise. The Kilmahonaig Journal[16] is one such. It is an account of three months spent near Lochgilphead by a Glasgow family in 1871; they fish, shoot, sail and row, attend church and walk, and receive a fairly steady flow of visitors. Their stay is enlivened by a ringside view of a romance, which comes to naught, between the local quayside porter ('a veritable negro, stalwart and strong') and a Miss Jessie, formerly servant to the notorious Dr Pritchard, the Glasgow poisoner, who had been publicly executed a few years previously for the murder of his wife. This journal was a family keepsake, and while some were designed for publication, most were not. There were those with a particular bent: sportsmen kept accounts of what they had shot or caught, where and when, and their experiences. Many were intended only for personal or family consumption, which may make them more authentic, although one needs to be careful: people may dress up their private accounts for their private pleasure. Those that do survive tend to present an unbalanced picture, that of the haves, rather than of the servants who accompanied them, but some views from below have come to light. There is the account of a trip to Dunrobin castle in 1832 by one of the Duke of Sutherland's footmen[17] and the remarkable Mary Allison's long letter to her niece about her and her husband's holiday in July 1881 with family at Butterbridge near Glencoe.[18] A storeman's wife, she counted her short holiday in days, not the weeks or months of the better-off.

Equally underrepresented are children's descriptions of their holidays. An exception, however, is the diary of an Edinburgh schoolboy, John Gulland.[19] Friday 31 July 1846 finds him taking the train to Portobello, where he and his sister spend the night and then go to bathe in the morning. The following year finds him on holiday at Melrose and visiting Abbotsford House, where he and a friend are signed in by an adult. David Hamilton has just published a journal kept by a seventeen-year-old girl while on holiday at North Berwick in 1894[20]; her great enthusiasm was golf. There is also fiction. Many writers found a holiday in Scotland a good context for a romance or a story. There are many sporting novels, of which Buchan's John Macnab still deserves a reread, or centred on life at a hydro, such as Compton Mackenzie's *Water on the Brain*[21] or life at a spa, as with Scott's *St Ronan's Well*, and so on. Regrettably there is no Scottish equivalent of Jane Austen's novel *Sanditon* on the early English seaside. Another twentieth-century source is the cartoon, none better than the tenement family the Broons, of 10 Glebe Street Auchentogle, whose doings have been part of Scottish Sunday reading in the *Sunday Post* since 1936. While they do visit the seaside, they appear to own a but and ben, or inland cottage, where they spend more time. And, a sign of the times, in the 1960s Grandpa is tempted by Sunny Spain rather than Rothesay or Aviemore; an attraction to which all too many Scots succumbed.

And then there are letters home and postcards, the last valuable for both sides, the picture and the message. The sending of postcards was a universal enthusiasm, not just a preserve of the better-off. Most series of postcard views in a given locality were taken and retaken almost every season, and catch both the staple sights and new attractions. Many of the messages, perhaps most, are only a line or two, of the 'wish you were here' variety, or what the weather was doing. But there are those with a cryptic comment that the recipient would have understood clearly but at whose meaning we can now only guess. Take the postcard, 'Monday morning at the Coast, Good bye to the boys', showing a crowd of ladies waving farewell to their husbands at they set off back by boat to their city offices. One of these was sent to Maggie Macdonald at Luss on 15 August 1904 with the handwritten question 'is this you weeping? I don't think so.' Scotland had its share of the comic and suggestive postcards; there were those of Cynicus, mocking local transport, or the cheeky cartoons of the Glasgow firm Millar & Lang. But many in their simplicity catch what the holiday experience meant. Quite a lot can be gleaned from the neatly written card (23 July 1907) from 'Eve', newly arrived at Canty bay (North Berwick) to her aunt at Cupar in Fife:

> We arrived a little late, and the luggage did not come for ages, and father had to go up to the station and see about it. Father and we three all went to the café and had tea & then we went for a walk round by the harbour. There are pierrots there. It is a simply lovely day here, only a little windy on the West beach. We saw Mrs Anderson & Muriel here. The house is just the same except there are more mirrors.[22]

If the humble postcard became and remained part of tourism in the twentieth century, as did the photograph, bought or taken on a box Brownie, a new form of record and of recollection was cine film. To be able to see activities in real time is a bonus, to catch dress and place. There are films made to promote holidays for children too poor to afford otherwise to have a summer break away; there are a series of films from interwar years made in black and white between 1928 and 1934 by the Glasgow Necessitous Children's Holiday Camp movement to raise funds; they show the slums from which these children were taken, and the places at the coast to which they went.[23] There are also family films, taken for private pleasure; one such is a set of clips taken at Elie in Fife in the early 1930s.[24] There are donkey rides, a hurdy-gurdy man, beach huts and a Children's Special Service Mission and they show how parents and children alike dressed for the beach. The grandparents are there also, but in their Sunday best; no dressing down whatsoever for them on what is still apparently a formal occasion.

What of the providers? The voice of the visitor is often heard, the voice of the visited seldom, people such as the hoteliers and their staff. An exception is the memoir published by James Caw at Crieff Hydro. His is a remarkable account[25] of forty years' service at a leading hydro, latterly as chief steward, and gives an informed account of the day-to-day challenges of running a big tourist establishment, including dietary issues, such as providing for Jewish or Catholic visitors. He mentions the big names who came to stay – the Frys of Bristol, the Rowntrees of York, Mary Slessor, Mr Quarrier of the Orphan Homes – but also changes within the clientele. While there were still patients, they no longer included those trying to 'get off the spree', as Caw put it (i.e. give up binge drinking). 'We never have', Caw noted in 1913, 'these tipsy cases now, though we have had in the past'; increasingly treatment of alcoholism was hived off to specialist institutions. Caw was more than an employee, as he clearly shared the religious and temperance ethos of the establishment at Crieff. But this is an exception; would that we had the diary of a seaside landlady, or apartment owner.

As distinct from travel accounts and tours, there is the value of the guide-book, which for Scotland was largely a nineteenth-century creation. There been published in 1776 Scotland's first road atlas, Taylor and Skinner's *Survey and Maps of the Roads of North Britain*, but from the turn of the century increasing numbers of guides to pleasure tour routes began to appear. Transport companies were active in this area, pioneered by a rather unlikely innovator, the Forth & Clyde Canal Company, which issued a guide in 1823 to the sights and scenes to be viewed en route between Edinburgh and Glasgow, 'all the interesting objects that are seen along the line of the two canals'.[26] Others quickly jumped on the bandwagon. John Harrison – like William McGonagall, a weaver poet and whose verse is of similar calibre – issued what he called sundry verses descriptive of the various watering places visited by the steam boats from Glasgow; Largs had, he said, colonies in the summer of sea bathing sojourners; ladies whose husbands 'come from town to see them once a week'.[27] Lumsden's *Description of the principal steam boat tours*, (dedicated to Sir Walter Scott) followed two years later.[28] The railway companies came rather later but with gusto to this form of publicity. The Highland Railway issued its first handbook in 1856, claiming to have scenery unsurpassed by any other railway company. These company guides were promotional; what might be termed non-partisan publications started with that of the brothers George and Peter Anderson of Inverness, who issued a *Guide to the Highlands and Islands* in 1843. Their guide was organised in several routes, three of which, reflecting their home territory, started from Inverness. This guide quickly went through three editions, and other publishers, scenting profit, followed suit. Some were local, such as Paterson's *Guide to Edinburgh*, and others were issued by railway and steamship companies.

In 1851 Thomas Cook had started a weekly flysheet *The Excursionist and Cheap Trip Advertiser*, which sold for a penny. Bulked up into a monthly publication, the *Excursionist* expanded its circulation from a few thousand in the early 1860s to 58,000 in 1867. The Tartan Tours featured prominently, with it made clear that it was entirely safe and proper for ladies to join them, which tours were projected for where for the coming season, and who would be leading them. In 1877,[29] for example, it was announced that a new series of tours to Skye would be led by one of Cook's most trusted lieutenants, W. E. Franklin of Newcastle (like Thomas, a fellow temperance campaigner). Cook was also quick to publish accounts from satisfied customers. 'How I went to the Highlands by a Cambridge man', which had first appeared in a Cambridgeshire newspaper, was reprinted in the *Excursionist* in June 1856. It was an enthusiastic endorsement of touring in Scotland with Cook. 'Hurray for the Excursion Trains say I! They are a fine invention for men like myself of small means and not much leisure. Had it not been for them, how should I have seen what I have seen?' Cook issued briefing notes to those who travelled with him, with practical advice, for example, on what travelling wear to take. Cook did not create tourism in Scotland, but tourism to Scotland was a core market for him and his firm.

The big three guidebooks for the visitor to Scotland were Murray's *Handbook for Scotland*, Baddeley's *Thorough Guide*, and Black's *Picturesque Tourist*, all of which went through many editions. Black's, for example, which was first published in 1839, was on its nineteenth edition by 1872. Pink specials or inserts with details of timetable changes were issued each year to top up the guides until a fresh revision was issued. Surprisingly, the Baedeker series did not issue a specific volume for Scotland, although the guide to Great Britain did include a section on Scotland.[30] All these guides were written in English. It is significant that foreign language guides to Scotland (or indeed Britain) hardly existed; with the solitary exception of a guide published in French in 1913 to the spas of Britain, Saroléa's *Travers Grande Bretagne*. Not a single Scottish spa, however, not even Strathpeffer, was thought worthy of inclusion. These guides are a cornucopia of information, not just about what to see, but where to stay and how to travel; successive editions show how resorts and their facilities were changing, and how tourist tastes were expanding. Sections were added on angling, cycling, mountaineering and golf; as Baddeley remarked in its 1906 supplement, in Scotland a place is not a place without its 'gowf'.[31] Much might done with a review of how subsequent editions in the same series changed; revisions brought not just new information but new perspectives. They are core sources of information on tourism, and were important players in the business of promotion; guides advised and shaped tourist itineraries.[32] Posters, prints, paintings and photographs fanned interest. Photographic firms such as the Aberdeen-based George Washington Wilson and Co.[33] started in the 1860s to issue albums of views for tourist hotspots: *Edinburgh, Dunkeld, Souvenir of Scott* and so on; individual views could be bought for pasting into travel journals. It was a virtuous interplay; views sold tourism, and tourism sold views. Glossy publications such as *Sights and Scenes in Scotland*, published by Cassell & Co. *c.* 1890 with over 400 views or the lavishly illustrated *Come to Scotland. The Bens and the Glens. The Hills and the Heather*, which was funded by the town and county councils of Scotland *c.* 1925 were part of the process.

As the volume of tourism grew, local worthies, often ministers, started to produce local publicity. An early venture was that of the parish minister at Callander, the probable author of a pamphlet descriptive of Callander and its neighbourhood, which the Wordworths were given in 1803, read with pleasure and subsequently lost![34] Literary men were quick to see the possibilities of supplementing their stipends. One such writer was the colourful and energetic Charles Roger (or Rogers), schoolmaster, minister, historian, editor and a man of energy: the Wallace Monument, which towers yet over Stirling, was his idea, which he drove to completion. On the other side, it has to be said, he bolstered his standing by claiming various higher degrees for which there is no corroboration, including a D.D. from St Andrews.[35] He was commissioned in 1852 by the local landowner, Major Henderson, to write a book at the developing Airthrey Spa. The result was a chunky volume, *A Week at Bridge of Allan*, first issued in 1851, and which sold out its first print run of 1,500 copies within eighteen months, or so Rogers claimed. At nearly four hundred pages long it was more of a handbook for visitors who were there already for the summer, setting out as it did a series of walks and drives in the vicinity, rather than a promotional tool to draw the undecided. Custodians of castle and cathedrals, as at Doune and Elgin, sold souvenirs and histories. Town councils took in hand the issue of short illustrated guides which listed shops and accommodation, amenities and activities. The Cheltenham publisher E. J. Burrow issued hundreds of pocket guides in the 1920s: that for Crieff was number 612 in that series. Local printers cashed in on visitor demand: R. S. Shearer of Stirling issued guides and panoramas to Central Scotland and the Trossachs.[36] This enterprising firm took out advertisements in North American publications such as the *Scottish American Journal* to offer their services to those interested in genealogy and family history. Specialist guides began to appear for particular clienteles. There were the shooting and fishing guides of Hall or Watson Lyall; those for hill walking including Walter A. Smith, for the Scottish Rights of Way Society, *Pentland Hills: their paths and passes* (first edition, Edinburgh 1885) and later in the 1920s *Hill Paths in Scotland, Drove Roads and Cross Country Routes*. Other guides appeared for sailing, golf and cycling, and in 1910 *Scotland for the Motorist*, a handbook for members of the Automobile Association, which carried a list of approved hotels and garages. *The Dunlop Road Guide to Scotland*, with its first edition in 1927, was one of many others to cater for the touring motorist. The boom in tourist information has been exponential and no tourist information centre is complete without its trails and walks. Some current publications and online sites go beyond information to evaluation, as with the *Rough Guides*.

The literature of tourism, from first-hand accounts to academic analyses, is immense and growing. Tourism history has emerged as a recognised and respectable discipline, with its own journal, something which was unthinkable even thirty years ago, when tourism was seen only as the soft end of social history, itself regarded as far from academically rigorous. The past twenty years have seen much published: academic studies such as that of Katherine Haldane Grenier, Eric Simpson, Douglas Lockhart, Kevin James, and local work on resorts such as North Berwick. And the flow shows no signs of diminishing. One can instance Archie Foley and Margaret Munro's *Portobello and the Great War*, which appeared in 2013. To these can be added some significant doctoral and dissertation work. It is unfortunate that there has tended to be rather a chill between academic historians on the one hand, and amateur or local on the other hand; the first regard local writing as obsessed with an accumulation of detail without context or perspective, and the latter (with some justice) recoil from academic writing as over obsessed with jargon and theory. Theory is a good servant, but a poor master, and sadly, as tourism has been recognised by a variety of disciplines as respectable academic territory, so it has attracted, particularly from literary and cultural theorists, far too much writing which preens itself on jargon and obscurity. The truth is that there is both bad academic writing and badly written local writing; just as there are good from both camps. And some do bridge the divide: T. C. Smout for example. This study is light on theory, though it does draw on some key concepts which are of real value, such as John Walton's crucible of conflict or the notion of contested territory. It accepts that tourism is not a neutral force; that economic gain has to be balanced with cultural impact. But at least the story of tourism in Scotland is one of long-term growth, although not without fluctuations due, for instance, to war. And this rise has been achieved in the face of very real competition from elsewhere in the UK, from Europe and other tourist destinations. Some sectors have suffered; many of the seaside resorts, as in England, saw from the late 1950s cheap air transport and guaranteed Mediterranean sun poach away much of their traditional clientele. But the performance of other traditional forms of tourism, and new niches, have more than compensated; tourism in Scotland is a story of sustained success.

Notes

1 Page, Stephen J. and Connell, Joanne, *Tourism. A Modern Synthesis*, (Andover, 2009), p. 4.
2 De Selincourt, E. (ed.), *Journals of Dorothy Wordsworth*, Vol. 2, p. 357 records coming across in September 1822 during her second tour of Scotland the detritus of a reading party of six Cambridge mathematics students in the inn at Tarbet.
3 Lord Cockburn, *Circuit Journeys*, (Hawick, 1983) p. 54.
4 Fairfoul's *Guide to Moffat*, (second edition, Moffat, 1879). The count was taken during the middle of August.
5 Fergie, John, *North Berwick, Wish You Were Here*, (Dirleton, 2013) p. 30. The Town Council organised this census over the weekend of 10–11 August 1918 and found there were in the town 3,311 visitors and 25,050 residents. The council minutes are silent however on why this exercise was commissioned and whether there was any follow-up.
6 Oban Visitors' Register, 19 August 1891.
7 For example, the 1881 census enumerators' books for Logie Parish (Bridge of Allan) noted amongst those who were temporarily resident in the parish (a category which included vagrants and construction workers) were 'visitors here for the sake of their health' or 'here for a change of air'.
8 1841 census: Abstract of the Answers and Returns, 1843 footnote p. 6.
9 Durie, Alastair, 'Tracking Tourism: Visitors' Books and their Value', *Scottish Archives*, Vol. 17 (2011), pp. 73–84.
10 Scott, Ronnie, *Death By Design. The True Story of the Glasgow Necropolis*, (Edinburgh, 2005).
11 *Inverness Courier*, 23 August 1843.
12 Sinclair, Sir John (ed.), *The Statistical Account of Scotland*, (Edinburgh, 1791–9) [Hereafter OSA], Parish of Inveraray, pp. 290–91.
13 *New Statistical Account of Scotland*, (Edinburgh, 1845) [hereafter NSA], Vol. 5, Ayr and Bute, p. 102. Parish of Rothesay, Rev. Robert Craig. Account written in June 1840.

14 *NSA*, (Edinburgh, 1845) Vol X Perth, Parish of Dunkeld and Dowally, p. 963, account written in February 1843.

15 Land Valuation Acts. The case for Andrew Philp for the opinion of judges under the Lands valuation Acts.

16 The original is a large leather-bound scrapbook, a copy of which has been deposited in the Argyll and Bute Council Archives at Lochgilphead.

17 Geddes, Olive, 'Stephen Place's Journal. A footman's visit to Scotland in 1832', *Scottish Archives*, Vol. 19 (2013), pp. 39–52. Place was one of thirty servants taken by the Sutherland family on a visit to Dunrobin in 1832.

18 Durie, Alastair J., *Travels in Scotland. A Selection from Contemporary Tourist Journals, 1788–1881* (Suffolk, 2012), pp. 206–233

19 Barclay, J. B., (ed.) 'John Gulland's Diary 1846–49: a transcript and commentary', *Book of the Old Edinburgh Club*, Vol. 2 (1992), pp. 35–115.

20 Hamilton, David (ed.), *A Girl's Golf in 1894: A North Berwick holiday diary*, (St Andrews, 2015).

21 Durie, Kate and Durie, Alastair, 'Earthly Paradise? The literature of the hydros', *Scottish Local History*, Issue 57 (Spring 2003), pp. 38–43.

22 Author's collection.

23 National Library of Scotland, The Scottish Screen Archive, 0705; Sadness and Gladness (1928), 0893 Sunny days (1931) and 0253 Tommy Trauchle's Troubles (1934).

24 Scottish Screen Archive, 8780, Shores at Elie.

25 Caw, James, *Reminiscences of Forty Years on the Staff of a Hydro*, (Crieff, 1914). He recalls Mary Slessor once when home on furlough bringing to the Hydro four black twin babies, saved from being killed.

26 *A Companion for Canal Passengers betwixt Edinburgh and Glasgow*, (Edinburgh, 1823. Port Hopetoun was the eastern terminus of the Forth and Clyde canal.

27 Harrison, John, *The Steam Boat Traveller's Remembrancer*, (Glasgow, 1824), p. 43.

28 Lumsden, James and Son, *The Scottish Tourist and Itinerary; or, a guide to the scenery and antiquities of Scotland and the Western Islands; with a description of the principal steam-boat tours*, (Edinburgh, 1825). See also Lumsden, James and Son, *Steam boat companion; and stranger's guide to the Western Islands and Highlands of Scotland*, (Glasgow, 1828).

29 *Cook's Excursionist and Tourist Advertiser*, 12 July 1877, Isle of Skye, 'Description from the pen of Mr W. E. Franklin'.

30 According to the editor of the 1901 edition [fifth edition] the section on Scotland was to be seen only as a stopgap until a special Scottish volume could be published.

31 Baddeley, M. J. B., *Thorough Guide to Scotland*, (London, 1908), p. 5.

32 Seward, Jill, 'How and Where to Go: the role of travel journalism in Britain and the evolution of foreign tourism, 1840–1914', in Walton J. K. (ed.), *Histories of Tourism* (Clevedon, 2005), pp. 39–54.

33 Durie, A. J.,'Tourism and Photography in Victorian Scotland: the contribution of G. W. Wilson', in Pringle, R. V., *George Washington Wilson Centennial Studies*, (Aberdeen, 1997), pp. 171–86.

34 Furniss, Tom, 'A Place Much Celebrated in England. Loch Katrine and the Trossachs before the Lady of the Lake', in Brown, Ian (ed.), *Literary Tourism The Trossachs and Sir Walter Scott*, (Glasgow, 2012).

35 He also claimed a LL.D. from Columbia College in New York, of which that institution knows nothing. The controversial career of Charles Roger is splendidly charted by Allan, J. Malcolm, 'Who was Charles Rogers?' *Forth Naturalist and Historian*, Vol. 13 (1990), pp. 97–106.

36 For example, *Guide to the Trossachs and Loch Lomond (including the story of the Lady of the Lake)*, (Stirling, 1915).

2 Tourism reaches Scotland

There is no doubting that before the nineteenth century the great majority of people south of the Border had negligible knowledge of the Highlands, or indeed of Scotland. They know 'as little of Scotland as of Japan', was Tobias Smollett's assertion in the novel *Humphrey Clinker*, which was published in 1771: one of his characters was convinced that to reach Scotland a sea crossing was necessary. As remote as Borneo or Sumatra, was Dr Johnson's view. One needs to take this with a pinch of salt. There was an increasing flow of Scots south on parliamentary or commercial business (as well as of cattle drovers), a degree of interconnectedness through marriage between the landowning elites of Scotland and England, a growing number of publications and prints. But there is no question that whereas before *c.* 1760 there had been but occasional travellers to Scotland – Ben Johnson in 1618[1] – from the 1760s onwards tourists began to arrive in increasing numbers. By the turn of the century Scotland had an embryo tourism industry, but not one prompted by any radical advance in transport. Although the roads were better, getting to Scotland was still a long haul and travelling around the country full of challenge.

It is often suggested that it was Walter Scott through his poetry and prose who created tourism in Scotland: Scotland is 'Scott-land'.[2] Scott's writings drew people to Scotland, and shaped where within Scotland they chose to visit. Reading Scott drew people to Scott-land: 'his books', says one recent assessment, 'contributed significantly to the remarkable increase in Scottish tourism.'[3] His writing helped tourism elsewhere, as at Kenilworth in England, for example, but Scotland was the prime beneficiary of Scott. 'Scott wrote the script for the promotion of Scottish tourism', conclude the Golds.[4] The effect of his novels and poetry was in the first place general, to sell Scotland as a romantic place to discover, sufficiently different to be intriguing, distant but not dangerous, a mix of the new and the already familiar. Academics disagree as to whether the role of Scott has been beneficial in terms of Scottish culture and identity, but it is not in dispute that an effect of his writing was to reshape Scotland's image to the benefit of tourism to Scotland and within Scotland. It was Scott who orchestrated the arrangements, 'tartan, tinsel et al'[5] for George IV's visit in 1822 to Edinburgh, the first visit to Scotland by any reigning British monarch for nearly two centuries.

What, however, will be argued here is that, for all his importance, Scott was less creator than reinforcement to a change already under way as Scotland was already on the map as a tourist destination. There was tourism before Scott: a growth gathering momentum from the mid-eighteenth century onwards, thanks to Ossian, as discussed below, scenery and geology. The flow was broader than is allowed; there were not just literary or scenic tourists, but the later eighteenth century saw the arrival of the sporting tourist, in the person of the Yorkshire squire Colonel Thornton, of whom more later. But the attractions were urban as well. Edinburgh, 'Auld Reekie', was on its way to earning a new title as 'the Athens of the North'[6] thanks to the Enlightenment literati (of whom Hume, Smith and Hutton were but three), and its classical New Town, which was much admired by visitors. But it was not just classical terraces that drew visitors: industrial sites were a draw. New Lanark, which was a convenient break point during the coach journey between Carlisle and Glasgow, offered the mills and Robert Owen's school as well as the Falls of Clyde. Carron ironworks awed Elizabeth Diggle: an infernal region, 'a whole town of smoke & fire & a thousand people at work, furnaces blazing on all sides, half seen through a black smoke'.[7]

Health has always played a part in travel, as a most fundamental desire of people is, if ill, either to be cured or at least to feel better. A whole business of therapeutic treatments grew up. Drinking goat's whey as at Arran or Dunkeld or Blairlogie was one much respected. Sometimes several therapies were combined. A physician in Stirling, Dr Lucas, noted in his diary on 27 June 1820 that numbers of people were leaving the town 'for the mineral waters at Dunblane, while the Blair is much frequented for goat whey'.[8] While Scotland had had in pre-Reformation times a tradition of pilgrimage with several notable shrines, as at Tain and many local healing sites, most were swept away by the Reformers, and often obliterated entirely. However, folk culture remained still committed to them, much more than the church would have wished, deeming them 'superstitious'.[9] A legitimate form of healing in Presbyterian Scotland was through drinking and bathing in spa waters. Here cure was a matter of medical science rather than by a miracle, and the therapeutic challenge to the physician was to match the patient's condition to the right kind of chemically infused mineral water: iron, sulphur or copper. But while some spas did develop in Scotland, perhaps some fifty or so as commercial undertakings, as at Innerleithan (St Ronan's Well) and Bridge of Earn or at St Bernard's Well[10] on the edge of Edinburgh, to which William Cullen sent some of his patients, none were of the scale or reputation to challenge the much better known and larger English or Continental spas. It was not for want of trying. Chemists of standing were engaged to verify the quality of the waters, including Dr Frances Home, who was commissioned in 1751 by the Earl of Home to test the spa waters at Duns. But for all his positive endorsement, that the waters were fully the equal of those at Tunbridge, and a list of patients benefited, the spa failed to develop. More successful for a while was that at Peterhead, which was pushed hard, and promoted by local interests. A pamphlet of seventy-nine pages[11] extolling the virtues of the mineral water regime there was published in 1793 by an Episcopalian minister, William Laing, who held a medical degree from Marischal College at Aberdeen and saw medical work both as a part of his pastoral responsibilities and a way of augmenting his income. But Peterhead was not to stay the course: an informed assessment in 1828 was that 'of late years it has lost its celebrity'.[12] There was always a deficit on the spas account; Scots travelled south in number to places in England such as Scarborough or Harrogate, or to the Continent, but they would have passed few English or foreign health seekers going north. People might have taken the waters while in Scotland, but that was not what drew them north.

What is important is that for a growing number of better-off people in Britain by the mid-eighteenth century, travel for pleasure had established itself as a significant enthusiasm. The question for them increasingly was not whether they would travel but where. For most, the first choice was the Grand Tour in Europe which was well established by the mid-eighteenth century, a journey of months or even years, to explore classical ruins and sites, the art and architecture of France, Italy and Greece. Some went also for their health, taking the waters at a Continental spa or perhaps overwintering in Southern France or Portugal. While ladies did go, it was overwhelmingly a flow of males, especially young men packed off for a period of cultural education, in the charge of a tutor or bearleader (guide): Adam Smith resigned his professorship at Glasgow University in 1764 for the much more profitable position of tutor in Europe to the Duke of Buccleuch's son. It has been argued that 'The Grand Tour of the eighteenth century was a form of cultural tourism with the aim of finishing the traveller's education... Going on the Tour was also considered essential for developing the traveller's personality. It was an individual and authentic experience far removed from the mass experience which the modern notion of tourism normally entails'.[13] What young men did, however, even when supposedly under the eye of their tutor was not necessarily quite as high-minded as their parents would have wished.[14] As Alexander Pope put it in his poem, *The Dunciad Book 4*

> he saunter'd Europe round,
> And gather'd every vice on Christian ground;
> ...
> The stews and palace equally explored.
> Intrigued with glory and with spirit whored

Some came back with paintings and statues, others with the clap. There are myriad journals of their experience, full of interest and anecdote. When Sir William Forbes visited a museum in Naples both the Episcopalian and the banker in him[15] were disgusted by being shown an exceptionally lewd statue and appalled by the extortionate fee demanded by the guide for showing it to him.

What started as an enthusiasm of the upper class became a growing addiction amongst the growing professional and upper middle classes. Their participation was assisted by the emergence of the short tour to the continent: a mini tour of six weeks suited those who did not have unlimited means or free time. Europe was the first choice for this increasing constituency of tourists. The flow across the Channel was, however, liable to disruption by war and hostilities, particularly those between Britain and France, which led to a temporary suspension of touring. But on every occasion, as Black has shown, when peace was concluded following a period of warfare, the numbers of British visitors boomed, as in 1763 with the Treaty of Paris: 'the English flock over daily', noted one Briton in Paris.[16] If war deterred travel to the Continent, it did not reduce the thirst for tourism. Certainly the Grand Tour which took years had to be shelved pro tem, but the short sortie, affordable in time or money to a growing number of travellers, was still viable, but now to the North of England or Scotland rather than to France, and this, it can be argued, temporarily and permanently turned the direction of travel away from the Continent to within Britain, Scotland or Ireland. The participants were perhaps not the grandest of tourists but the lesser grand. Malcolm Andrews[17] has described how, during periods when the Continent was shut, British travellers started to explore the more remote parts of their own country, a process fanned by changing taste in landscape, for the unimproved and rugged as opposed to the manicured lands of lowland estates. Beneficiaries of this cultural shift included North Wales, the Lake District and even Ireland. By the end of the eighteenth century the Lakes of Killarney, the Giant's Causeway and the Glens of Wicklow had become internationally recognised tourist sites.[18]

It would be a simplification, however, to see the rise of Scotland as merely the result of a taste for travel thwarted of its preferred pathways in Europe.[19] There were positive reasons why some tourists, not just those frustrated of their first choice, began to look to Scotland, pull factors which made Scotland attractive but in rather different ways from the Continent. What emerged was not a tartan grand tour. There were some similarities: Scotland did have ruins, abbeys rather than temples, even if not Greek or Roman; it did acquire classical new towns, which were much admired; and there was a new culture of the Scottish enlightenment to lay alongside the fascination of a living feudalism in Gaeldom. Nor was Scotland as respectable as its Presbyterian face suggested, as it was possessed both of drinking dens and brothels.[20] What was different to the European model was that visitors to Scotland came only for visits of a few weeks, even months, but only from April through September and not over the winter: the Scottish climate saw to that. What did help was Scotland's reputation as a safe place in which to travel: Elizabeth Diggle had no qualms about undertaking a six-week tour in 1788 accompanied only by her aunt and a servant. That was bold, but not unique. A few years later on her various tours in the North, Mrs Murray needed no gentleman companion as an escort, just her servants. She did boast, however, that of the nine females to visit Staffa in 1800, she was the only one to go valiantly alone, as she had done: 'an unprotected weak woman'.[21] The image of Scotland was changed. By the 1760s and 1770s Scotland was coming to be seen not as a place only of poverty and rebellion, but of respectability and economic advance; the Highlands as remote and romantic but not rebellious. Robert Clyde has well described how the image of the Highlands and the Highlanders came to change from rebel to hero, from threat to pet.[22] This was in stark contrast to attitudes only thirty years previously when the Highland army had reached Derby. It was not just the English who had rejoiced in the rout of the Jacobite cause at Culloden in April 1746; many Lowland Scots had no love for the clans and their depredations. One Edinburgh merchant complained in February 1746 to a correspondent in Perth about 'lying at the mercy of a parcel of lawless, robing Highlanders' during what he called this 'plaguey rebellion'.[23] But within a generation after Culloden, attitudes had altered. Significantly, when the young French aristocrat Alexandre de Rochefoucauld and his companion Maximilien de Lazowski visited Highland Scotland in 1786 they found locals quite prepared to boast that they had fought with Prince Charles, an innkeeper at Fort William and a boatman on Loch Linnhe; the latter rolled up his sleeve to display a long scar: 'my memento of Culloden', he said, whether truthfully or not.[24] The lost cause had been sanitised, romanticised and made ready for the tourists. Another accidental by-product was that a Jacobite landowner held in captivity after Culloden returned from the South to Pannanich in Aberdeenshire to develop a spa on his estate which he saw (as did others) as a safer road to prosperity than rebellion.[25]

And then there were the poems of Ossian, translated from Gaelic or (as some would argue) created by James Macpherson in the early 1760s,[26] which became widely popular throughout Europe with the reading classes, whose numbers were steadily growing; Napoleon carried a copy of the poems in his knapsack. The Ossianic cult helped to convert the Highlands into a place a fascination, of myth, of heroic deeds and romance. It drew visitors. Literary tourists were new entrants to the world of travel and their first appearance in Scotland was with Ossian. Ossian was to be a continuing fascination, which inspired both Scott and Wordsworth, and planted a tradition of travelling to marry place with prose or poetry. The new interest in travelling to the north was further fanned by local landowners. At Dunkeld, the 2nd Duke of Atholl had already laid out a pleasure ground in the later 1750s. Designed as a wilderness garden, the Hermitage had a network of walks, a grotto, rustic seats and viewing stations above the Black Linn falls of the River Braan. After MacPherson burst on the scene, an Ossian's Cave was constructed as 'part of the 3rd Duke's scheme to heighten the visitor's thrill and imbue the area with a mystical history'.[27] In 1782–83 his son, the 4th Duke, added what became the most famous feature of the Hermitage, Ossian's Hall, a small temple with oil paintings, including one of the blind Ossian singing to the music of his harp. The Hall and its coloured mirrors, which caught the sparkling waters of the falls, became an obligatory calling point for all visitors in the area. The local minister at Dunkeld reported in 1795 that 'it is one of those places which every foreign tourist hastens, on his arrival in Scotland to see, nor does he return disappointed'.[28] The minister exaggerated. There were those who disliked the hall and the mirrors. Though she enjoyed every step to the Hermitage, and was delighted by it, Sarah Murray reported that some tourists found the mirrors absurd.[29] But the numbers certainly came and guides had to be appointed. There were three at Dunkeld in 1814. Their duties included making sure that no flowers were picked, gates left open, or dogs allowed. Robert Heron arrived at Dunkeld as it was getting dark and reflected that he 'was entering the land of Ossian's heroes'.[30]

While some came to see and sketch[31] the scenery as nature had created it, mountains, lochs and waterfalls, Scottish landowners were not above contributing their own embellishments to aid and amuse the tourist: walks, shelters, follies and the like. At Loch Katrine, Mrs Drummond of Perth 'erected booths of wicker work in the most convenient places for the accommodation of strangers who visit this wild and picturesque landscape'.[32] The policies at Inveraray Castle – the Duke of Argyll's pleasure ground and plantations – were visited by increasing numbers of tourists. The local minister commented that 'such is the resort of travellers to it that in 1790 a hundred have viewed it in the space of one week, and in 1792 that number has been doubled in the same space of time',[33] Given how remote Inveraray was, and difficult to reach in the pre-steamship era, these figures suggest that tourism was already a significant flow; the Duke had to build an inn to accommodate those whom he could not put up at the castle. Not all were satisfied: Burns, having been turned away from the castle in June 1787, penned the following scathing lines about the lack of attention paid to him at the Inn

> There's naething here but Highland pride,
> And Highland scab and hunger:
> If Providence has sent me here,
> 'Twas surely in his anger

Figures like these may be just the tip of the iceberg, but allow a guess that by the 1790s the annual numbers of English and other tourists in Scotland may have been by then in their thousands, rather than as previously in their hundreds. The practicalities of travel to Scotland meant that few, if any came for less than a month or two, which multiplied the impact. A new stream was also making its appearance as Scots were beginning to explore their own country. Heron had noted in 1792 how Edinburgh emptied during the summer or in his words 'was commonly deserted by all the migratory parts of its inhabitants'. He added that the tour of the Highlands had become fashionable, within the last ten or twelve years.[34] Henry Cockburn recalled that in either 1797 or 1798 he and two other boys had made a tour in a gig from Edinburgh to Inverness and back by Fort Augustus, quite a venture for three eighteen-year-olds.[35] Thomas Baxter of Dundee undertook what he called a Highland 'jaunt' in August 1811 with two friends, and was astonished by the view at Taymouth, where 'I had always thought there was nothing but Poverty and barrenness'.[36] The notion of a jaunt suggests that these forays were shorter – a week or two – than those of visitors from England or the Continent, but it all added to visitor numbers.

Scotland was increasingly visited and written about. The handful of traveller's accounts relating to Scotland – less than half a dozen in the 1750s – mushroomed to more than fifty by the early nineteenth century. The most famous of these was the tour of Johnson and Boswell, and the most quoted that of Thomas Pennant. Not all visitors to Scotland were literary and cultural tourists. There were already signs of what was to become a major part of Scotland's portfolio for the tourist, namely sporting tourism, as Chapter 5 will show. For the British upper classes, field sports were top of their agenda: hunting, shooting and fishing. Game shooting (of which grouse, pheasant and partridge were the main quarry), fox hunting and deer-stalking were long established enthusiasms. But whereas by the later eighteenth century in Lowland Scotland, landowners had increasingly controlled and limited access to their land, keeping their sport for themselves, in the Highlands there was a much more relaxed attitude: wild game, whether deer or grouse, was not seen to have any commercial value. But that was to change. Growing awareness in the South of the good sport to be had on Scottish moors led to an increasing number of sportsmen – mostly young men – making their way north for a few weeks of walking the moors. The sporting tour of the Yorkshire squire, Colonel Thornton, which was published in 1804[37] but was actually a composite of several sporting forays in the 1780s, did much to alert southern sportsmen to the potential of the north. By the end of the eighteenth century there was a stream of sporting tourists from the south, with whom Scott was familiar. 'They came here occasionally as sportsmen to shoot moor game, without any idea of looking at scenery'.[38] Mrs Murray found in August 1796 at Dalnacardoch Inn in Glengarry north of Pitlochry a crowd of sportsmen 'come to the Highlands to shoot'.[39] They seldom paid at that time for their sport; but commercialisation, and the letting of moors was to set in from the 1820s, partially at least in response to the rapidly rising numbers of itinerant sportsmen. While it was just a few, there were no great problems; as for example, Scott's neighbour, the Cornish gentleman who had settled in Selkirkshire for the sake of the fishing.[40] But the grouseshooting in the North became a growing attraction, with some Highland inns packed to overflowing on the eve of the Glorious Twelfth. In his journal for 1846 Lord Cockburn considered that the autumnal influx of sportsmen was a very recent occurrence; in his phrase they are 'not to be counted in ones, pairs or coveys, but by droves or now flocks'.[41] But the scouts had already arrived at the turn of the eighteenth century. In no other country in Europe was sporting tourism such an important element in the tourism portfolio. Mountaineering had also established a foothold, not yet from England, but locals. Etched on a window at Tarbet inn, as one visitor found in 1817, but dated October 1777, was some advice in rhyme from a Thomas Russell of Glasgow to those thinking of climbing Ben Lomond: 'Trust not at first too adventurous a pace'.[42]

If the growth in scenic and literary tourism to the Highlands was apparent, another new form of tourism was making a dramatic impact, and exciting contemporary comment. What burst upon the Scottish scene in the 1780s was sea bathing for all classes as pleasure, an English invention, originally promoted as good for one's health. While it had been gathering momentum from the early 1700s in England, first on the south coast at resorts such as Margate, it soon worked its way north, and a sketch of Scarborough beach in 1745 shows several bathing machines. Scarborough was a spa which attracted 'crowds of Scottish gentry'[43] according to Withers in 1733, who may well have bathed there, and certainly would have become familiar with the claims made for this saltwater therapy. Yet there seems to have been a hiatus of some thirty or forty years, for reasons which are not clear, apart from a short-lived venture at Leith in 1750, before saltwater baths and sea bathing reached Scotland for anything other than a medical purpose. Recent work on the correspondence of Dr William Cullen, a noted Edinburgh physician, show him to have been recommending sea bathing, sometimes on its own, sometimes in conjunction with spa waters, as early as the 1760s; in June 1772 he wrote to Lady Gordon to advise a remedial course of sea bathing combined with the use of chalybeate water: 'we think this can be obtained better at North Berwick than Peterhead'.[44] The young Walter Scott was quartered at Prestonpans in the summer of 1778 for the 'sake of the seabathing'. Other places which Cullen mentions in connection with sea bathing were Arran and Scarborough. An indication that sea bathing was becoming more important is confirmed by a proposal made in December 1784 to St Andrews council for a bathing house: the supporting memorial stated that the town had been 'much resorted to for some years past by persons from the country around for the benefit of sea-bathing'.[45] Elizabeth Diggle, when in Edinburgh early in May 1788, noted the advantage to the city of sea bathing 'but a mile off'. It may not have been until that decade that the Scots, other than invalids, discovered the seaside and sea bathing, but once they took the plunge they did so with enthusiasm.

Contemporaries talked of a 'salt water mania', of a 'rage for watering places', of beaches now much resorted to for sea bathing', and, as at Portobello, of a number of 'gay or commodious dwellings erected for bathing quarters'.[46] Some were still bathing for their health – as the dying Burns tried in 1794 – but more and more for pleasure. A young Glasgow man noted in his journal in July 1791[47] that nothing now would 'satisfy either married or unmarried or the aged and young but a trip for the summer to the Sea coast'. He called the new enthusiasm a 'saltwater mania'. That sea bathing in Scotland was a recent arrival is confirmed time and time again by ministers in their parish reports, using phrases such as 'of late' or 'recently'. But there would appear to be distinct characteristics to the early Scottish seaside. It was only Scots who were to be found there, not visitors from England or elsewhere. And it would seem that there were Scots from all social classes. Lady Anstruther might have her private bathing station at Elie, but the seaside was open to all. The Scottish physician Dr William Buchan, author of the best-selling *Domestic*

Medicine, added an appendix in 1786 to the ninth edition on waters and bathing; 'It is', he stated, 'now fashionable for persons *of all ranks* [my emphasis] to plunge into the sea... people resort in crowds every season to the seaside and plunge into the water without the least consideration'. It helped, of course, that some of the better beaches were within walking range of the cities, as was true of Edinburgh with Portobello and Leith, Dundee with Broughty Ferry, and Aberdeen, where, in the words of the local paper, there was 'an excellent beach very easily accessible, [which] renders it peculiarly convenient for salt water bathers'.[48] Entrance to the spas could be controlled; access to most beaches could not.

The picture of tourism in Scotland at the end of the eighteenth century is therefore of an industry beginning to develop. Numbers were sufficient to prompt the building of hotels and the renovation of inns, and the provision of seaside lodgings and property to rent. Guides were in place at country houses and their pleasure grounds, and also for hill climbing. But it was to be boosted in the first two decades of the nineteenth century by three things: Continental war, Walter Scott, and better transport, with improved roads and particularly the coming of the steamship. War on the Continent with the Revolutionary and Napoleonic wars largely closed off Europe to British visitors for twenty years or so. And Scotland, as elsewhere in Britain, benefited. 'Since the Continent has been shut to us, Edinburgh is as much visited by every dashing citizen who pretends to fashion as Margate or Tonbridge' claimed the London journal *The Quarterly Review* in 1809.

A second factor was Scott, and there is no doubt as to the impact of Scott in the early nineteenth century and for a considerable time thereafter. There is no more powerful illustration and corroboration of the immediate impact of Scott's writing on tourism than the way that the publication of *The Lady of the Lake* in May 1810 led to a remarkable surge in tourists over the following months and years to Callander and the Trossachs. Dr Lucas of Stirling noted in his diary on 28 August 1810 that many strangers were 'passing through the town in their way to the Trossachs, a very wild romantic part of the country'.[49] And what was producing this 'mania', as he dubbed it, was Scott's poem. Within weeks of its appearance, travellers were making their way north. Mrs. Grant of Laggan had warning early in June that two English ladies of her acquaintance were set on a trip to Loch Catherine (Katrine), and mid-September found her accompanying them from Stirling to the Trossachs, 'where all the world are going to disturb the wood-nymphs and emulate Walter Scott'.[50] There is even some statistical evidence – unusually for tourism of this period – drawn perhaps from an inspection of the visitors' register at the inn. 'Five hundred chaises have been here this summer', Mrs Grant reported from the inn at Callander.[51] Sir John Sinclair was of like mind as to the increase of tourists and its cause. In November he wrote to Scott after a visit to Loch Katrine to acknowledge that 'you have increased the number of visitors beyond measure'. He went on – not for nothing was he known as *Statistical Sir John* – to state that his was the 297th coach in the course of the year 'when there had never previously before been above 100'.[52] Sir John's objective in writing to Scott was to persuade him to set a sequel to *The Lady of the Lake* – to be called *The Lady of the Sea* – in Sinclair's native Caithness in the hope of attracting like numbers of tourists to that remote locality.

While Loch Katrine and the Trossachs stand out as prime beneficiaries of Scott, there were other places in Scotland which also benefited, though none perhaps to the same extent. Some of these visitors by chaise or coach will have travelled not on their own but in families and parties, and so the influx was substantial, particularly when concentrated in the summer months. While some were from England, others were Scots, discovering their own country. The changed image of Scotland attracted English visitors; the changed image of the Highlands no longer repelled Lowlanders. Scott did not just work his spell on English and foreign visitors, but on Scots who for the first time were turning their sights on their own country, rather than going south or to the Continent. Contemporaries recognised what value there was to Scott's writing. Places Scott wrote about, or used as settings for his poetry or prose, attracted visitors, from whom money could be made. Guides, innkeepers and coachmen were all fans of Scott. And places that Scott had not written about wondered whether he could be persuaded to feature their locality. That writing could sell a place to visitors was a lesson that others drew: Washington Irvine heard in August 1817 from Scott of an aged woman at whose inn 'with but little custom' he was pausing for refreshment. Her attention to him was first-rate, but what lay behind it was that she had heard that he was the gentleman who had written 'a bonnie book about Loch Katrine'. Could he not write a little about their lake also, she begged, as it had done the inn at Loch Katrine a 'muckle deal of good'?[53] As with all marketing, there was – unconsciously – in Scott a degree of gloss; 'Scott-land is a Baedeker to an imaginary land'.[54] But in all destination marketing, the dream is always worth more than the reality, the means less important than the end; if the visitors come, then massaging is justified, truth a secondary consideration. And never more than at this time: when a first generation of people were being encouraged to travel for pleasure. Even if not all Scott's contemporaries shared that view. There is the anecdote to be found in James Hogg's *Malise's Journey to the Trossacks* about a crusty Highlander who complained that 'a Mr Scott had put all the people mad by printing a lying poem about a man that never existed – "what the d-was to be seen about the Trossacks more than a hundred other places – A few rocks and bushes nothing else"'.[55] Perhaps, but Scott made those rocks, rather than some other, a place to visit. And it could not be gainsaid that his writing had made a very substantial difference. Curiously Scott never wrote about the Scottish seaside, which sold itself without him: not for him a novel such as Jane Austen's unfinished *Sanditon* (1817). Nor much about spas, other than St Ronan's well.

Whether it was Scott alone that drew a visitor, there is no doubt that for decades a knowledge of Scott coloured for many visitors their time in Scotland, and was an essential part of their experience. Charlotte Bronte's time in

Edinburgh was, in her biographer's words, 'homage to Scott'. There was however a group who loved Scott but never visited Scotland, of whom the best-selling English novelist Charlotte Yonge is a good example. The appeal of Scott was especially strong for Americans and Europeans, for whom enthusiasm for Scott lasted longer than it did for the locals, as has been argued by Lockwood[56] and others. Harriet Beecher Stowe was an enthusiast for the enchantment of Scott.[57] This degree of connection is seen time and time again, with an example being that of an unknown English diarist who came to Scotland in successive summers. During his first short eight-day Scottish tour in August 1817,[58] the recently published *Rob Roy* was clearly very much in his mind when he visited Glasgow. The Cathedral he describes as 'a place rendered immortal by being designated the Laigh Kirk in the novel of Rob Roy'. In the following year, as part of a 'Peep at the Highlands' he made a point of visiting Rob Roy's celebrated cave, 'where it is said that Walter Scott composed part of his tale called Rob Roy'. But reality, as is not uncommon, did not always match expectation, especially for those who were just keeping pace with fashion. A Swedish lady on a tour through the Trossachs found that her neighbour, a Belgian count, was not inspired but completely bored. When she asked him why he had come, he replied that 'it was the modish thing to do'.[59]

By the time of peace on the Continent in 1815 after Waterloo, Scotland was firmly established as a tourist destination, whose attractions could compete well with the reopened Continent. But it was to receive a further fillip in the form of better transport, particularly through the coming of the steamboat, of great significance to a country with such a long coastline, so many estuaries, firths, rivers and inland waters. The roads of pre-modern Scotland have often been stigmatised as dismal, but there was to be a marked improvement in the later eighteenth century.[60] There were the turnpikes, with better gradients and surfaces; over 3,000 miles of turnpike road were open in Scotland by 1810, three-quarters of which had been constructed since 1790. Landowners and county authorities contributed to improved roads, new bridges, alignments and embankments. Milestones and signposts were erected to guide the traveller. Hand in hand with this was the development of a network of posting inns and stables where horses could be changed or chaises hired. And while accommodation when off the beaten track was still basic, it was much improved on the main routes and in the towns. Of course, what was at work was a virtuous interplay: the better the roads and the accommodation, the more visitors came; the more they came, the more investment in facilities was stimulated. Tourism in Scotland was in an upwards spiral.

Notes

1 Groundwater, Anna, 'Ben Jonson's Performance of Union. A walk to Scotland, 1618'. Lecture given to the Royal Society of Edinburgh, 8 December 2014.
2 This phrase was used by the American traveller Bayard Taylor in 1844, *Views Afoot; Or Europe as Seen with Knapsack and Staff*, (New York, 1859) cited by

Lockwood, Allison, *Passionate Pilgrims. The American Traveler in Great Britain, 1800–1914*, (London, 1981), p. 70.

3 Withey, Lynne, *Grand Tours and Cook's Tours*, (New York, 1997), p. 55.

4 Gold, J. and Gold, M., *Imagining Scotland, Tradition, Representation and Promotion in Scottish Tourism since 1750*, (Aldershot, 1995), p. 83.

5 Prebble, John, *The King's Jaunt. George IV in Scotland, August 1822*, (London, 1988). See also Patrick Cadell, '1822 and all that', *Scottish Archives*, Vol. 16 (2010), pp. 41–50.

6 A phrase first used of the city in the 1820s.

7 Durie, Alastair J. (ed.), *Travels in Scotland, 1788–1881*, (Suffolk, 2012), Elizabeth Diggle, Tour, Letter 18, 26 June 1788, p. 32.

8 Stirling Archives, PD 16/4/2 *Diary of Dr Lucas*

9 Buchan, Dr William, *Domestic Medicine*, (Glasgow, 1819) p. 681: 'Every parish has still its sainted well which is regarded by the vulgar with a degree of veneration, not very distant from that which in papist and Hindoos we pity as degrading.'

10 Taylor, J., *A Medical Treatise on the Virtues of St Bernard's Well Illustrated with Selected Cases* (Edinburgh, 1790). On the general history of spas in Scotland see Durie, Alastair, 'Medicine, Health and Economic Development: promoting spas and seaside resorts in Scotland c. 1750–1830', *Medical History*, Vol. 47 (2003), pp. 195–216.

11 Laing, William, *An Account of Peterhead: Its Mineral Well, Air and Neighbourhood*, (London, 1793). In 1804 he followed this up with *An Account of the New Cold and Warm Sea Baths at Peterhead*, (Aberdeen).

12 Professor Thomas Thompson, 'On the Mineral Waters of Scotland', *Glasgow Medical Journal*, Vol. 1 (1828), pp. 130–31.

13 Berghoff, Hartmut and Korte, Barbara (eds), *The Making of Modern Tourism*. (London, 2002), p. 4. According to Chard, 'The Sublime to the Ridiculous; the anxieties of sightseeing', the Grand Tour is a concept formed by reference to a specific practice of travel in Europe over the period – roughly – 1600–1830.

14 Littlewood, Ian, *Sultry Climates. Travel and Sex since the Grand Tour*, (London, 2001).

15 Brown, Iain G., 'Grand Tourists in General and Particular', *Scottish Archives*, Vol. 19 (2013), pp. 145–517.

16 Black, Jeremy, *The British and the Grand Tour*, (London, 1985). See also Mullen, Richard and Munson, James, *The Smell of the Continent. The British Discover Europe*, (London, 2009).

17 Andrews, Malcolm, *The Search for the Picturesque: Landscape, Aesthetics and Tourism in Britain, 1760–1800*, (Stanford, 1989).

18 Williams, William H. A., *Creating Irish Tourism. The First Century*, (London, 2010), Chapter 5: 'Picturesque Tourist Sites in Ireland'.

19 Lord Breadlabane noted in 1759 that it 'has been the fashion this year to travel into the Highlands, many have been here this summer I suppose because they can't go abroad (Andrews, p. 200).

20 See *Ranger's Impartial List of Ladies of Pleasure in Edinburgh*, (Edinburgh, 1978 [1775]).

21 Murray, Sarah, *A Companion and Useful Guide to the Beauties of Scotland*, (Hawick, 1982), p. 138.

22 Clyde, Robert, *From Rebel to Hero: The Image of the Highlander*, (East Linton, 1995).

23 Durie, A. J., (ed.), *The British Linen Company Papers, 1745–1775*, (Edinburgh, 1996), p. 24, Ebenezer MacCulloch to Alexander Christie, 6 February 1746.

24 Scarfe, Norman, *To the Highlands in 1786. The Inquisitive Journey of a Young French Aristocrat*, (Suffolk, 2001), p. 181.

25 Cormack, A. A., *Two Aberdeenshire Spas*, (Aberdeen, 1962), p. 18

26 Andrews, Malcolm, *The Search for the Picturesque*, (Stanford, 1989), pp. 203–6.
27 National Trust of Scotland, *The Hermitage*, (2013).
28 OSA XX, p. 411.
29 Murray, *Companion*, p. 55: 'On entering the Hermitage, I was astonished. The contrast between the room, the beautiful cataract, and its scenery, is beyond description striking.'
30 Heron, Robert, *Observations Made in a Journey through the Western Counties of Scotland in the Autumn of MDCCXCII* [1792], (Perth, 1793), p. 157.
31 Murray, *Companion*, p. 145; 'on the pommel of my saddle hung a bag containing drawing instruments'.
32 OSA XI Callander, p. 579.
33 OSA V Inverary, p. 290.
34 Heron, *Observations*, p. 325 'The frequent resort of gay company to the North [is] for the purposes of pursuing game or viewing its scenery'.
35 Cockburn, *Circuit Journeys*, p. 7, entry for 12 April 1838.
36 Durie, *Scotland for the Holidays*, p. 41.
37 Brander, Michael, *A Hunt Around the Highlands*, (Bath, 1973). Scott was very unimpressed by the amount of equipment and supplies that Thornton took for his safari. 'Some of us do know where to find a bit of game, [but] having in our retinue neither two boats nor a skiff to travel by seas, nor a gig, two baggage wagons nor God knows how many horses for the land service.' (Scott, Walter, *The Edinburgh Review*, Vol. 5 (1805), p. 399)
38 Ibid.
39 Durie, Alastair, '"Unconscious Benefactors": grouse-shooting in Scotland', *International Journal of the History of Sport*, Vol. 15, No. 3 (December 1998), pp. 38–9.
40 Lockhart, D. G., *Memoirs of Sir Walter Scott,* (London 1900), p. 343: Scott to George Ellis, 27 August 1803.
41 Cockburn, *Circuit Journeys*, 19 September 1846, p. 195.
42 Glasgow City Archives, TD 637, Journal of a Tour to the Highlands.
43 Brodie, A., 'Scarborough in the 1730s – spa, sea and sex', *Journal of Tourism History*, Vol. 4, No. 2 (August 2012), pp. 125–53.
44 Royal College of Physicians of Edinburgh. The Cullen Project. The Consultation Letters of Dr William Cullen. www.cullenproject.ac.uk A Mrs Barclay was advised by Dr Cullen in June 1776 that 'a part of the benefit of Peterhead is by the sea bathing'[ID 3842].
45 Simpson, Eric, 'East Fife's Open-Air Swimming Pools – safe places for dooking', *Scottish Local History*, Vol. 67 (summer 2006), p. 5.
46 *Statistical Account of Scotland*, Vol. 18, (1796), Parish Of Duddingston, pp. 361–62.
47 Durie, *Travels in Scotland*, Adam Bald. A Ten Days' Ramble to the Sea Coast, 16 July 1791.
48 *Aberdeen Journal*, 5 October 1789.
49 Stirling Archives, PD 16/4/2 *Diary of Dr Lucas*. He further noted in August 1813 that there were again numerous parties of pleasure passing and re-passing through the town, but 'that the rage or madness of going to see in the Trossachs this year seems to be much abated'.
50 Grant, J. P., Memoir and Correspondence of Mrs Grant of Lagan, (London, 1844), p. 269.
51 *Memoir and Correspondence of Mrs Grant of Laggan*, edited by her son, J. P. Grant, (London, 1844) Volume 1, pp. 267–9: Letter CVII, Stirling 17 September 1810.
52 Grierson, H. J. C., *Letters of Sir Walter Scott, 1808–1811*, pp. 419–20: Scott to Joanna Baillie, 31 December 1810.
53 Irving, Washington, *Abbotsford and Newstead Abbey*, (London, 1835), p. 186. Irving says that this took place at Glenross, which is not identifiable. Glencorse is a

possible candidate, being in country near Edinburgh that Scott knew well, but there is no loch.

54 Kelly, S., *Scott-Land. The Man Who Invented a Nation*, (Edinburgh, 2010), p. 2.
55 'The Spy', 1 June 1811, cited in Bohls, E. A. and Duncan, Ian (eds), *Oxford Anthology of Travel Writing* (Oxford, 2005), p. 178.
56 Lockwood, *Passionate Pilgrims*, especially pp. 65–78. See also Katherine Haldane Grenier's important study, *Tourism and Identity in Scotland: Creating Caledonia*, (Aldershot, 2005), pp. 53–5.
57 In her *Sunny Memories of Foreign Lands*, (Boston, 1854), letters written during her tour of Europe in 1853, when she reaches Scotland (Glasgow) in April 1853, she emphasises how much Scottish views, Scottish ballads and songs, the 'enchantments of Scott' had been part of her childhood.
58 Glasgow City Archives, MS TD 637/1 *First Tour to the Highlands, 1817*, and *[Second Tour] 1818*.
59 Kramer, Lotten von, *Among Scottish Mountains and Lakes*, (Stockholm, 1870), p. 58.
60 Durie, Alastair, 'Movement, Transport and Travel', in Foyster, Elizabeth and Whatley, Christopher (eds), *A History of Everyday Life in Scotland 1600–1800*, pp. 252–72.

3   Tourism and transport

Transport and tourism are intertwined; better transport feeds tourism, and tourism feeds transport improvement. What better transport offers may be cheaper travel, or shorter travel times, but not to be over looked is the value of regular and scheduled services, without which, for example, Cook's week-long tours, which were calculated to the last penny and the last minute, could not have functioned. Travel in earlier times was plagued by roads made impassable by mud, or ferry services paralysed by rough water, or shipping pinned in harbour by adverse winds. The better-off could afford to take their time, but for the tourist with limited time, and a fixed budget, the improvements in transport which gathered momentum from the mid-eighteenth century were a boon; they got the tourist and holidaymaker more value for their money, widened their choice of destination, and opened up new resorts. But improved transport also could expose those resorts whose main asset had been proximity: for Glasgow folk, as we shall see, there developed the option by sea of holidaying on the Isle of Man, or by rail to English resorts such as Blackpool and Scarborough. It was a two-edged sword: it could bring tourists in, but also allow people to travel away. It heightened competition, resort against resort, region against region and country against country.

Nineteenth-century writers, living as they were in an age of transport revolution, tended to regard the state of travel in the previous era as very difficult and restricted. Yet either on foot or by horse the determined could travel in premodern Scotland. The Rev. James Allan,[1] a peripatetic Presbyterian minister, more motivated than most and perhaps protected by providence, was able to travel around in 1689, even in the depths of winter. He does complain about ill ways and bad weather and in particular about 'the devil's bounds' between the Spey and Dundee but he gets there. Though most visitors preferred to use either a horse or coach, there were those who chose to walk for pleasure, which was a new and strange enthusiasm in Scotland; common folk had long walked to find work or as a part of their livelihood, droving cattle or peddling, but not for pleasure and scenery. Visitors could and did walk very long distances: during his tour in June 1818 Keats reckoned on completing twenty miles each day before dinner.[2] Coleridge did even better; thirty to thirty-five miles a day for eight days during his walking tour in the Highlands in the summer of 1803 after breaking away from the Wordsworths. Social conventions had to be observed even when on the road – one English visitor on her way north in 1788 had come across a gentleman on a journey with his two footmen following behind. Walking continued to be a preferred mode for some tourists, and of course in the more remote or hillier areas there might be no alternative. Hill walking for pleasure developed as a distinct form of leisure activity in the later nineteenth and early twentieth centuries,[3] as did climbing with the establishment in 1899 of the Cairngorm and Scottish Mountaineering Clubs; both activities are still very popular, with long distance walking on trails such as the West Highland Way presently very much in vogue.

It was true that in the later eighteenth century away from the beaten tracks and major roads, navigation could be a problem for the tourist, gauging distance a matter of guesswork, and finding accommodation uncertain. Travelling by carriage or coach was difficult, especially north of Perth; rough surfaces made Mrs Murray's advice good sense – take a good lynch pin and complete repair kit.[4] Crossing water by way of ford or ferry carried risks, especially when the ferrymen, waiting for custom, had spent their waiting time in the local inn. When the Wordsworths toured in 1803 their horse was – understandably – terrified by its brutal treatment at the hands of the ferrymen at Connel and unsafe near water thereafter.[5] The Queensferry crossing from Edinburgh to Fife was often a difficult stretch of water, and some tourists chose to take a longer but all-land route north by way of Stirling. But improvements came in the form of better roads, notably but not only through the new turnpikes, the availability of guidebooks, and the creation of a network of inns and hotels where food and rooms were available. The new county roads and turnpikes provided better surfaces, and new bridges were built, as across the Tay at Perth in 1766. Also important was the evening out of gradients, the straightening out and levelling of roads to avoid sharp descents and ascents, which made far less physical demand on horses, as with the long embankment over at Oxenfoord south of Edinburgh, whether with grain or coal carts or passenger coaches, than the old up-and-down and winding roads. Hand in hand with that went the provision of milestones with distances to the next stopping place, many of which are still to be seen. By the early nineteenth century, Scotland was mostly well served by its roads system, though dust in the summer and mud in the winter were the bane of travellers. And in the bigger cities, even those with the new layouts of planned thoroughfares and wide terraces, congestion was becoming a problem. But tourists could travel with much more ease. Elizabeth Diggle's carriage carried her five hundred miles in Scotland during the summer of 1788 without any great mishaps. Coaching became a form of regular movement: by the mid-1830s there were 24 mail and 316 coach services in Scotland. A network of posting inns serviced the traveller by coach or carriage or the rider. Longer-distance coaching was to be wiped out by the railway, and the advent of the motor car draw away the few wealthy who had preferred still to travel in their own horse-drawn carriage, but tourist brakes ['four in hand'] were still run by private operators from railway stations and hotels in localities such as Oban and Pitlochry until after the First World War. The Blairs, hoteliers in the Trossachs, had several large excursion coaches which were twenty-six-seaters, and had exclusive rights to the forecourt at Callander station for their coachmen, resplendent in grey top hats and red coats, to wait for new arrivals. Theirs, the last working stable in Scotland, was sold off in April 1931.[6]

Much is rightly made of the contribution of the railways to the development of tourism in Britain. Yet for Scotland, it was the coming of the steamboat after c.1815 as much as or more than the railway that transformed travel and tourism in Scotland, given its geography: a long coastline with many islands, firths and inland waters. The coming of the steamboat, pioneered in Britain on the Clyde in the second decade of the nineteenth century, was to transform water transport. The Minister at Dunoon summed up the impact in 1844: prior to steam navigation, access from this parish and the neighbouring districts to the low country and towns on the Clyde was 'tedious, uncertain and sometimes dangerous'.[7] The Glasgow Historian, Robert Reid or 'Senex', looking back to his childhood, remembered how difficult it was for a Glasgow family to holiday on Bute: their voyage in a small wherry, complete with servants and household necessaries from the Broomielaw in Glasgow to Rothesay in 1778, took eight hours (as against three by the steamers) and was very tedious for a four-year-old.[8] But now no longer did contrary winds or flat calms keep boats in harbour, and departures could now be scheduled with a degree of certainty. Not so perhaps arrivals, as the early paddle boats were slow and unreliable, but that improved as the technology developed. The first passenger service in Scotland, indeed Europe, was run in 1812 between Glasgow and Greenock by Henry Bell, whose statue is still to be seen on the front at Helensburgh, and within a few years, steamboats were to be found on all the river and sea estuaries of Scotland, east coast and west. Dorothy Wordsworth in her second tour of Scotland in 1822 took a steam boat from Newhaven to Alloa, and several more in her travels on Loch Lomond and in the Clyde estuary before returning to Glasgow, where there was a great bustle in the harbour and 'puffing of steam boats'.[9] In the west the boats worked their way out from the more sheltered waters of the Clyde to longer distance travel to the Hebrides, where they were known by the Highlanders as 'black boats of smoke'[10] up to Oban, across to the Isle of Man, Ireland and London. These boats helped the growth of tourism in both coastal resorts, providing they had a suitable landing spot in the form of a pier, and on inland waters. The first inland steamer was the *Marion* on Loch Lomond in 1816; others quickly followed for Lochs Tay and Katrine. It is important not to underrate the importance of this advance in water transport for tourism, especially the boats on the inland waters; while the island boats carried cargo and people alike, and made mass tourism possible for Scottish islands such as Bute and Arran, the main traffic on lochs such as Loch Lomond was of tourists. In August 1828 there was a tragic accident when a boat carrying passengers from the shore at Tarbet to the waiting steamer capsized, with eleven drowned, amongst whom were a doctor and his wife from South Glasgow

newly wed who had enjoyed but two months of married state,
for in Loch Lomond they met their fate.[11]

While the railways were to leech away some of the traffic to the coast, river
and sea services were to remain vitally important to island tourism, and
nowhere more than in the Clyde region. The annual exodus at the Glasgow
Fair in July saw every boat, even some retired, pressed into holiday service.
The doun the watter phenomenon is discussed in depth in Chapter 5. The
efficiency of the steamer network allowed holidaymakers and day trippers in
the west of Scotland to travel widely. It was possible, for example, (with an
early start) to take a day trip from Glasgow to Campbeltown on the remote
Kintyre peninsula. The network of piers allowed the holidaymaker in the Clyde
any number of day excursions in the area; some eighty were available from
Dunoon alone in the 1890s to places such as Inveraray, Oban and Ayr. For the
visitor, watching steamers coming to and fro was also part of resort entertainment, spiced up when two steamers were racing to berth first, and thus
scoop up those waiting to travel on. The loss of steamer services was dis-
astrous, as happened briefly in July 1906 at Millport when, after renovation of
the piers at the Council's expense, the steamer companies and the town
authorities fell out over the higher level of pier dues being asked. 'The siege of
Millport', as it was known, led to a collapse in advance summer bookings,
and a substitute motor launch service was unsatisfactory. Fortunately and
necessarily the dispute was resolved fairly quickly.[12] The volume and variety
of steamer traffic on the many Firth of Clyde routes has tended to dominate
attention, but there were steamers on the Forth, and the Tay, and elsewhere,
which also in the summer carried holidaymakers and tourists. The Galloway
steamers visited Alloa and Stirling upriver, ran to Elie and Aberdour in Fife
and offered cruises to the Bass Rock and North Berwick. Special sailings
from South Queensferry allowed sightseers to follow the construction in the
1880s of the Forth Bridge. The building of the new naval base at Rosyth,
which started in 1905, was another draw. The steamship companies showed
themselves enterprising in stimulating tourist, day tripper and excursion
demand. Indeed the very idea of the excursion was an innovation pioneered
in Scotland by the steamboats. Day pleasure trips – the early boats did not
sail at night – was an idea which they may have copied from coaching, and
outings down the Clyde from Glasgow to Port Glasgow or Greenock were
soon popular. Days out, say to the races, were an eighteenth-century initiative,
but the pleasure outing was an innovation of the steamboat companies:
William Daniel in 1818 detailed how in good summer weather boats from
Glasgow, carrying up to five to six hundred people, were visiting Port Glasgow
and Greenock, some to sea-bathe, and returning that evening: what he called
'a mere excursion of pleasure'. Such business was to become a mainstay of
railway companies. Another contribution was the way that regular steamer
services allowed the growth of summer commuting; moneyed families going
to Arran or Fife with father returning by steamer on the Monday back for

two or three days' business. The railways also fed this kind of traffic from inland resorts such as Callander, the so-called carriage folk. There had always been a tradition of the urban wealthy retiring to the country for the summer; what was new was the regular return of the businessmen to keep an eye on their commerce while the family continued in their holiday quarters.

In most minds and in many areas the railways are synonymous with the rise of tourism in Britain. To be served by rail made tourist resorts; to be bypassed was to be side lined. It was the volume of holiday traffic that they could carry, the regularity of service and the speed, which effectively shrank Britain in terms of which places could be reached in a given time. They wiped out longer distance coaching: in 1880 the main road north from Perth to Inverness was said be overgrown with grass in places, as was true of the Great North road at Grantham, the railways having taken all the traffic. Resorts shifted up the gears, thanks to the railway: Dawlish and Teignmouth in South Devon, Llandudno and Rhyl in North Wales, Silloth in Cumberland, Newcastle in Northern Ireland and many others. Nowhere more clearly illustrates the value of a rail service than Blackpool; essential to its development was the coming of the railway in the 1840s, which opened this small watering place to a huge influx of holidaymakers from the Lancashire cotton towns.[13] But there was no equivalent in Scotland to Blackpool of a mass resort made by the railway. Certainly the railway was greatly to aid longer-distance travel from the South, but mostly it strengthened flows to existing resorts such as Ayr or North Berwick rather than put entirely new ones on the map. Spa resorts such as Moffat and Strathpeffer were all firmly established as health resorts before they got their own branches. The railway certainly helped the better-off to travel with their luggage and servants, and their stations saw a spike in activity as June lets gave way to July.

But arguably what the resorts felt most, inland or coastal, was the impact of weekenders and day excursionists, tempted by cheap fares. They came by steamer to the islands and the firths, by train and later horse brake and motor coach to inland communities. This caused stress; John Walton has coined the phrase 'crucible of conflict'[14] to describe the clash of lifestyles and behaviour at English seaside resorts, and it holds as true for Scotland as for England. It was not just the number of excursionists, but the behaviour of the arrivals, out for a good time; not all were rowdy but many were. There were complaints from the locals, whether all–year-round residents or respectable summer visitors, whose peace was disturbed. The *Argyllshire Standard* in June 1871 disapproved strongly of the riotous and disorderly behaviour of a number of excursion parties, complete with their own bands, which had landed the previous Saturday by the steamers; what particularly offended polite society was the level of drunkenness amongst women and men alike. But, the paper concluded, this was all too typical of present-day excursions to Dunoon. The same complaint is repeated in the local press throughout Scotland: 'disgusted of Dunoon' had many sympathisers elsewhere. There were several issues which offended the respectable: lack of respect for the Sabbath; mixed bathing rather than observing the middle-class conventions of either separate beaches for men and women, or different times for bathing; not bothering to change in boxes or behind screens, or even bathing without costumes. A letter from Largs in 1868[15]

> viewed excursionists as a curse to this as to every other watering place on the coast, all owing to the conduct of a few composing them. No later than yesterday I observed from eight to twelve full grown young men bathing opposite to the Broomfields, one of the most fashionable promenades here, walking about without the slightest attempt to conceal their persons, putting every feeling of modesty at defiance.

Drink was often the aggravating factor; a correspondent from North Berwick complained in July 1873 of the way that every weekend parties of excursionists poured into town with the sole idea of swilling strong liquor, converting the quiet streets into a miniature Donnybrook (a notoriously rowdy Dublin horse fair). It was a problem that was encountered everywhere in Scotland, inland as well as at the coast, and did not resolve itself quickly. In 1932 a local schoolteacher at Glencroe wrote to the County Clerk about the behaviour of the summer hordes who came by cycle or charabanc. 'Men and women in various states of undress parade about the road and hillside. Men absolutely naked, stand on the banks of the River Croe and do their utmost to attract the attention of passers-by whilst all sorts of immorality are practised on the lower slopes of the hillsides, and in full view of the public and of young children'.[16] The County Clerk had no remedy to offer.

Excursionism was to be a major source of traffic for the railway companies in Britain and one which they (unlike their European counterparts) promoted with enthusiasm: for holidaymakers, for works or masonic outings, for Sunday school treats – for any organisation that could muster a train load. It was with a Saturday temperance train that in July 1841 Thomas Cook made his first move into the tourism business. And it was not just lines in tourist locations that benefited; there was the outflow of excursionists and holiday-makers from the industrial and manufacturing towns which the railway companies could exploit. One of the earliest railway companies in Scotland to take an active interest in the early 1830s was the Glasgow & Garnkirk, a coal line, which offered evening, afternoon and day trips from Glasgow to the then (as now) rather unattractive town of Airdrie. But it was able to sell trips, which suggest it was the sheer experience of travelling – rather like a flight on Concorde – and the wayside views rather than the destination which were the attraction. Other railway companies, big and small, were quick to join in: a nearby company, the Wishaw & Coltness, a coal line running through bleak territory, suggested in 1834 that its newly executed and extensive tunnel was well worth a visit.[17] The volume of holiday traffic boomed: in 1840 the Glasgow, Paisley and Greenock Railway Company, then in its first year of operation, was caught unawares and ran out of engines, swamped by demand on

Paisley's August Holiday. Railway companies became increasingly interested in summer traffic when coaches and engines of every vintage were pressed into service, and extensive sidings (of which little remain) had to be provided for the temporary stabling of stock at the resorts. Tourism was something which increasingly the promoters of railway schemes mentioned in their company prospectuses. That for the Peebles Railway in 1852 pointed to the many strangers 'health seeking and for recreation' who would use the line.[18] Tourist traffic was not the principal justification, except perhaps for the Highland lines, where sporting traffic was so significant, but it was a useful additional source of revenue to the staples of fish, or farm or coal traffic for lines such as the Leven & East of Fife. The provision of passenger services in 1907 on the remote Campbeltown & Machrihanish Light Railway, a coal line, in Kintyre proved an astonishing success; golfers and day trippers could leave Glasgow, enjoy the links or the beach at Machrihanish, and be back in Glasgow that night. But once the pit closed in 1931, the line was no longer viable, or else Scotland might have had a narrow-gauge venture to rival the Ffestiniog. Tourism helped railways, but holiday traffic alone was not enough; significantly various railway schemes which aimed at the tourist market alone, such as a mountain railway up Ben Nevis like those up Snaefell and Snowdon never got off the ground; the economics were not viable.

Excursions were a valuable supplement to the passenger traffic brought on standard services and all resorts experienced the influx of day trippers, even those inland, sometimes in numbers that almost overwhelmed them. Not all locals welcomed the railway's coming because of the hordes – some with drink in them – that would be brought. Wordsworth, in his opposition in 1844 to a proposed line to Windermere, was not alone in his objection to the working classes invading his privacy. But mostly the railway won, and during the summer life was changed in the receiving resorts. In June 1856 was opened the first stage of what would become the Highland Railway to Inverness, a line from Perth to the small community of Birnam. The line had stopped short of Dunkeld because the Duke was unwilling to allow its continuance north through his grounds. That summer saw excursion after excursion train arrive. One Saturday there were so many visitors, over a thousand, that there were not enough guides to take them through the Duke's pleasure grounds. The Duke himself led a party of 350 workers from a Perth factory, mainly girls, and joined in with their dancing on the green opposite the Birnam Hotel while waiting for the train to depart.[19] When the railway pushed north in 1863 to Pitlochry and then Aviemore, so the excursion trade withered at Birnam, but by then it had become well developed as a tourist destination, with lodging houses and hotels for the upper and middle classes.

Excursionism has had a bad name, and some certainly were more than cheerful – drunken and rowdy, particularly works outings when too often 'drink had been taken'. The Caledonian Railway excursion in 1899 for its staff to Carlisle[20] resulted in eighty-eight drunks being locked up in Carlisle. Excursionism carried the opprobrium then of hen or stag parties today. And in Scotland it seems to have been more of an issue. Thomas Cook thought that in his experience that sobriety of excursionists in outings from England was 'remarkable, but that the same could not be said of the some of the working class excursions of Scotland where day trips were often occasions of drunken revelry'.[21] Yet not all were like this, it depending on who was in charge of the outing. John Hope's Temperance excursions were a model of good behaviour, and it would be a mistake to tar all with the same brush. Many were very respectable and passed off with no trouble at all. Take the case of Peebles, for example, a favourite destination after the coming of the railway in July 1855. It was a small county town with a population of just over 2,000 in 1861, four licenced hotels, two pubs – and only three public toilets! The resources for the control of public order were minimal: only one sergeant and six constables for the whole of the county. Yet Peebles was able to cater for some very large excursion parties of over a thousand people, including one in 1864 of 1,700 people, an outing of working-class Catholics from Edinburgh. Trouble was feared but the priests kept their flock in check, apart from a few troublemakers, and the whole day passed off cheerfully.[22] Most excursions were more often than not without disturbance, and for the participants just a good and cheap way of enjoying a day out. Typical of these is an excursion from Peebles on Friday 11 July 1884 during the Innerleithen holidays. There were 544 on the special from Peebles, which was a fair proportion of the town's population, and of whom 187 had got on at Walkerburn at 5.45 a.m. About half went only to Edinburgh, either spending the day there, or to Leith for a sail, or Portobello for bathing. The remainder went to Stirling, where they had engaged a hall for dancing, having first visited the Wallace Monument. They left Stirling at 6.30 p.m., reached Edinburgh at 8.20, and were back at Innerleithen by 10. Some bought extension tickets and stayed overnight in Edinburgh to visit the Forestry Exhibition being held in the grounds of Donaldson's Hospital. The local paper commented that the whole body behaved themselves in 'a gentlemanly and lady-like manner, and all seemed highly pleased with their trip.'[23] But this form of travel was hugely successful, though the scale of movement and the pressure of this traffic meant the timetabling could and did slip. And while incidents involving overloaded excursion trains were sadly common in Britain (the worst British railway accident of the nineteenth century, a Sunday School outing with eighty dead, was at Armagh in June 1889), Scotland seems largely to have escaped. That is not to say that all was perfection: Perth Station, nowadays just an empty cavern, was then the hub for sporting traffic, a bedlam of passengers, their luggage, servants and dogs – and too few porters. Timekeeping on the branch lines was poor – though, to be fair, not perhaps as bad as in Ireland, where all timings were very approximate, as captured in the music hall song, 'Are you ready yet, Michael?' Nevertheless one English party in Scotland summed up their summer experience in 1876: 'we always found Scotch trains very late'.[24] The leisurely nature of branch line operations in Scotland is well caught and caricatured in a Cynicus postcard: 'Our Local Express. North

Figure 3.1 One of a series of postcards satirising the lack of urgency in Scottish branch line operations. (Author's collection)

Berwick' which shows the engine being pulled by a donkey train, and the passengers helping to push, while the crew play cricket alongside.[25]

Tourism could make money for railway companies, and the summer takings, which reached their climax in August for the Highland Railway, for example, were what determined the year's profits. The seasonality, as for the hoteliers, was a challenge: too much traffic in the summer, particularly during Glasgow Fair and the other Trades weeks, but too little in the winter, when there was little or no tourism. A new type of travel, associated with sport rather than holidaymaking, which began to help business was the movement of supporters and spectators to watch their football or rugby team, and from the later nineteenth century specials were being run for sporting occasions. The development of international sport was a real bonus: there were thirty-one extra trains from Wales to Edinburgh for the 1934 Scotland–Wales rugby match – with Welsh-speaking staff temporarily brought north from Swansea to help. And so the railway (and steamship) companies did what they could to promote traffic through promotion and publicity. All the bigger companies had their own excursion and travel departments, which sometimes had an uneasy relationship with travel agencies such as those of Thomas Cook or Henry Gaze, with whom they both colluded and competed. They organised and promoted trips, with cheap fares, to special events: exhibitions, processions, state occasions, the opening of the General Assembly of the Church of Scotland in Edinburgh, through handbills and leaflets and newspaper advertising. Many issued guidebooks to the scenery through which their lines passed. And what was also to emerge at the end of the nineteenth century was the colour railway poster, which developed into an inspired art form, combining image and text.

One of the earliest for Scotland c.1910 (artist unknown) was the Caledonian Railways Company's restrained poster of Bridge of Allan, a scenic view over the 'brig' looking east towards the Wallace Monument. Most, as one might expect, show scenery and sport, beaches and mountains, hills and high-landers, but there are exceptions: Norman Wilkinson did superb views for the London, Midland & Scotttish Railway (LMS) in the 1930s of Grangemouth Docks and of Shipbuilding on the Clyde.[26] To advertising was added some support for local facilities to appeal to tourists; the enterprising John Anderson of the Callander & Oban arranged for mountain guides at Crianlarich to take climbers up Ben More. Golf, especially in Scotland and in Ireland, attracted interest from the railway companies. There were halts provided adjacent to the courses, and golfers' specials to take businessmen after work for an evening round: the North Berwick branch in East Lothian was dubbed the 'Golfers Line'. On occasion railway companies promoted golf courses, as at Newcastle in Ulster, but in Scotland the companies went further, building luxury golfing hotels as at Turnberry, Cruden Bay and Gleneagles: the hope was to capture not just the travel profits of the first-class passengers en route but the profits of their stay at the hotel. Cruden Bay proved a financial failure, and the hotel was eventually demolished, though the golf course survives: the other two hotels prosper yet. What the railways were also to provide were camping coaches in sidings at rural stations. The Scottish region of BR offered a choice of thirty-five locations in 1956 at places such as Aberlady, Culross and Kil-many;[27] Gullane, where the station waiting rooms were also available as holiday apartments, was graced in 1963 by two Pullman coaches converted to holiday use.[28]

The coming of the bicycle – the safety bike of the 1880s rather than the cumbersome penny-farthing – as a form of individual transport is seldom accorded much attention. Yet it did much for leisure, if not necessarily as much for tourism. It allowed freedom from the straitjacket of railways or steamship timetables for short-term impulse trips away, and it is a matter of regret that as yet there is no comparable study of cycling in Scotland as there is for Ireland.[29] While cycling had started as an upper- and middle-class activity –Queen Victoria had a tricycle – it became an artisan enthusiasm for both sexes. A writer in the cycling journal in Scotland, *The Scottish Cyclist*, reported that on Saturday afternoons the Fenwick Road out of Glasgow was 'thronged with girl cyclists', and noted in 1906 that 'it is rapidly becoming universal amongst all classes except the very poorest'. There were those who raced, those who went on club outings, and those that holidayed, taking with them tents and camping equipment. The left-wing Clarion Club held a week-long discussion camp each year during the Glasgow Fair in southern Kintyre; sixty men and women in eight tents in July 1898 where they ruffled local feathers by their lack of respect for the Sabbath.[30] Typical of the kind of cycling holiday taken by many was the week-long trip taken in July 1893 by two brothers, who were millers, from Motherwell to the North of Scotland, a remarkable 695 miles in seven days. They were touring for pleasure, spoiled only by an encounter with some drunken railway navvies, but there were others concerned only with distance records, with Land's End to John o'Groats a top challenge. On their arrival at that hotel, the McGregor brothers looked through the Visitors' Book at the hotel there and 'read the accounts of the great rides against time done by road scorchers from Land's End'.[31] There were organisations to look after their interests when travelling, of which the Cyclists Touring Club, (originally founded in 1878 as the Bicycle Touring Club) was the foremost and of which they were members. To serve its growing membership, to which female cyclists were admitted, of 44,000 in 1897, it erected road signs and boards to warn against steep descents ('Ride with Caution'), issued guidebooks and introduced a system of recommended hotels and repair shops, an idea which the Automobile Association was to follow. Its handbook also included an agreed tariff for food and accommodation; the Queensferry Arms in South Queensferry, handy when waiting for the ferry to Fife, promised in 1895 a light breakfast of tea and toast for 1/3 or a full cooked affair with chops or steak for only six pence more. A few of the original CTC signs – a two-foot spoked wheel with interior wings – can still be seen, as at the New Inn in Rhuddlan in Denbighshire, or at the bottom of King Street in Stirling. The cyclists also travelled abroad, Holland with its flat terrain being understandably a particular favourite. While in town cyclists had to avoid horse drawn traffic-carts and carriages, and in the bigger towns had vans, trams and horse buses to contend with, in the countryside they mostly had the road to themselves. At some tourist attractions there would be horse-drawn brakes, but the main problem was not so much other traffic but the conditions of the road surface and camber. Tram lines were a growing problem as the tram networks pushed out from the big cities, from Edinburgh to Cockenzie, Glasgow to Balloch, Dundee to Broughty Ferry (the last advertised as 'Scotland's most beautiful tramway'[32]); great for the day tripper, but a hazard to the cyclist whose wheel could get trapped in the rails. But a far greater danger was to arrive within a relatively short time with the advent of the petrol-driven motor car, and its kin: the motor cycle, the char-abanc and the motor caravan. The first cars appeared in the mid-1890s, and their numbers in Britain quickly rose from over 8,500 in March 1904, when vehicle registration was introduced, to 32,000 by March 1907, of which 2,697 were in Scotland. Motor cycle numbers were even higher. While some – vets and doctors – used their vehicles for their work, the car became for many moneyed people a way to travel faster and further, and the touring car became a frequent visitor both in established tourist areas in the Central Belt but also in those which had been remote. The motorists were not always welcome; they were dangerous to themselves (there was no compulsory driving test until 1935) and to others: unwary pedestrians, other road users, and animals; their driving at speed threw up either mud or dust on bystanders, and wore out road surfaces for which local taxpayers had to foot the bill. Small wonder that there was a campaign launched against the reckless motor driver immortalised in Kenneth Grahame's Toad of Toad Hall 'who drive over and kill your children, your men and women, your dogs, your chickens, who spoil your houses with dust, and with dust and stink, poison the air we drink'.[33] The Automobile Association was set up to do what the CTC was doing for cyclists, issuing guidebooks, erecting signs, establishing a network of recognised hotels and garages. But it added one important function: road scouts to warn members of speed traps lying ahead! The Scottish Automobile Club had nearly a thousand members by 1908, a substantial proportion of car owners in Scotland.

What did the coming of motor transport mean for tourism? It is clear that very quickly summer touring in Scotland by motor car became popular amongst the well-off, particularly on the eve of the Glorious Twelfth, with sportsmen from England heading to shooting-lodges. One witness to the Royal Commission on Motor Cars in November 1905 spoke of having witnessed as many forty-two cars passing Moy Hall on the Perth to Inverness road in a single day in August. Sir John MacDonald, an eminent judge and President of the Scottish Automobile Club, had himself visited Pitlochry during the touring season to find it 'crawling with motorcars'. The Secretary of the SAC also gave evidence and was convinced that for the majority of Scottish hotels and inns, the motor car had increased custom. He cited the case of one country inn '25 miles from any railway' which had previously been without any customers for days on end, but now was averaging about eighty persons a week.[34] But there was a downside: as early as 1908 roads authorities in Stirlingshire and Perthshire, through which so much traffic passed, were complaining about the damage being done to their roads, by what were described as heavy touring cars, some from England. It was not just the number of such cars but their speed which was cutting up road surfaces, for which not the visitors but the locals had to pay.

The loss of revenue from those who would previously have travelled first class by train was a serious problem for the railways, though they did fight back by offering back to carry cars long distance, or to avoid, as did the Highland Railway, more difficult stretches of road and ferry crossings. A photograph from June 1909[35] shows a Wolseley Tourer loaded on a railway waggon in Strathcarron station for carriage to Kyle of Lochalsh, which avoided both indifferent roads and an awkward ferry crossing at Stromeferry. The coming of the motor car altered how the wealthy travelled to and within Scotland, and where, and as hotelkeepers noticed, the pattern of stay. Tourers by car stayed only a few nights at most before moving on, whereas those who came by train tended to longer stays. For tourism in general the motor car, the motor bus and the charabanc were nothing but good news; for other forms of transport the story was rather different. Motor transport, with chauffeurs and drivers rather than coachmen and grooms, for travel and tourism was progressively to take over from horse power, a process completed when the last horse-drawn tourist service in Scotland between Stronachlachar and Callander was withdrawn in the summer of 1937; it was as complete a change as the displacement in agriculture of the horse by the tractor after the Second World War. The railways put up more resistance, adjusting where they could to new patterns of travel by putting on, for example, cycle carriages. And they were still the first choice for most. But the motor bus was eating into their traffic, and the evening tours the bus companies could offer in the summer were very popular amongst a working-class clientele. Charabanc tours offered an ever increasing range of day trips from resorts. But even before the First World War, bus tours to resorts in England were becoming popular. In the nineteenth century better transport helped tourism to Scotland, notably the transatlantic steamships, which carried increasing numbers of Americans; in the twentieth better transport started to carry increasing numbers of Scots – not just the upper class – away from Scotland. While ownership of even a second-hand motor in the inter-war years was beyond most people's pockets, motor bikes were within range of artisan budgets, and they allowed a much wider exploration of destinations within and beyond Scotland. Recently discovered photograph albums show a series of motor cycle camping trips made by a Glasgow joiner through Europe in the late 1930s to France, Germany and Switzerland, the last in August 1939 fortunately completed before the outbreak of war.[36]

The more that people could travel cheaply, the more people would, and it would not be Scotland necessarily that was the beneficiary, as was to be underlined much more starkly with the coming of cheap air travel in the 1960s. This proved a very mixed blessing, as was true of the associated development of direct transatlantic flights to and from Scotland; more visitors came, but more Scots of all classes holidayed abroad, which was good for Scots holidaymakers but not for some of Scotland's once popular resorts.

Notes

1 Barrett, John R., *Mr James Allan. The Journey of a Lifetime*, (Forres, 2004), p. 120: 'I met with some who had empty horses, from whom I got one betwixt the ferries and sent back that which I had. I had two miles to go on foot to Newmore after crossing the ferry of Inverbrackie, for I could not get a horse for hire. But got a boy who carried my boots & clock the most of the way.'
2 Walker, Carol Kyros, *Walking North with Keats*, (New Haven, CT, 1992), p. 162.
3 See, for example Smith, Walter A., *Hill Paths in Scotland*, (Edinburgh, 1926).
4 Murray, *Companion*, p. 11.
5 Wordsworth, Dorothy *Recollections of a Tour made in Scotland, 1803* (Introduction by Carol Kyros Walker, New Haven, CT, 1997), p. 140.
6 *Callander Advertiser*, 18 April 1931, 'Severing a link with the past'.
7 NSA Vol. 7 Argyleshire, Parish of Dunoon, p. 608. He cited the experience of a colleague on Rothesay, who had twenty years previously taken nearly three days to make a good passage from Rothesay to Greenock, whereas it now took but two days.
8 Senex, *Glasgow Past and Present*, (Glasgow, 1851), p. 414.
9 De Selincourt, E., *Journals of Dorothy Wordsworth*, Vol. 2 (London, 1952) pp. 378–89. Dorothy added 'that steam boats are always in a hurry and take noise and commotion along with them'.
10 Translation of an elegy by the Gaelic poet Allan MacDougall on Allan MacDougall of Glengarry, drowned along with his two daughters when the steamship the *Stirling*

Castle was wrecked in 1828. Cited in Robbins, Nick S. and Meek, Donald, *The Kingdom of MacBrayne*, (Edinburgh, 2006), p. 8.

11 Poem by an Edinburgh publican, Willison Glass, cited by A. Graham Lappin, *The Loch Lomond Steamers*. Vale of Leven website.

12 Paterson, Alan J. S., *The Golden Years of the Clyde Steamers*, (Newton Abbot, 1969), pp. 196–202.

13 Walton, John K., *Blackpool*, (Edinburgh, 1998), Chapter 3, 'Blackpool in the Railway Age'.

14 Walton, John K., *The English Seaside Resort. A Social History*, (Leicester, 1983), Chapter 8, styles of holidaymaking: conflict and resolution.

15 *Glasgow Herald*, 1 July 1868.

16 Durie, Alastair J., *Scotland for the Holidays*, (East Linton, 2003), p. 19.

17 Durie, Alastair J., 'Tourism and the Railways in Scotland', in Evans, A. K. B. and Gough, J. V., *The Impact of the Railway on Society in Britain. Essays in Honour of Jack Simmons*, (Aldershot, 2003), p. 202.

18 Marshall, Peter, *Peebles Railways*, (Oxford, 2005), p. 26.

19 This section draws on Anne Cameron, 'The Development of Tourism in Dunkeld & Birnam', Undergraduate Dissertation, University of Glasgow, Department of Economic History, 1997.

20 Burnett, John 'Some Perspectives on Railways and Railway life', in *Scottish Life and Society, Volume 8, Transport and Communications*, p. 187.

21 Cook, Thomas, *Twenty Years on the Rails*, (Leicester, 1861), p. 21.

22 Duncan, John, 'The Peebles Railway', PhD, Open University, 2004, Appendix 7.

23 *Peeblesshire Advertiser,* Saturday 12 July 1884.

24 Freeman, John George, *Three Men and a Bradshaw*, (London, 2015).

25 Another card with the same scene, for the Dumfries & Moniaive branch, carries the couplet 'First-class passengers keep your seats, Third-class passengers get out and push.'

26 Furness, Richard, *Poster to Poster: Railway Journeys in Art. Volume One. Scotland*, (Gloucester, 2009).

27 Mullay, Alexander J., *Scottish Region. A History 1948–1973*, (Chalford, 2006), p. 63.

28 Hajducki, Andrew M., *The North Berwick and Gullane Branch Lines*, (Oxford, 1992), p. 129.

29 Griffin, Brian, *Cycling in Victorian Ireland*, (Dublin, 2006).

30 *Campbeltown Courier*, 23 July 1898.

31 I am grateful to Mrs Isobel Robertson for permission to quote from this journal, which is called 'Wheel wanderings', and is currently held in Stirling University Library.

32 Cited in Simpson, *Wish You Were Still Here*, p. 81.

33 Plowden, William, *The Motor Car and Politics, 1896–1970*, (London, 1971), p. 81.

34 Smith, Robert J., *Precis of Evidence given on behalf of the RAC to the Royal Commission on Motor Traffic*, dated 17 November 1905.

35 Grieves, Robert, *Scotland's Motoring Century*, (Paisley, 1999), p. 56.

36 Family papers, courtesy of Ms Jacqueline Young.

4 Forms of tourism

There developed a complex of tourist flows in Scottish tourism, varied by class and by interest, and drawn by different aspects of Scotland's tourist portfolio. While time and income were key determinants of the volume of tourism, the choice of which holiday stream in which to participate was shaped by a variety of factors. Significant, as will be shown, were class and gender, age or (ill) health, scientific or sporting enthusiasms, literary and cultural fashion. But there were some lesser and quirky flows. A different legal framework in Scotland had led to marriage tourism from England since the 1750s, at Gretna, Coldstream and other places just over the border. There was even a little divorce tourism, because divorce was cheaper in Scotland.[1] One notorious case was that of Lord Paget. who wanted to get himself divorced so he could marry Lady Charlotte Wellesley (sister-in-law of Wellington). The guilty couple *plus his wife* eventually had to head to Edinburgh because Scots Law allowed the husband to be divorced on the ground of adultery alone, which English law did not. In October 1810 the *Examiner* reported, 'Such is the consequence of a jaunt to a Scot's[sic]*Watering Place*! Talk of Brighton or Margate indeed.' The *Morning Chronicle* commented that 'Lord P and Lady P and Lady AW have all *by pure accident* taken up their residence in Scotland lately.'[2]

From the 1820s onwards the honeymoon couple became a familiar sight in Scotland and their proud signatures a feature of hotel registers. A solicitor from Wolverhampton bumped into a friend with his new bride in Edinburgh in August 1868 on their way to the Castle, but he would not disrupt their privacy by calling out to them.[3] A honeymoon that went sour was that of an Irish cad, or so the press labelled him, Major Yelverton, who had gone through in August 1857 a form of marriage in Edinburgh with a Miss Longworth, they having met in the Crimea where she had been nursing. At the end of September they went on a honeymoon tour on horseback through the Highlands, signing hotel and castle registers as man and wife. On return however, she 'blooming after her Highland jaunt',[4] things were to sour. Yelverton threw her over for a rich widow, arguing that the form of marriage he had gone through with Miss Longworth was not valid. It was fought through the courts but Maria Theresa Longworth lost, to the dismay of her many supporters.

Scotland had a wide range of attractions, whether scenic or historic, seaside or spa, sport or literature. But not all drew the same clientele in terms of class, income or gender. Some forms consistently did: sporting tourism in the form of grouse-shooting, deer-stalking or salmon fishing was generally and still remains a male, upper-class, moneyed sport. A Royal enthusiasm, this drew wealthy English, Continental and American participants. By contrast, golf in Scotland at the tourism resorts, it is argued, straddled social class, and mountaineering also fits this model. Some streams changed in terms of their social composition over time. The Scottish seaside started as an upper-class health fashion, with bathing machines and beach huts, but changed quite quickly to take in middle- and working-class visitors, which caused considerable social tensions. The seaside was a place not of integration but rather of layering of classes and behaviour. While the practitioners in field sports were male, they increasingly brought their families with them, which prompted a need for better accommodation and a range of evening and other activities to keep them amused. Some resorts remained more select, others more popular, but over time the upper classes largely abandoned the Scottish seaside for the Continent, either the Riviera or an upmarket spa. Some of the middle class began to follow suit, and then the working class post 1960.

The rise of tourism during the nineteenth century in and to Scotland seems to have an air of inevitability about it, thanks to rising incomes, more free time and better transport. But while it is true that tourism was developing as an industry, and that demand for travel was booming, it is worth underlining that there was no guarantee that Scotland would be the main or sole beneficiary. Government took no part in shaping where people chose to go; it was a highly competitive industry in which resort competed against resort, region against region and country against country. The better-off had always had choice. But in the nineteenth century an increasing proportion of the population did have more choice, as part of the leisured class, particularly the 'middling sorts', and their sights were not set only on their own country. Some started to follow the lead given by their social superiors and to look not just to England but to the Continent. There had, of course long been the Grand Tour, the flow of aristocratic and moneyed people to France, Italy and Greece, for culture and education, health and amusement, a movement in which upper-class Scots had participated, a journeying for months or even years. It is sometimes implied that the Grand Tour came to end *c.*1830, and in one sense it did. What had once been a leisurely experience only for the elite widened with the coming of the railways to take in a broader clientele drawn from the middle and professional classes whose travelling was much more focused. The Patersons from Montgomerie in Ayrshire, who travelled to France and Italy in 1848–49 were but one family among this new constituency of tourists. A staunch United Presbyterian family, they were taken aback in Paris by how different the French observance of Sunday was; 'I never saw anything like the way the Sabbath is profaned – all the shops were open – everything was more gay than on a weekday'.[5]

This encroachment on what had been their exclusive territory met with considerable hostility from those who had once had Britain, the Continent and Egypt to themselves. It was resented by people such as Babbington, an English snob who complained in October 1864 that he had gone to the North East of Scotland during the spring equinox when he had hoped to be quite certain of escaping all Southern tourists. But he had had no such luck, either in Scotland or indeed Egypt.

> What beasts the English are – The middle orders when they go touring! These railroads are the great curse of this country. How I wish we lived in the good old days when men had to fight their way from Edinburgh to London with pistols at their saddle bow and snobs [very illegible] were kept in their proper places, when one might ascend the Great Pyramid without finding a lady practising her quadrille steps on the top which I almost did.[6]

The nineteenth century saw the growth in Britain of a prosperous middle and professional class. Bankers, doctors, lawyers, clerics and the annuitant or person living on private means were increasingly familiar figures on tour and at resorts, especially after the channel crossing ceased to be quite such a daunting prospect, thanks to the new steamers. And they were the constituency who might well think of a holiday on the Continent, at a spa, or the Riviera. Or even further afield, as a new form of pilgrimage revived, that of Protestants to Palestine (the Holy Land), or the Land of the Bible. But for Catholics there was to be no Lourdes in Scotland, not even a Knock, merely Carfin, a minor grotto near Motherwell, which opened in the 1920s. Pilgrimage was not significant in Scotland, whereas honeymooning, as we have seen, was.

While culture, scenery and sightseeing shaped where many tourists went, the search for health was behind much travel. The reality was that, while more and more people had the means to look for cure or alleviation, orthodox medicine's capacity to respond was still very limited. While nineteenth-century surgery was advancing dramatically after the arrival of anaesthetics and asepsis, so that once highly dangerous procedures became commonplace, medicine's curative armoury remained limited. . For non-surgical conditions, there was no such transformation, even if you had money. Diagnosis was better, but cures limited. Public health programmes helped, and vaccines were developed against some diseases but not TB, no disappointment greater than Koch's tuberculin in 1891 of which so much was hoped but which proved a spectacular failure. The result was a large and growing constituency of health seekers, either genuinely unwell or the 'sick well' prepared to travel and to try new curative regimes either in Britain or on the Continent, or further afield. Much of present-day health tourism is cosmetic – for example, dental work in Hungary – but in the nineteenth century it was to find remedies for afflictions such as gout and rheumatism, or the alleviation of chest and lung conditions. Or just for a tonic to a jaded system. It was good business for the transport companies and the health resorts alike. Indeed, it was suggested, tongue in cheek[7] that the railway companies had bought up the medical profession to get them to persuade their patients – with means – to travel for a change of air. What was also welcome was that health tourism was spread throughout the year; there had long been a tradition of wealthy Britons overwintering on the Riviera ('les hivernants') at places such as Mentone and Nice, but to this was added in the later nineteenth century a growing traffic of invalids in Switzerland, where the dry high Alpine winter air was believed to have healing properties for TB.[8] The sick of Europe hunted around, trying this and that – mountain air, spa waters, dietary regimes – some of which were quack, others pseudo-scientific, and a few of which seemed to work for some sufferers, perhaps through the placebo effect. The questing around of the moderately well-off is caught nicely in an autobiographical account by a lady painter ('J. D. A.')[9] of some years' travel around Europe in the early 1890s. She had a chronic if unspecified weakness and sought relief through almost every medical regime on offer: hydropathy, magnetism, homeopathy, vegetarianism, bread regimes, goat's milk, grape and beef dietary cures, baths of every kind – hot, cold, mud, brine and pine. And so on. Her search took her to Geneva, Marienbad and other European spas, to health centres in Scotland and England, and to Deeside, where she had been assured that the air itself was usually a cure. But not in her case.

As is clear from her experience, the medical marketplace was full to over-flowing with competing therapies, treatments and regimes, of varying value, with thousands of resorts stridently competing against each other. In France alone in 1893 there were nearly 400 recognised spas.[10] Not all European spas were large and high class: there were many lesser centres which were much more sober. Some centres specialised in just the one medical therapy; others had a portfolio. How to choose was therefore very difficult, and not surprisingly an immense medical literature emerged to aid their selection. Some reports, such those by Macpherson, Weber or Madden[11] were impartial surveys of which resorts and climates were best for a given condition. Others were more partisan, written by doctors with a local practice, and as such to be taken with a pinch of salt. The *Lancet* savaged a promotional publication in 1891 on *Baden Baden as a Watering Place*, which had been written by a consulting physician there – Dr Fry at the Sanatorium – as having been written with a 'confident dogmatism, but a slender foundation of assured fact'. There were new treat-ments, new facilities and new locations, which tempted the sick: North Africa, Malta or the Azores. Madeira, now on the tourist map thanks to the steam-ship, was regarded as particularly good for bronchitis – 'it has been 'long known as a haven for weak lungs'– with its absence of wind and 'absolute freedom from dust'.[12]

Not coming for their health, but for cultural reasons, was a new mass flow, that of North Americans. There had always been American visitors to Britain, prepared to risk the 3,000 miles' sea voyage by sail, which might take up to six weeks, but the arrival of the transatlantic steamers, which eventually cut crossing times to under a week, transformed the situation. Instead of handfuls, from the 1860s tens of thousands came each year to Europe, with Britain their first port of call, and the Old World became for many the destination for a once-in-a-lifetime grand tour. And it is clear that while some were rich – the multimillionaire Gordon Bennet, Jnr, owner of the *New York Times* and sponsor of Stanley's expedition to find Livingstone, and his ilk – many were not: what Barbara Lockwood[13] calls a new type of traveller – clerics, university school teachers and students. The steamship allowed people of lesser means to 'do Europe' in their version of the Grand Tour, assisted by publications such as Rolfe's *Satchel Guide to Europe*, first published in 1872 and which had gone through forty-five editions by 1915, intended as a guide for the 'vacation tourist who can spend but three or four months abroad'.[14] It was much used by schoolteachers, college parties and the like, perhaps even clerks. Janet Gair, who was on holiday in Scotland, sent a postcard of Edinburgh and the Forth Bridge in August 1907 to Annie Hopkins at the post office in Kansas City. Her message was 'enjoying every minute – Wish all the P.O clerks could have such a fine holiday as I am having this summer. Do not work too hard.'[15] Shearers of Stirling, who had published a guide to the Trossachs which included the story of Scott's *Lady of the Lake*, received letters of thanks from American teachers who had bought it while on holiday in Scotland. 'I find it has been very helpful in teaching the poem', wrote one New York teacher. The 1915 edition also included a letter from a German schoolmaster from Dusseldorf who was ordering some additional copies as he would like his class to read the book.[16] War presumably torpedoed that.

It is not possible to put a figure on how many Americans visited Europe each year but the sudden outbreak of war in August 1914 caught, or so it was estimated, at least 100–150,000 Americans in Europe. Some were rich, such as Cornelius Vanderbuilt, who was motoring in Austria, but most were not. Some were German Americans visiting relatives, others were Afro-American musicians on tour, but many were female school teachers. There was panic, and the American government was forced to take an active role in bringing back these stranded tourists. They came back, but not their luggage; travellers returning to New York said there was baggage piled to the height of two storeys in front of Cologne cathedral. And not until 1919 was the American tourist again to be seen in Europe. We cannot know how many of these 1914 tourists had visited Scotland as part of their tour, but it would have been a significant proportion. Most of the Americans made land first in Ireland and then crossed the Irish Sea, taking in sights in Britain before they passed onto the Continent. And this was no new pattern. As *Chamber's Journal* remarked in October 1887, 'we in Britain see almost without exception every American who leaves his country.' We do know that thousands did come to Scotland in the later nineteenth century. As one American responded when asked if he had liked Scotland 'I should think I did. It is Switzerland with a clean population and without a tribe of robbing hotel keepers.'[17]

There are no official statistics to confirm how many Americans came to Scotland but a useful barometer is to look at the numbers of American visitors who signed the visitors' register at Abbotsford, Sir Walter Scott's home, which was high on the must-see agenda of the educated American. Thomas Cook made room in 1873 in his fast-paced promotional tour of Britain and Europe for American educationalists to visit Abbotsford; he himself signed the register there on 7 July – 'Thomas Cook, London with a party of 137 American Teachers'. What the registers show is that there was a twenty-fold increase in American visitors between the 1840s and the 1880s, from a hundred or so to a couple of thousand annually. There were the big names: Jefferson Davis in July 1869, and Ulysses S. Grant in May 1883, and any number of American clerics, but also growing numbers of tour and college parties; in August 1898 the house received a group of ladies from the newly established Pomona College near Los Angeles. What the registers also show are downturns, notably in 1893, when the number of Americans at Abbotsford fell by three-quarters, a fall which other sources confirm to have been general throughout Scotland. The *Railway News* in September 1893 reported that there appeared to have been a very great 'falling off' in the number of Americans travelling North, and the *Scotsman* newspaper confirmed this: 'In a good season some-thing like 10,000 Americans will pass through Edinburgh; this year 1,000 will be the number.'[18] A variety of factors were blamed, not least the Chicago Exposition, which it was thought kept many tourists at home. After the English, the Americans were the largest flow of tourists to Scotland.

By contrast the number of visitors from the Continent were low: far more English and Scots went to the Continent than ever came to Britain from the Continent, as unbalanced a flow as the lack of British visitors (as opposed to emigrants) was to America. There were odd years when the numbers of French or German visitors picked up. The *Oban Times* in August 1901 noted that there had been a pleasant French invasion of Scotland this year. 'In Oban and the highlands generally, French tourists with their polite ways have certainly appeared this summer in larger numbers than have ever before been seen, and they are welcome guests.'[19] This influx appears, however, to have been excep-tional, not that we can determine with any precision the true number of visitors from the Continent or indeed England in any given year. No count was kept at the Scottish border as to who was visiting from where. We know more about individual visitors through their travel accounts than how many, as with Felix Mendelssohn from Prussia in 1829, or Krystyn Lach-Szyrma from Poland in 1820–1824, Hans Christian Anderson from Denmark in 1847, Garibaldi from Italy in 1854 and Jules Verne from France in 1859. There are, however, some pointers as to how many came from where. Analysis of the addresses given by those visiting Abbotsford in the nineteenth century shows that the number of European visitors was but a fraction of those from North America. In 1868, for example, of the 6,229 callers at the house, nearly half were from Scotland, one third English, but only 119 (1.2 per cent) were from Europe.[20] It may not be entirely safe to generalise from a particular destination to a general pattern throughout Scotland, but Abbotsford was high on the agenda for the cultured European visitor, and if anything may have attracted more than its fair share of Continental tourists. Theodore Fontane from Germany, with two friends, called at Abbotsford in August 1858, regarding the drive to Scott's house as 'a kind of pilgrimage, a duty which I had fulfilled, a step to which my heart urged me'.[21]

Travel agencies did fan the American flow to Europe, and that of Britons to Europe and the Middle East, but they had little success in stimulating any matching flow from France or Germany. But travel agencies were important in the growth of tourism, particularly perhaps for that first generation of travellers who had not travelled before, and who welcomed all the planning being done for them. And Cook did that, with tour timetables, travel and accommodation all pre-arranged, and a reliable tour escort with them, perhaps Cook himself or one of his sons, or a trustworthy agent such as W. E. Franklin of Newcastle, a temperance enthusiast like Cook himself. It was a formula that worked and of which many took advantage. Cook himself estimated that in his first decade of operations in Scotland between 1841 and 1851, he had frequently taken as many as 5,000 visitors in a season, drawn from every part of England.[22] The *Scotsman* reported on 4 July 1861 that the first of Mr Cook's summer excursion trains had arrived in Edinburgh, bringing with them an aggregate of no less than 1,400 or 1,500 excursionists in three parties: one from Leeds, a second from Penzance and the South West of England, and the third from Newcastle. Some visitors to Scotland, of course, went their own way, by hook and crook rather than Cook, as Trollope put it.

The role of Thomas Cook has tended to overshadow the work done by other agencies, such as John Frame or Henry Gaze, and that of the railway companies, each of whom had their own excursion departments. In part this is because Cook's records have survived, whereas those of competitors such as Gaze and Frame, which became bankrupt, have not and as a result history has simply ignored these firms. But Gaze's did operate a big programme of excursions within Britain and tours to the Continent, (see Figure 4.1[23]). It did considerable business in Scotland, where in the 1890s it had more offices than Cook, at Dundee, Greenock and Aberdeen, for example.

According to Brendon, 'the House of Cook dominated the Edwardian travel scene',[24] and if one man was responsible for the rise of Victorian tourism it was Thomas Cook; he made, as Simmons said, 'the largest single contribution of any man to the growth of this new industry, and fully earned the titles given him: the Field Marshal of Tourism, the Emperor of Tourism. William Chambers, Lord Provost of Edinburgh, congratulated Cook in October 1865 on his 'gigantic system of excursion parties'.[25] The firm's profits rose from about £5,000 a year in the 1870s to £20,000 a year in the late 1880s and £119,000 annually between 1909 and 1913. Of course he and his firm caught a rising tide, but his organisational and promotional skills, and those of his sons, the reliability of his staff and the capacity to reinvest revenue in the business were positives; not for him, because of his Baptist background,

4

CALEDONIAN AND LONDON & NORTH-WESTERN RAILWAYS.

HENRY GAZE & SONS, 142 STRAND, LONDON,

CONTINENTAL TOURIST AGENTS OF THE COMPANIES,

Have arranged, in connection with the Excursions from the North to London, advertised on the other side, the following

CHEAP CONDUCTED TRIPS

To PARIS & BACK,

STARTING FROM GLASGOW AND EDINBURGH, THURSDAY, 16th JULY, AND LEAVING LONDON, FRIDAY AND SATURDAY, 17th AND 18th JULY, 1896.

Via Dieppe from Victoria (L. B. & S. C.) 8.50 p.m., or London Bridge (L. B. & S. C.) 9.0 p.m., Via Calais from Charing Cross 8.15 p.m., or Cannon Street 8.20 p.m.

EACH TICKET INCLUDES—

RAILWAY AND STEAM-PACKET JOURNEY FROM SCOTLAND TO PARIS AND BACK.
HOTEL ACCOMMODATION AND BOARD IN PARIS, consisting of MEAT BREAKFAST; DINNER at the Table d'Hote; BED-CHAMBER, Light and Service; commencing with Breakfast on the morning after departure from London, and terminating with Dinner on the fifth day.
ESCORT OF A COMPETENT CONDUCTOR who will travel from London to Paris via Dieppe.
THREE DAYS' CARRIAGE TRIPS for visiting the principal sights of Paris.
OMNIBUSES to the Hotels in Paris: COPY OF GAZE'S GUIDE BOOK; ENTRANCE FEES, GRATUITIES, HOTEL FEES, &c.

TERMS PER TICKET FROM EDINBURGH OR GLASGOW.

THIRD CLASS BETWEEN SCOTLAND AND LONDON—BEYOND AS UNDER:—

WITHOUT DRIVES.				HOTEL.	RAILWAY.		WITH DRIVES.		
* 4 Day. Dieppe.	* 4 Day. Calais.	* 5 Day. Dieppe.	* 5 Day. Calais.	Class.	Class.	Section.	Via Dieppe.	Via Calais or Boulogne.	
£ s. d.	£ s. d.	£ s. d.	£ s. d.				£ s. d.	£ s. d.	
3 18 0	4 2 0	4 4 6	4 8 6	A	Third	A	4 18 0	5 2 6	
4 2 3	4 9 6	4 8 9	4 16 0	A	Second	C	5 2 3	5 7 6	
4 5 6	4 9 6	4 14 0	4 18 0	B	Third	B	5 4 0	5 8 6	
4 9 9	4 17 0	4 18 3	5 5 6	B	Second	D	5 8 3	5 15 6	
4 18 9			5 7 9	B	First	E	5 17 3		

* Accommodation terminates with Dinner in Paris on fourth and fifth days respectively.

These Tickets are available for 16 days.

Class A Hotel Accommodation, used for Sections A and C, is inferior to Class B, used for the other sections.

RETURN JOURNEY.—The homeward Tickets are available at any time within Fourteen Days by the Night Services—via Dieppe, from St. Lazare Station 9.0 p.m.; via Calais, from Nord Station 6.0 p.m., or via Boulogne, 6.0 p.m. The return to the North may be completed by any Ordinary Train within Sixteen Days.

PASSENGERS MAY PROCEED TO THE CONTINENT ON FRIDAY, SATURDAY, OR SUNDAY EVENINGS.

HENRY GAZE & SONS HAVE ALSO ARRANGED FOR THE FOLLOWING

CONDUCTED TOURS:—

To ANTWERP and BRUSSELS, leaving London, FRIDAYS, 17th and 31st July.
" SPA, LIEGE, and THE ARDENNES, leaving London, SATURDAY, 25th July.
" THE RHINE and BELGIUM, leaving London, SATURDAY, 18th July.
" THE BLACK FOREST and SWITZERLAND, leaving London, FRIDAY, 17th July.

For full particulars see Gaze's Conducted Tour Programme.

GAZE'S INDEPENDENT TRAVEL TICKETS.

THIRD CLASS BETWEEN SCOTLAND AND LONDON—BEYOND AS UNDER:—

From LONDON to	1st Class.	2nd Class.	3rd Class.
	£ s. d.	£ s. d.	£ s. d.
Paris, via Newhaven and Dieppe, Excursion, ...	3 4 3	2 15 3	2 11 0
Paris, via Dover and Calais, Excursion, ...	...	3 2 6	2 15 0
Antwerp, Brussels and back, via Harwich, ...	3 11 6	2 14 0	2 10 4
Amsterdam and back, via Harwich, Hook of Holland, and the Hague, ...	4 0 11	3 3 7	...
Harwich, Hook of Holland, Cologne, Aix-la-Chapelle, Brussels, Antwerp, Harwich, London, ...	5 0 1	3 14 6	...
Same Tour, including Hague and Amsterdam, ...	5 6 0	3 19 0	...
Dieppe, Paris, Geneva, Lausanne, Fribourg, Berne, Thun, Interlaken, Neuchatel, Paris, Dieppe, and London, ...	8 4 4	6 11 4	...

GAZE'S CONDUCTED TRIP PROGRAMME

free on application, or post free for stamp, contains details of the Season's Tours to ANTWERP, BRUSSELS, and PARIS; HOLLAND, THE RHINE, and BELGIUM; BLACK FOREST and SWITZERLAND.

Together with extended Tours in GERMANY, AUSTRIA, ITALY, NORWAY, &c.

Passengers for the above, or any of Gaze's Tours, may secure Tickets at either of the following Agents—

D. DUNCAN, 63a Princes Street, EDINBURGH. J. SAMUEL, Booking Office, Railway Station, STIRLING.
D. MARTIN, Cathcart Street Station, GREENOCK. W. GREIG, Booking Office, General Station, ABERDEEN.
J. M'NEE, Booking Office, Railway Station, DUNDEE (West). J. M'CROW, Railway Booking Office, PERTH.

GLASGOW—J. LONIE, Booking Office, Central Station.

McCORQUODALE & Co. Limited, Printers, Glasgow and London.

Figure 4.1 Gaze handbill for 1896, showing the range of the firm's tours to Scotland and from Scotland (Author's collection)

the temptation to spend on grouse moors or yachts or the other symbols of wealth. His early reputation was made by tours in Scotland, the first of which was in 1846, and his parties, sometimes conducted by him personally, were to be in Scotland two or three times a year thereafter and Scotland remained a main theatre of operations. It was of Cook's tourists that John Henry Newman complained. Staying at Abbotsford in July 1872 he was greatly irritated by them peering through the windows even at six in the morning. Whether it was a Cook's party we know not, but for Newman (and many of his class) any middle-class tourist was a 'Cookite'. It can be argued that Scotland made Cook: it was there that he tried out the model of the conducted tour which was to be so generally successful, and Scotland established Cook's reputation, which was well able to survive the scandal of the golden eagle shot by him or one of his party on Iona in 1861. It was never clear who was actually responsible, and it seems unlikely that Cook ever carried a firearm, but he was the one attacked by *The Times* as an 'Eagle Murderer'!

Thomas Cook & Son was prepared to take an interest in any kind of event to which crowds could be drawn from a distance: Bank Holiday events, Queen Victoria's Diamond Jubilee, English football cup finals, the Olympic Games of 1908, public executions in Paris,[26] and it could provide for any kind of independent traveller to almost any destination at any time of year. But its particular strength lay, as it had done since its foundation in the 1840s, in the conducted tour, with transport and accommodation precisely choreographed. It catered for those who wished to tour within Britain or to Europe or to the Middle East or indeed India and the Far East. The fashionable destination of Egypt, as far as tourists were concerned, was the firm's monopoly: 'Cook simply owns Egypt' was one American verdict in 1897, and in 1891 a third of its staff (978 out of 2,692) were employed there. It had offices and agencies throughout Britain, in Europe, and in North America, in South Africa, Australasia and even Japan. Its memorial window to the dead of the First World War, uniquely for a British business, was to carry the names of German and Austrian employees as well as those who were British or French. Its hotel coupons were widely accepted – by forty-five hotels in Algeria alone in 1911 – and its banking department was able to provide what now would be called a traveller's cheque, an aspect of the business which was highly profitable to the firm as well as useful to the tourist. As a company, Cook's was well aware of the value of publicity and promotion, and had a widely read magazine, *The Excursionist*, later Cook's *Travellers Gazette*, which showed the level of destination marketing and promotion to attract the growing travelling elite to its programme of tours within Britain and abroad. It also published guidebooks to key destinations. There was a well-staffed and well-paid accountant's' department at the Head Office in London. In short, this was a progressive and efficiently run company. Paternalist it may have been: John Cook (son of Thomas) required younger members of staff (those under twenty-five) to ask his permission before they married, but to work for the firm was a sought-after position.

To summarise, the nineteenth century saw an immense expansion in European tourism. Scenery and culture, as they always had, drew ever increasing numbers of British travellers, as did climate and cure, travellers drawn from not just the wealthy elite. This flow was supplemented from mid-century onwards by a new influx of American vacationers, arriving in the early summer, schoolteachers and the like, doing Europe on a modest budget in what was a once-in-a-life-time holiday. There was growth in winter tourism, especially to Switzerland, which became both a sanatorium and a playground, thanks to tobogganing and skating. For the well-off, the possibilities were almost infinite, depending on taste – a cruise in Norwegian fjords, a month at a German spa, a stay on the Riviera, where the royalty of Europe gathered, including Queen Victoria. She disapproved strongly of the casino at Monte Carlo, (as the contemporary triplet had it, 'Cannes is for living, Monte Carlo is for gambling and Mentone for dying') but joined with enthusiasm, despite her age and rank, in the battle of the flowers at Grasse.[27]

Scotland tapped into the new American passion for vacationing. Its literary shrines at Abbotsford and Alloway were flagged as essential viewing, a tour through the Trossachs mandatory, and Edinburgh a required point of stay. But Scotland was more than scenery and history, important though these were: for many English visitors, especially young men, Scotland was a sporting play-ground, for grouse and deer, trout and salmon. But there were also those who were interested in its natural history, geology and botany, following in the footsteps of Dr Joseph Banks, and his visit in 1772 to Staffa. Dr Edward Daniel Clarke, later Professor of Mineralogy at Cambridge University, visited there in 1797 to study the local rock formations.[28] Geology students were regular visi-tors to Oban to examine 'breccia', a compound of fused and broken rocks found extensively in the area. Charles St John was one of many whose wildlife sketches captivated Victorian audiences. There were the enthusiastic amateurs. Manchester Botanists' Association was enthralled in December 1876[29] by a talk by three of its number on their excursion that July to the Grampians in search of rare Alpine plants, which, having found them, they then collected, thus, of course, making them rarer still. University reading groups were another kind of summer visitor to be found in places: Oxonians or Cantabs, as Thomas Grierson[30] scornfully remarked, 'who under the imposing term "reading" think of little else than amusement'. Cuthbert Bede agreed with him, pointing at their allegedly necessary reading paraphernalia of fishing rods, gun cases and riding whips.[31] At Oban, a favourite haunt for reading parties, the names of seven different Oxford and Cambridge colleges were recorded in the visitor lists for 1891.[32] Many of these scholars stayed for at least three weeks, some even residing for the whole summer. These reading parties comprised four to six students who generally took a house for the duration of their stay.

Nineteenth-century tourism in Scotland was a kaleidoscope: excursion parties tied to a schedule, families off to the coast or inland for the summer, young men on their way to the hills and the moors, clergymen recharging their batteries, honeymooners, day trippers and weekenders.

The variety is well caught in W. C. Dendy (italics my emphasis)[33]:

> The roof of the Sunbeam is crowded with a group of smiling voyagers. There sit a brace of the true *devotees of beautiful nature*…close to them stands their contrast, the *mere holiday tourist*, gazing around like an automaton, looking at everything and seeing nothing. And there is a *very spicy sot*, incessantly plying at his flask of Glenlivet, yet no more inspired by the blue hills of Lorn, that rise in majesty before him than with the russet molehill of Primrose in front of his London villa. There is the petit-maitre from London, the *mere routine excursionist*, decked out in all the exuberant fashion of Regent Street; now with lacklustre eye, poring over the dirty leaves of his itinerary, and teasing the man at the helm with idle enquiries….There is the *wandering fisher* with his wicker and fly rod…*the stone cutter* with his wallet and hammer and he is come to pummel the side of Ben Nevis for pebbles, or Ben Macdhui for the choicer cairngorm. There is the *flycatcher* with his green net for the ensnaring of gnats…, and the *botanist* with his tin basket.. There is the *desecrating vagrant*, boasting of his immortal name done in black paint on Schloss Drachenfels: and now his highest pride is to carve his initials on one of the holy tombs on Iona, chip off a morsel of moulding from the prentice pillar in Roslin, and filch one of Macalister's stalactites in the spar cave of Strathaird. There is the double-*refined gallant* in lavender kids, pestering the *girls* with his flummery and all the *dowagers*.

What stands out emphatically is that tourism, in one or other of its many forms, was no longer the preserve of the moneyed few. It had become part of the experience of almost every section of society, particularly industrial, urban and professional Scotland, with only the very poor and the farming community left out. The change was evident to those in the industry. A steamboat proprietor in 1861 who ran services on the west coast of Scotland said that once only a few wealthy tourists had come to see Iona and Staffa, but that he now saw 'large numbers of the middle and humbler class of society coming out this way'.[34]

It should be remembered that some had little or no choice in where they went: children or servants, for example; or when they went: workers with but a week's holiday in July. Southern sportsmen often took their head keeper with them when they came north to act as their loader, a kind of 'paid holiday.'[35] Children and servants went to where their families or employers chose. A census taken at Stonehaven in August 1898, cited by Simpson[36] found that of the 1,433 visitors in the town, no less than 165 were maids, brought to look after the 298 children under fourteen. They did have time off, and the pleasure of a change of air.

Clearly the lower the income the less choice that people had, and lack of disposable income tied poorer people to holidaying in their immediate vicinity, with the poorest reliant on church or corporation or charity for an outing, or perhaps they were able to stay with friends and relations in the countryside. In 1881 Mary Allison and her husband, a storeman in Glasgow, spent their week away in Cowal with her older sister, a holiday that cost them only their steamer fares.[37] This kind of holidaymaking, although below the radar, must have been prevalent in a country where so many city dwellers were recent migrants from the countryside and still had kith and kin there. An outing away had become a birthright for nearly all Scots.

Notes

1 Muirhead, Andrew, *Reformation, Dissent and Diversity: The Story of Scotland's Churches 1560–1960*, (London, 2015), pp. 89–91.
2 Wilson, Ben, *Decency and Disorder: The Age of Cant 1789–1837*, (London, 2007), p. 147.
3 Durie, *Travels in Scotland*, p. 204.
4 National Archives of Scotland. CS 46/73/8. The keeper of Doune Castle produced the Visitors' Book for 1857 which showed their signature as 'Mrs and Mrs Yelverton'.
5 Journal of Mary Paterson, Travels in France and Italy, 1848–9. Original in private hands.
6 Glasgow City Archives TD 1/913: Babbington letters, 15 October 1864.
7 Hughes, Thomas, *Tom Brown's Schooldays*, [1857] (Penguin Popular Edition, 1994), pp. 30-1: 'I have been creditably informed, and am inclined to believe that the various Boards of Directors of Railway Companies,' "those gigantic jobbers and bribers", while quarrelling about everything else, agreed together some ten years back to buy up the learned profession of Medicine, body and soul. To this end they set apart several millions of money, which they continually distribute judiciously among the Doctors, stipulating only this one thing, that they shall prescribe change of air to every patient who can pay, or borrow money to pay, a railway fare, and see their prescription carried out. If it be not for this, why is it that none of us can be well at home for a year together? It wasn't so twenty years ago, – not a bit of it.'
8 Barton, Sue, *Healthy Living in the Alps: The Origins of Winter Tourism in Switzerland, 1860–1914*, (Manchester, 2008).
9 [J. D. A], *Curiosities in Cures being the Experiences of a lady in Search of Health*, (London, 1895).
10 Mackaman, Douglas P., *Leisure Settings: Bourgeois Culture, Medicine and the Spa in Modern France*, (Chicago, 1998).
11 Macpherson, John, *The Baths and Wells of Europe: Their Action and Uses with Notices of Climatic Resorts and Diet Cures*, (London, 1873); Madden, Thomas More, *The principal health resorts of Europe and Africa for the Treatment of Chronic Diseases*, (London, 1876).
12 Brown, A. S., *Guide to Madeira and the Azores*, (London, 1903), p. 6.
13 Lockwood, Allison, *Passionate Pilgrims: The American Traveler in Britain, 1800–1914*, (London, 1981), p. 283.
14 Rolfe, W. J., *A Satchel Guide to Europe* first edition, (Boston, 1872), preface p. vii.
15 Author's collection.
16 *Shearer's Guide to the Trossachs*, (Stirling, 1915), p. x.
17 A'Beckett, Arthur and Sambourne, Edward, *Our Holiday in the Scottish Highlands*, (London, 1875), p. 42. This might be set along aside Sydney Smith's remark: 'I look upon Switzerland as a kind of inferior Scotland.'
18 *The Scotsman*, 'Great Diminution of Tourist Traffic in Scotland', 24 August 1893.

19 *The Scotsman*, 10 August 1901.
20 Durie, Alastair, 'Tourism in Victorian Scotland: the case of Abbotsford', *Scottish Economic and Social History*, Vol. 12 (1992), Table 3, p. 49.
21 Fontane, Theodore, *Across the Tweed. Notes on travel in Scotland* 1858, (London, 1965), p. 204.
22 Thomas Cook, *Travelling Experiences, Leisure Hour*, (London, 1878).
23 Author's collection.
24 Brendon, Piers, *Thomas Cook. 150 years of Popular Tourism*, (London, 1991), p. 245.
25 Testimonial to Thomas Cook, 30 October 1865.
26 The Paris office supplied special buses for their clients to see the public guillotining of Allorto and Sellier in 1889 at the height of the Paris Exposition.
27 Nelson, Michael, *Queen Victoria and the Discovery of the Riviera*, (London, 2001).
28 *Oban Times*, 7 April 1883.
29 Oldham Field Club, 1876, *A Botanical Excursion to the Grampian Mountains*, (Manchester, 1876).
30 Grierson, Reverend Thomas, *Autumn Rambles Amongst the Scottish Mountains*, (Edinburgh, 1850), p. 147.
31 Bede, Cuthbert, *A Tour in Tartanland*, (London, 1863), p. 163.
32 White, Alexander, *A Summer in Skye*, (Edinburgh, 1912), of Oban: p. 68 'Reading parties from Oxford lounge about, smoke, stare into the small shop windows and consult "Black's Guide".'
33 Dendy, W. C., *The Wild Hebrides*, (London, 1859).
34 Durie, *Scotland for the Holidays*, p. 141, citing *Cook's Directory and Guide to Scotland* 1861.
35 Jones, David S. D., *Gamekeeping, An Illustrated History*, (Shrewsbury, 2014), p. 89.
36 Simpson, *Wish You were Still Here*, p. 13.
37 Durie, *Travels in Scotland*, pp. 210–33.

5　Distinctive features of Scottish tourism

This chapter asks whether there were there any features of Scottish tourism which were unique or exceptional in either British or European terms. Clearly enjoyed though it was, the Scottish seaside does not qualify. As Walton has rightly argued, this was an 'English invention',[1] and while places in Scotland described themselves as the Torquay or Margate of the North, even (in North Berwick's case) the Biarritz, this was never reciprocated, say by Brighton entitling itself the Rothesay of the South. Scotland's spas were essentially second or third division. The Loch Ness monster, now confirmed as an inspired PR fiction of the 1930s[2] was more of a tourist draw than Moffat or Strathpeffer.

A number of possibilities have been identified for analysis, such as the role of Scott. This can be widened to ask if literary tourism has been more of a driver for Scotland than elsewhere in Europe, given a strong supporting cast, amongst whom are Stevenson and Barrie. What of battlefield tourism, notably that at Bannockburn and Culloden, the latter the best defined site in Britain, rivalled only pre-1914 in Europe by Waterloo with its Lion Memorial? One can ask what part in the promotion of Scotland was played by Queen Victoria. Where she visited, people followed. When in 1860 she visited Grantown-on-Spey, the next summer Strathspey was thronged with visitors. Incidentally, while there she stayed at the Grant Arms, the first time that she had overnighted at any commercial residence, as opposed to staying with a local dignitary. Balmoral was a draw for many tourists and certainly the Irish felt that the lack of any Royal Residence in Ireland was a distinct disadvantage: 'if we could but induce a member of the Royal family to live amongst us, we would soon find that Ireland would become an even more favoured tourist resort than Scotland'.[3] But they had no success in that.

The focus here is on three features: the first is the movement dubbed 'Doun the watter', the exodus from Glasgow each July of the working class by rail and steamer down the Clyde. The second is the hydropathic hotel movement, in which Scotland was disproportionately interested, and the third sporting tourism: arguably through grouse and golf Scotland became the birthplace of sporting tourism, participants and spectators.

There was no similar river traffic anywhere in Europe to rival 'Doun the Watter'. Created by paddle steamers in the 1820s (later screw and turbine), it

Figure 5.1 'Captured. The Arrival of the Loch Ness Monster at Inverness'. Comic
postcard *c.* 1935 (Author's collection)

meant in the summer an extraordinary volume of passenger traffic. Steamers
had been important to holiday traffic elsewhere in Britain, as from London to
Margate, where they, however, soon lost their place to the railways, and from
Cardiff across to North Devon destinations such as Ilfracombe. There were
steamers on the Firths of Forth and Tay, and of course on the inland waters
including Lochs Lomond, Ness and Katrine. But nowhere in mainland Britain
was there so much holiday traffic by water as there was from Glasgow and
Greenock to Dunoon and elsewhere on the Lower Clyde and or for so long;
not until the 1960s did it begin to wane. Steamers distributed holidaymakers
to piers throughout the Clyde estuary, to Bute and Arran, up to Oban and
beyond to the Hebrides. The movement was started in June by professional and
moneyed families moving out of the city for the summer, with paterfamilias
returning each Monday. It was accelerated by works and other excursions,
further augmented by tourists passing through Glasgow for the islands, and
brought to a peak during the Glasgow fair, an eight-day holiday in July when
all who could leave, did. And while there were many alternatives – camping
and climbing in the Campsies (and later hutting at Carbeth), sailing on Loch
Lomond from Balloch, apple picking in Clydesdale, or even a stay at an east
coast resort, many/most Glaswegians chose to go west by water: some 'all the
way' from the Broomielaw in the heart of Glasgow, others from the Lower
Clyde. An article in Chamber's Edinburgh Journal in 1852 described how
'smoking, sputtering and flapping their water-wings, scores of steamers ply in
endless succession'.[4] Huge numbers were carried in a single day. It was great
business, – if hectic- –over which the steamer companies fought; on one day

alone, Fair Saturday in July 1850, the Glasgow Herald estimated that no less than twenty thousand people left the Broomielaw by boat. And the numbers were to build only to higher and higher levels, with new steamers launched and older boats pressed into service to handle the luggage, with fierce competition on the most profitable routes, e.g. Glasgow to Rothesay, competition that overstepped the safety line on occasion, with racing between rival boats leading to actual collisions. The railway companies invested in new downriver faculties to draw off the traffic from the upper Clyde – the Glasgow Fair holiday of July 1894 had seen a dozen steamers (of the forty or so on the Clyde) operating from the Broomielaw to the coast, and even then the numbers swamped them. But more and more Glasgow travellers were taking the train to the coast and then crossing to Arran or Rothesay by sea, which took less time, and it was to tap into this trade that the railway companies invested in new railhead faculties at Greenock, Gourock, Fairlie, Ardrossan and Wemyss Bay. The Caledonian dominated this business, and company records show that the eight steamers of the Caledonian Steam Packet Company carried between them over a million passengers in both 1892 and 1893.[5] Some of those were locals, but most, especially in the summer, were visitors and tourists, and it was to challenge them that the Glasgow & South Western invested heavily in rebuilding Wemyss Bay in 1903 (it is the best of all Victorian hubs). High summer was the height of excursion traffic, and all the Clyde resorts benefited: the head waiter of a busy tourist hotel[6] was asked when he slept.'I sleep in winter', he replied. After the summer traffic, some boats were laid up or serviced during the winter.

Why was so much holiday traffic funnelled down the Clyde? Geography played a key part. Whereas Edinburgh had Portobello, a beach on its doorstep within walking range, as was true for Aberdeen and Dundee, the Glaswegian had to go several miles further down the Clyde, or further afield, to find suitable places for sea bathing. Some could be reached by rail, or by a combination of rail and water, but islands like Arran or Bute, or the Campbeltown peninsula required a steamer voyage. The first part of the sailing from the Broomielaw on a hot summer day in the 1870s was not very pleasant: the upper Clyde was a big dirty sewer and ships' paddles churned up the sewage. But going all the way saved the transfer, which would be awkward with children and luggage, at Greenock from train to steamer. Once down below Dumbarton the industrial Clyde was left behind, and fresh sea air enjoyed. It is hard to appreciate just how dirty Glasgow was in Victorian times, with factory, foundry and works chimneys belching out smoke; Tennant's stalk at the chemical works was reputedly the tallest chimney in Europe in the 1850s, 'continually pouring his sooty treasures into the region of the clouds'.[7] Other industrial cities were, of course, as bad. There were better areas in Glasgow and fine parks, but in the poorer areas, Nathanial Hawthorne observed, the children seemed to have been unwashed from birth and gathering only a thicker coat of dirt until their dying days.[8] Small wonder that the trip by water down the Firth was seen as a blessing. Walter Wilson, a Glasgow entrepreneur, used to organise an annual outing for poor

Figure 5.2 Industrial Dundee, as seen with only a degree of exaggeration. (Postcard;
author's collection)

children. To celebrate Queen's Victoria's Golden Jubilee on 21 June 1887 he
chartered no less than five steamers for a day trip to Rothesay and additional
places on regular services, all in all carrying from the Broomielaw 15,000
children, who were fed and watered in the public park with milk and cakes.[9]

The boats from Glasgow tended to cater for a less well-off clientele. 'The
cheap steamers are the working man's highway to the sea air', said James
Caldwell, MP, in 1890.[10] And the benefits of this were widely appreciated. 'It
is almost impossible to estimate the blessing that this pleasure ground is to
Glasgow. It raises one of the densest dirtiest and most immoral conglomerates
of humanity to stage above many of the finest cities of the Empire', rhapso-
dised a writer.[11] Another labelled the Clyde as 'the great sanatorium of the
east as well as the west country', but one which during Fair week had an ill
reputation for drinking. None were worse than the Sunday boats: anathema
to the Sabbatarians (and still unwelcome to many in the Western Isles) for
their disregard of the Sabbath. Not until the turn of the century did Sunday
sailings become respectable. Before then, there was confrontation. In August
1853 the landowner at Garelochead refused to allow a Sunday steamer to
land at his pier; only after a pitched onslaught with potatoes and coal did the
passengers get ashore.[12] But the offence was compounded by the fact that
Sunday boats were, in one writer's words, simply floating pubs. In Scotland
the Forbes Mackenzie Act of 1853 meant that only a genuine (or bona fide)
traveller could get a drink. Two Glasgow publicans hit on the idea of putting
on Sunday sailings – booze cruises – which too often finished in drunken and
riotous behaviour until legislation intervened. In evidence to a Select Committee on Intemperance in March 1878 the Lord Provost of Glasgow referred
to the Sunday steamers as a 'means of recreation'. Large numbers of Glasgow
people went out by them on afternoon excursions, with the result that during
the summer the weekend population in Glasgow was considerably smaller
than on weekdays.[13] He added that there were one or two steamers that sailed

on the Sabbath and he believed that 'the principal business that they do is supplying drink on board.' In response a temperance syndicate had the *Ivanhoe* built. Significantly, its cruises to Arran and elsewhere started not from Glasgow but down the river at Craigendoran; the advertising insisted that 'as this steamer does not sail to or from Glasgow, passengers would be able to rely on having a pleasant sail without the Ordinary Rabble common on board Clyde steamers during the Glasgow Fair'.[14]

It should not, however, be thought that all of Glasgow holidayed down the Clyde. The volume of those wanting to holiday particularly during the Fair week was simply beyond the capacity of the steamer fleet to move, or the receiving communities to absorb. Rothesay was but a town of a few thousand permanent residents, swollen five-fold during July. The overflow went elsewhere in Scotland and indeed to England. Even though steamers could carry 1,000–1,500 people three times a day to Rothesay, the volumes at peak times were too great. It was the railways that absorbed the surplus from what was the second city of the Empire, taking tens of thousands to Blackpool and to Scarborough, where there was a 'Scotch Week'.

Real conflict and social tension came not between the culture and attitudes of English visitors on the one hand, and the locals on the other, but between different Scottish social groups at the seaside over behaviour: another example of John Walton's crucible of conflict.[15] It was not the English visitors with whom the Laird of Dunollie (near Oban) was irate when he found their party in his grounds. As he explained to them, 'Glasgow Fair had lately been held and so many excursionists had invaded the place committing all manner of damage.'[16] There were a number of flashpoints, over drink, over damage, over Sabbath-breaking, where there was clear conflict between local custom and tourism. But the tourism objected to was generally that of the Scottish excursionist, not the foreign visitor. It was Scots who took up cudgels on occasion amongst themselves. There was a confrontation over the payment of pier tolls at Rowardennan pier on a July Saturday in 1881 between the pier agent of the local hotelier, who held the collection rights, and a group of 150 botany students from Glasgow and Edinburgh Universities. Having failed to collect any dues, the hotelier – ill advisedly – tried to recoup his losses by overcharging the party for their refreshments, which resulted in further bad feeling and some smashing of windows.[17]

The search for health has always been an incentive behind travel. Diet, goat's whey, good air, exercise and waters were all part of mainstream medicine As everywhere in Europe, as we have seen there was in Scotland a tradition of healing waters and spas, places where people went to drink a water impregnated with iron or some other salt. Amongst those with some reputation were Moffat, Bridge of Earn, Bridge of Allan and Strathpeffer, where there was sufficient clientele for there to be accommodation, amusement and facilities. But as already noted, most were small, such as that at Pannanich, attempted by a local laird, and few achieved either long life or anything approaching a reputation. 'We have failed', regretted one commentator in

1862, to attract 'that class of visitors who in the summer season congregate so thickly at the famous baths of Germany'.[18] Scottish spas were third division, even Strathpeffer, into which such effort was poured. In August 1911 there were eight hotels there, of which the largest was the Ben Wyvis, with 140 rooms; the next, (and the most recently opened) was the Highland Hotel with 137 rooms, and there were another 43 villas, lodging houses and cottages which catered for summer visitors. The resort was well promoted by the Highland Railway Company, and there was ample specialist literature written by medical experts to endorse the value of the waters.[19] Fortescue Fox, the well-known advocate of British spas, was a particular supporter, was a co-author of the guide to Strathpeffer spa, and his son, later editor of the *Lancet*, married a local minister's daughter. Yet examination of the list of visitors published in the *Ross-shire Journal* for the first week of August 1911 shows that there were only 841 visitors staying in the village, of whom half were Scottish, and half not. There were a few colonial visitors, a missionary family or two, and one solitary Continental tourist, a Mr Louis Cassak from Paris. Not a single American can be found, though there was a villa called 'New York'. It is unlikely that, given the location, there were many day trippers The summer numbers were certainly large in relation to the resident population of the village – a mere 425 in 1911– and the dependence of the community on the summer trade must have been nearly total. It did draw a clientele from a distance – many of the English addresses were 'London', which might reflect both the opening of the Highland Hotel and the new Spa Express from London. But the summer numbers were small in scale relative to the kind of Continental resort with which Strathpeffer tried to compare itself. Those at Vichy or Baden-Baden ran to tens of thousands, not the few hundred who came to this Northern Scottish spa.

The problem was not the quality of the waters, though the absence of any thermal springs was a handicap, but lack of enthusiasm; those who did believe in spa treatments tended to go to the Continent or to England, where there was a richer culture to enjoy. Some did single out for criticism the lack of patronage by any of the Royal family. But for whatever reasons the spas of Scotland gently subsided in their dull respectability.

What was to enter the health scene in the 1840s from the Continent was hydropathy,[20] one of a number of challengers (homeopathy was another) to mainstream medicine. As the previous chapter has explained, in a society of increasing wealth for some, there was increasing frustration amongst the sick

Table 5.1 Visitors staying in Strathpeffer in August 1911 (Source: *Ross-shire Journal*)

Type of Accommodation	From Scotland	From England	From elsewhere	Total
Hotels	133 [32%]	254 [61%]	21 [7%]	418
Other	267 [63%]	140 [33%]	16 [4%]	423

and unwell as to how little medicine was progressing in terms of cure or alleviation. The physicians were still bloodletting, as their medieval counterparts had done, or using drugs of doubtful benefit, or, more beneficially, advocating changes in diet and lifestyle or recommending the waters at a spa. So any new therapeutic system which claimed to be able to cure rheumatism, gout and much else found a willing clientele. What made a spa was the chemicals in and other qualities of its spring water. The key curative activity was the daily drinking of several pints and then bathing in it. Hydropathy (or what we would now call hydrotherapy) was different. What mattered was not the water but what was done with the water in the form of a variety of showers and baths, complemented by massage, good diet and exercise. A distinctive technique in the early days was wrapping the patient in a damp sheet for hours. As with the spas, weeks of treatment were needed. Hydropathy offered no miracle cure but treatment through a controlled regime under the supervision of a resident doctor. And in Scotland, hydropathy meant a regime of no alcohol. The cold water cure was a cure using only water, which made it very attractive to the burgeoning temperance movement; 'twins by birth' was how one enthusiast for both causes, James Haughton of Dublin, described them.[21] From the ranks committed to temperance in Scotland was to come real support for hydropathy and hydropathic establishments, as patients, practitioners and investors, with United Presbyterian supporters particularly prominent, perhaps, according to Muirhead, the most temperance-minded of the major denominations.[22] Radical therapeutics and radical theology went hand in hand: Evangelical Union members, Plymouth Brethren and Baptists were keen participants, as also were the Quakers in Ireland. Non-establishment thinking in theology also carried over into medical radicalism, as well as politics, and their support allowed proportionately many more hydropathic establishments in Scotland than was true elsewhere in the UK: Ireland had only two, and North Wales only one, at Llandudno, and while England had more, many were either small specialist establishments or high-class hotels trading on the cachet of hydro.

The early hydropathic institution (or Hydro) was a place of cure, supervised by a resident physician, who might or might not be medically qualified. A few were: Dr Paterson at Rothesay and Dr East at Dunoon. Some were lay enthusiasts, such as William Hunter of Gilmorehill, by trade an upholsterer, who moved to Bridge of Allan; he was later to call himself 'Dr' on the strength of a doubtful degree from an American hydropathic medical school. Others were ministers, notably Alexander Munro of Aberdeen and Forres. Over time their successors were medically qualified; and hydropathy mutated its way to respectability as hydrotherapy. It lost the wet sheet and acquired instead the Turkish bath and the Scotch douche, made fewer claims as to what it could cure, became acceptable rather than radical, and increasingly became a place for the right sort of company and culture, rather than cure.

The first hydros in Scotland at Rothesay and Dunoon were small, converted villas equipped with baths and showers, looking after not more than a handful of patients. Munro's premises in the west end of Aberdeen at Lochhead, opened in 1860, added in the following year a sixty-foot Turkish bath, complete with minarets, which must have been in extraordinary juxtaposition with the surrounding granite terraces. In this early phase the movement in Scotland lagged a long way behind what was happening in England, where there were some very big establishments set up at Matlock, Ben Rhydding and Malvern. It went up a gear however in 1865, when Clunyhill Hydro (near Forres) opened. This was a purpose-built establishment, much larger than those before in Scotland with some ninety rooms. Expensive to construct and equip, it was financed by the new device of limited liability company and shareholders; and it drew on a clientele which was not just local. They came, according to visitor lists, from Glasgow, Newcastle and indeed Gibraltar: a stay at a hydro was recommended for those returning from the colonies to help them re-acclimatise. Forres was conducted on strict temperance lines: 'no spirits, beer or wines' reported the local paper. It was under the charge of Dr Munro, an Evangelical Union minister who was lured away from Aberdeen, where he had been running the Lochhead hydro. Editor of various Journals of Health, he was a big name in the hydropathic movement, which helped to draw a clientele to Forres. It was certainly a profitable enterprise. For many years its dividends ran at 10 per cent, to be later cut back to half that, in order to reduce borrowing. Other hydros came into operation at Crieff, Bridge of Allan and Melrose. The last was the creation of a wealthy Dunfermline draper. John Davie was a United Presbyterian elder, temperance reformer (he claimed to have been instrumental in the formation of the first total temperance society in Scotland) and a man of many causes, who poached Dr Munro from Forres to manage the business. Seven new Scottish hydros were opened between 1865 and 1875, but momentum converted into mania, with twelve more projected between 1876 and 1882. It was too many. There was a high mortality amongst these new ventures: two ran out of money during construction, as at Oban and several more became insolvent and were resold at heavy loss to the original shareholders: £180,000 is one calculation. Some, such as the Coats of Paisley, could afford the loss; many smaller shareholders could not. The Atholl at Pitlochry which had cost £80,000 to build, fetched a mere £25,000 in 1886. There were those who picked up bargains, such as Andrew Philp, who bought Dunblane Hydro in 1890 for a mere £20,000 to add to an already extensive portfolio of hydropathic shareholding. He was a director of Waverley Hydro at Melrose, and controlling owner of the Glenburn at Rothesay; and also had two English ventures at Harrogate and at Conishead. His first venture in the hotel business had been a temperance hotel in Kirkcaldy and temperance remained a lifelong commitment of his. This allowed to him to work happily with Thomas Cook, who himself had entered the excursion business through his temperance work. Cook and Philp shared the same values: Cook made Philp's Cockburn Hotel in Edinburgh his GHQ when in Scotland, and Philp acted as agent for Cook in Scotland. Active into his late eighties, he was no dry stick: 'Possessed of an inexhaustible fund of Scots wit and Humour', said one contemporary.[23]

Philp prospered whereas others had not. The hotel business has always had a disproportionate casualty rate, but why so many hydros got into difficulty in the early 1880s was the result of a mixture of factors, of which overcapacity was one element. Their palatial buildings went over budget, their off-season takings were far less than expected, causing them to be labelled butterfly hydros, standing almost empty for most of the year. But there was also the fallout from the failure of the City of the Glasgow Bank in 1878, whose unfortunate shareholders had unlimited liability. That hurt the very class of people who were the staple clientele for the hydros. But once the dust had settled and the wreckage cleared, the reality is that the Scottish hydros then traded very successfully. The older hydros had been unscathed, the more recent under new management did well. But there was a change in the ethos of the hydros. In fewer and fewer was the medical department the key section and the resident doctor gave way to a manager. Genuinely ill patients were replaced by the sick well, people suffering from overwork, overindulgence and stress, then called 'brain fever'. The culture of the hydro became much more geared towards exercise and entertainment: tennis and golf outside, dances, concerts and tableaux vivants inside. The hydros were able to extend their season with Christmas and New Year festivities and the picture pre-1914 was healthy in terms of numbers and of profits. Serious fires struck several but they were rebuilt. More and more the hydros were becoming simply large luxury hotels, known for their food, their facilities and their culture. The term hydro became diluted, especially in England, where it was increasingly applied to luxury hotels without even any medical baths or staff.

And there was some slippage from the temperance regime. Not at Crieff with its strongly Christian regime, bolstered by the special funds which allowed a subsidy to ministers and missionaries. It was to remain temperance until 1971, when for the first time, it obtained a table licence. It was the last standard-bearer of the temperance cause which had faded during the twentieth century; organisations like the bands of hope, temperance hotels and alcohol-free hydros were a thing of the past. And indeed church membership was in sharp decline. Crieff could hold its niche, but there was little room for any other there. Bridge of Allan Hydro had long lost its hydropathic identity, and the vegetarian regime there of Mrs Hunter in the 1890s had alienated its clientele, and it, along with the Atholl Palace was snapped up by Sir Henry Lunn in 1914 with a view to converting both into sporting hotels. The Scottish railway companies had their golfing centres at Turnberry and Cruden Bay with Gleneagles under construction; Lunn felt that was the way the wind was blowing. But the outbreak of war in August 1914 torpedoed his schemes.

The First World War saw some hydros converted into military hospitals. Their baths and other facilities were seen as useful therapeutic tools, Dunblane for naval officers and Craiglockhart became Slateford Military Hospital. Others offered temporary relief to schools evacuated from the East Coast of England; Queen Margaret School at Scarborough moved to the Atholl Palace at Pitlochry after the German navy had shelled the English resort in

December 1914. One girl found in the visitor's locker that she had been allocated a large empty whisky bottle that a guest had left behind! The reality is that not all the clientele were as teetotal as the establishment regimes. For those hydros that remained unrequisitioned there was reasonable business, especially Crieff and Callander, which marketed itself as safe from the Germans – 'sixty miles inland'. At the end of the war those hydros that had been requisitioned were handed back, but even though there was compensation, the lack of maintenance during the war meant they were in poor condition. Craiglockhart briefly reopened, but was sold as a Catholic training college. Moffat, after extensive renovation burnt down in 1921, but it was already clear by then that it was no longer a paying concern. To all too many by the 1920s the hydros were too staid, too respectable, and they were faced as all hotels were with a change in visitor habits. Fewer guests came for a month, more – thanks to the touring car – for a few days only. But some did do well. Crieff continued to be the standard-bearer of the old regime with its continuing commitment to temperance. Christian conferences were a staple. By contrast Peebles, which was equally or even more successful modernised: hot water basins in every room, an American bar, first-rate conference facilities and excellent tennis courts. Not for it the old temperance regime. A new family dynasty had taken over at Peebles, that of the Calazels. Family-run businesses have not always had a good press, the feeling being that they fade over time, but Peebles is a striking exception to this rule, surviving the difficult interwar years with barely a tremor. Indeed were Peebles' balance sheets the only indicator that we had of economic conditions in Scotland one would never infer that there had been severe depression. It declared dividends of 10 per cent or thereabouts during the 1920s, and an astonishing 30 per cent in the mid- and later 1930s.

We could follow the hydro hotel story on further, but essentially by the twentieth century hydros were – with the exception of Crieff – hydropathic establishments only in name. And indeed most were phasing out the name 'hydro' from their title as synonymous only with stuffiness and gloom; fit for maiden aunts and the clergy. In Ivor Brown's words (of the Atholl Hydro) 'the Hydropathic became the Hydro, then the Hydro Hotel, even, last step of all, the Hotel, the Luxury Hotel, the Palace'.[24] The golden years of the hydropathic hotels had been in the later nineteenth century, but even by then, in the great majority of cases, they were no longer hydropathic in the strict sense of the word, no longer a medical institution but a recreational and leisure facility. It was a movement which was failing from within even as it was apparently reaching its highpoint. Ironically, with the current interest in wellness, the term hydro or spa and hydro is making a comeback, as top-end hotels add swimming pools, steam rooms, saunas and massage and other treatments to their attractions, pampering, not curing their clientele. A common combination is spa and golf hotel. And it is to sporting tourism we now turn.

Scotland developed a high profile as a sporting playground.[25] There was yachting, cycling, hillwalking and mountaineering. Mountaineering had a long pedigree. The opening of the West Highland railway 'had caused a great increase in the number of visitors to the top of Ben Nevis. Last week over 500 visitors ascended the Ben, there being on the summit one gentleman of 81 years and a child of three months!'[26] For the elite, Scotland meant grouse and deer, and salmon fishing. For a wider group it was golf. The English clergymen who knew Scotland, according to Donald Macleod, only as land from which grouse came, could equally have described it as the home of golf – in England the golf was known as the 'Scotch game'. The sports were very different: grouse-shooting was for the wealthy elite, practised in seclusion on the moors, and deer stalking a solitary sport, sealed from any gaze. But golf was much more democratic, brought together very different classes, and was played in public. The shot having a bad day on the moors was exposed only to his peers (and perhaps his wife); the golfer might be ridiculed by the public. A game-keeper might offer advice on how a drive should go, but he would never find himself shooting beside his employer; nor did working-class keepers ever graduate to join the guns, whereas an amateur golfer from London might well find himself in direct competition with a golf professional, an artisan.[27]

As already indicated in Chapter 2, some sportsmen had already found their way north in the later eighteenth century. But this essentially was only for their pleasure, and to the landowners over whose ground they shot this sport was without profit, as the visitors were usually allowed to shoot without any charge. But that was to change: grouse-shooting, deer-stalking and salmon fishing all became commercialised. Demand for Highland sport rose as access to the North improved, thanks to the railways; and also widened, thanks to the development in the 1860s in grouse-shooting of a new technique of using an army of beaters to drive the birds to the guns in butts; the young and fit could still 'walk up' with dogs, but for the older and less mobile shot, driving was a godsend. Many landowners saw the opportunity of improving their estate income, which in some cases was a top priority, through either renting moors or in extremis selling ground. The process of the commercialisation of High-land sport seems to have become established in the 1830s. Catherine Sinclair, writing in 1840, could look back to a few years previously when, according to her, parties of English sportsmen had come north by boat to Dundee or Aberdeen for grouse-shooting in the Perthshire or Aberdeenshire hills in the belief that such sport there was free; they were soon disabused.[28] In 1837 an Inverness-shire gunsmith, Snowie, issued his first list of shootings to rent; the modest list of eight moors had grown thirty years later to several hundred. This sporting agency brought together Highland proprietors and southern sportsmen, and Snowie himself spent each May in London to advise those interested. The effect was soon noticed; Lord Cockburn noted in September 1846 that he had met with a party of Irish sportsmen at Glenshee: 'this autumnal influx of sporting strangers is a very recent occurrence in Scotch economy. Almost every moor has its English tenant.'[29] More ground was made available to rent for sport, but demand outstripped supply, with the happy result that rents began to rise sharply. Evidence gathered by the *Quarterly Review* in 1865 suggested that in the last thirty years, rents had risen at a minimum three-fold, in many by a factor of ten, and in some cases, depending on the quality of the moor, by even more; the shootings at Glen Urquhart which had been let for £100 in 1836 were now priced at £2,000 p.a. Small wonder that sporting tourism in the North was hailed by the *Edinburgh Review* in 1857 as 'a stream of gold, quite wonderful in the extent and rapidity of its growth. [bringing] an enormous amount of London money'.

Of course, there were costs to be set against the stream of sporting revenue: for game to be 'preserved' and the sporting ground or water to be cared for, gamekeepers, stalkers, ghillies and water bailiffs. Moors that were looked after – vermin and predators killed, heather burnt and grit put out – held better stocks of grouse – four or five times the unkeepered level and that converted into higher rentals. Conservation of grouse meant continuing war on its predators. The red kite, for example, was once quite common but was exterminated because of its reputation as a killer of young grouse. Lodges had to be provided, especially as families rather than just males started to arrive for the season, some quite grand; draughty castles such as Balmoral were renovated. But money smoothed the way, as did permanent and seasonal employment (as beaters say), and there was no serious objection to the enthusiasm for grouse. Deer forests were another matter, and generated much more friction about the power of the landlords and the use of land for sporting pleasure. But demand created supply and one estimate in the early twentieth century, was that there were 197 deer forests, with about one-third of the land in the crofting counties devoted to deer, and 3,000 grouse-shootings. Some were kept in hand but many were let. The total income from grouse was £1.5 million, or £5,000 per moor as against £300,000 for the deer forests at an average of £15,000 per forest.[30] Averages, of course, conceal wide variations, but they do underline that these sports were only for those with deep pockets.

Highland estates wanted the sporting income, and returns from sporting rentals were more reliable than those from sheep, cattle or crofters. Evidence to the Deer Commission in 1893 showed that in the Dunrobin district land in deer generated seven or eight times what the same ground in sheep could produce. And if in crofting, even less. Few Highland owners could afford to disregard the possibilities, but to put more land into sport, as the Sutherland estate did – no less than 212,000 acres by 1892 from sheep walks to deer forests – meant clearing crofters, and letting loose the cry 'deer for men'. In Sutherland shooting and fishing rents, as Annie Tindley has pointed out 'were by the 1890s the most lucrative and stable source of income the estate had'.[31] It was a great pity that much of this income was blown by the 3rd Duke on his mistress, whom he had married. On his death she came into huge monies, including, after an expensive court case, no less than £750,000 to buy her out of the Sutherland estates which he had bequeathed to her. But the presence of crofters was complication. At an auction of Scottish sporting estates held in London in June 1885, a marketing plus for one estate near Inverness (Glengloy) was not just that it was well stocked with game but that it was 'possessed of neither tenants, paupers or crofters'.[32]

The financial need of Highland proprietors made land available in increasing quantity for sport. But why was demand so buoyant and who wanted Highland sport? And why? The quip of J. S. Blackie was that 'London brewers shoot the grouse and lordlings the deer.'[33] Certainly many sporting estates were either rented or bought by southern sportsmen and amongst the tenants of deer forests were Alfred Bass and Samuel Whitebread. Overseas millionaires bought in, including the controversial American W. L. Winans, discussed below. But successful Scottish industrialists also took shootings: there was the Aberdonian papermaker Pirie, Lithgow from shipbuilding and Colville of steel fame. For them to have a Highland estate was a mark of success. There was Balmoral with the Royals but Balmoralism predates Balmoral. Moreover, not all the incoming English were titled. There were numbers of the rising professional and commercial classes looking north. Some rented, others took up residence, and for some, there was a process of migration and assimilation over several generations. The Joynson family, owners of the Glassert estate near Aberfoyle, illustrate a pattern which was more common than has been allowed, from summer sporting tenants graduating to estate owners and permanent residents. A sightseeing tour of 1833 in the Trossachs by Edward Joynson from Cheshire, drawn by Scott's *Rob Roy*, was followed by the leasing of shootings. In the later 1840s, there was the rent of a house for the summer at Glassert and eventually two generations later, the purchase of the family home there, and a final move north, by which time they were part of local society.[34]

Why were Highland sport and a sporting estate so popular, despite their cost? Grouse-shooting and deer-stalking were elite sports. The grouse was a wild bird which could not be bred, strong in flight, first game bird to come into season, but mere love of the hunt was not the sole reason for their popularity.[35] Stalking was a physically demanding activity for the few. Grouse-shooting on the other hand was lighter in its physical demands, thanks to the new technique of driving outlined above. The latter was a young man's activity; the former possible for the less fit and older. These elite activities carried cachet and status and there was a romance about the Highlands which Northern English moors, good as they were, could not match. It was a unique tartan sporting package, with various add-ons to appeal to those not shooting. Ladies might spectate or join the guns for lunch but there was also visiting and sightseeing, dinners and balls in the evening, Highland Games at Ballater or Cowal. And church on Sunday; there were even tin tabernacles – grouse kirks – such as the Earl of Breadalbane's kirk at St Fillans, which were open only during the shooting season for English guests. It was a cultural cocoon and the Highland moors were both private and safe; there was no risk of any repetition of the sad experience of the Vyner family, whose son Frederick was murdered by Greek bandits in April 1870.[36]

The Highland sporting estate also served as a form of social climbing, bringing together new money and the social elite. For them it was a way of networking, a form of business hospitality. The returns for most tenants were not financial – the host had so many expenses – but in the reciprocals. To be able to offer Highland sport was a great asset, and few who were offered declined the invitation. The knowledgeable Evan Mackenzie considered that 5,000 out of the 6,000 of those who travelled north by rail in 1895 for the grouse shooting in the Highlands were guests. Another contemporary put the figure far higher at 39,600.[37] Not all necessarily enjoyed the experience: the musician Arthur Sullivan was invited in 1871 by a friend from Manchester, J. H. Agnew, a cloth manufacturer, for three days' grouse-shooting in Scotland – where is not specified. The first day, as he reported to his mother, was ruined by the weather – eight hours of walking up and down 'these awful endless hills they call moors, and never a bird of any sort we could get near. I was drenched through without by the rain, and soaked inwardly by the whisky. I never thought I could have drunk so much raw spirit and it had about as much effect as cold water.'[38]

But most did enjoy their sport. If hosts enjoyed the prestige of having a sporting estate, the growth of sporting estates did create tension. There was the question of ground being cleared for deer and the raiding of crofters' ground by deer in hard weather, which provoked a riot in Lewis in November 1887, a virtual land war, which required the sending of a Royal Navy gunboat. There was also conflict over access. No one in Victorian times expected an unfettered right to roam over farm land or moor, which is much more of a later notion. But mountaineers, hill walkers ('stravagers and marauders' as they dubbed themselves), ramblers, botanists and others came to resent the way in which large areas of moorland and deer forest country were kept private, and entry to them denied by the landowners or sporting tenants, not just during the stalking or shooting season, but all year round. There were skirmishes, as in August 1847 when the Professor of Botany at Edinburgh Universityand seven of his students at Glen Tilt were confronted by the Duke of Atholl, nicknamed the 'Tourist baffling Duke of the impassible glen'.[39] Other estate owners were equally unwelcoming. There is a photograph in the Scottish Mountaineering Club Journal of a notice *c.* 1900 posted by one estate: 'Tourists are requested to keep on the path; otherwise they are liable to be inadvertently shot by Sportsmen and keepers when stalking'.[40] W. L. Winans, a thoroughly disagreeable man, was fiercely litigious over any access and notoriously had a Glasgow naturalist who was merely collecting butterflies thrown off his estate. He also litigated against a crofter whose pet lamb had strayed onto his ground.[41]

Rights of Way Societies began to put pressure on, as did mountaineering clubs, but progress was slow. Access legislation was attempted in Parliament on several occasions in the 1920s and direct action did occur, notably in England in April 1932, when there was a mass trespass organised by the Communist-inspired British Workers' Sports Federation at a moor in the English Peak District. Four hundred men and women, largely from Manchester, assembled in the Peak District with a view to trespassing onto Kinder Scout, the highest point in the Peak District. They did this to proclaim that 'that God gave the land to the people'.[42] There was confrontation with the ground's gamekeepers and arrests were made. Not until 1939 was a weak Access to Mountains bill passed. Much more was achieved after the Second World War in 1949 with the creation of National Parks (but not until 2000 in Scotland) and the passage of an Access to the Countryside Bill.[43]

There was also a growing challenge, mostly from those on the radical and socialist or nationalist left, to the whole idea of the ownership of so much ground by the few. Sporting estates were in the firing line, particularly the deer forests which were so large. Why, the critics asked, should so much ground be reserved for the pleasure of so few? In the Highlands of Scotland it was a further aggravation that some of the new owners were either English or foreign. Edward Carpenter singled out as of particular offence the way in which 'we have grouse moors and pheasant covers, with their concomitant evils let to rich Americans and titled grocers'.[44] Queen Victoria and the Royal family were always welcome at Balmoral, but as we have seen, W. L. Winans was especially and deservedly unpopular. But these tensions were held in check.

Like Highland field sports, golf too underwent huge expansion in Scotland in the late Victorian period. It had a long provenance, played since mediaeval times, particularly on the east coast. In 1617 a local landowner claimed that the links at Dornoch 'doe surpasse the feilds of Montrose or St Andrews'.[45] The latter was such a hotbed of golf that it was described by Alexander Munro in 1695 as the 'metropolis of golfing'.[46] Rules were devised, a key stage in the conversion of a pastime to a sport. But growth was relatively slow and in 1879, or so Price estimates, there were only forty-three golf courses in Scotland, of which two were for ladies. The real expansion came thereafter with at least 223 golf courses opened between 1880 and 1909. What fed this boom was cheaper clubs and balls that made golf more affordable, although it was never free; even the new municipal courses had to charge, and participation by the poorest layers of society was negligible. Putting, perhaps, golf, no. St Andrews Town Council, according to Simpson, built one of the earliest public putting greens in 1914. There were artisan clubs, however, and the middle classes, male and female, young and old, took to golf with gusto. It was a game which offered play all the year round, except in the worst of weather, and through the handicapping system allowed people of quite different skills levels to compete against each other. More Scots were playing golf, and they were joined during the summer months by increasing numbers of visitors. No tourist resort, coastal or inland, was complete without a golf course. Callander opened its in 1890, and very progressively allowed women to play in its club championship. This forced nearby Bridge of Allan, a fading spa, into following suit. If the town were to maintain its reputation as a summer resort, a course had to be provided, which it was in 1895, with Old Tom Morris, the famous St Andrews golf professional and four-times winner of the Open, as the architect. Hydro hotels either had their own short courses or arranged special terms with a local course for their guests. The role of railway golfing hotels has already been discussed in Chapter 3.

The question of Sunday play was a point of friction. Mostly it was completely unacceptable. The *Bridge of Allan Reporter* carried a story in April 1896 that two gentlemen staying at the Hydro had had a Sunday game of golf on the local course (which the Hydro owned). The hydro's directors immediately denied that this had been done with their permission. The Editor commented 'that the Golf course is in connection with one of those unimpeachable institutions known as hydro establishments which are patronised by the unco good of all denominations. Alcohol is forbidden and any man who asked for hot water for shaving later at night is looked at askance... One can understand how absolutely necessary it is for the proprietor of this Golf course to disclaim all complicity with these Sabbath breakers.' But even before the First World War some private clubs had begun to relax the ban on Sunday play; an Aberdeen businessman recorded in his diary for Sunday 2 March 1899 that he had that day played golf at Cruden Bay and 'shocked the natives quite a bit I expect'.[47] The thaw continued in the interwar years, with those courses owned by town councils slowest to change: not until 1958 did Sunday golf arrive at North Berwick's municipal courses.

Golf drew visitors to quite distant resorts. Machrihanish on the west coast of the Kintyre peninsula was laid out by Old Tom Morris in 1876, and was claimed some twenty years later in a nicely nuanced phrase to be 'almost world famous'. What was important was the way that golf became an integral part of holiday experience in Scotland, either casual or competitive, family or mixed foursome, Scots or English. Girls and women took part; the Ladies Golf Club at North Berwick had 300 members by 1894. Golf had taken off in England too, but as a rule it was more expensive; the English golfer who came to Scotland tended to find it both good and relatively cheap. And come they did to play, from the middle and the top drawers of English society. One Edwardian guidebook boasted of North Berwick in 1903 that 'the Speaker of the House of Commons, the Lord Mayor of London, statesmen, Archbishops, bishops, ministers of all denominations, judges, lawyers, merchants all go to the links when they come to North Berwick'. Lord Kitchener is reported to have first tried his hand at golf there.[48] Other Scottish clubs had a similar holiday influx: about one-third of Dornoch's membership in 1909 was from London.

Relations were good between visitors and locals, and in many resorts matches were organised between residents and summer arrivals. What helped was that the monthly tickets which the visitors bought at many courses were much more expensive relatively than the annual subscription; milking them kept the cost down for the locals. In 1909 at Rothesay where the annual subscription was 21/-, a day ticket was 1/-, weekly 2/6, and monthly 7/6.[49] And the visitor, however important, got no special privileges; at Dornoch it was a matter of principle that there was no queue jumping whoever you were. In that Scottish golf was democratic. Moreover visitors spent, and spent well: on equipment and lessons, on clubs and caddies, and doubtless at the nineteenth hole. Small boys could find lost balls and caddying was how several big names from humble origins found their way into golf: James Braid from Elie, son of a ploughman, was one such. Another was Willie Anderson, a licenced caddie on the links at North Berwick in 1890 at the age of eleven. After emigrating to the USA he had a stellar career as a golf pro, winning four US Opens, before dying tragically young at the age of thirty-one. Caddying was also a useful fallback for fishermen when the fishing was poor, and in the 1920s unemployed men, living in tents, touted for custom at the railway station at North Berwick. Golf professionals made their living at their courses, often combining club-making with teaching,[50] and there was also money to be made by playing exhibition matches; Young Tom Morris (aged thirteen) made £15 by playing in an match at Perth in 1864; his father's win at the Open in the previous year had netted him only a share in the prize money of £10. Stake or challenge matches became popular; one in 1899 played over 72 holes was for a purse of £200. What helped fund these contests was that they attracted hundreds of spectators, paying gate money: small beer, perhaps, as against the huge crowds who now follow golf, but a harbinger of things to come. Golf, like other sports, was well covered in the local and national press; sport sold papers, and papers sold golf. Golfing journalism became a recognised sub-species, and some writers played to a high standard; in 1890 at Prestwick, John Ball from Hoylake was the first amateur and first non-Scotsman to win the Open Championship.

With grouse and golf, therefore, Scotland had some claim to be one of the leading sporting playgrounds of Europe. Or so at least, the social elite, actual and aspirational, of Britain would have thought, an endorsement shared by others of their class and income in Europe and North America. There were many other sporting options available elsewhere, but Highland grouse and deer carried a social cachet without rival. By contrast, the river steamer trade down the Clyde was primarily a Scottish working-class phenomenon. The hydropathics fitted in between in social terms. They were the preserve of the respectable middle classes, and drew their popularity from a particular cultural strand then strong in Scottish society, the temperance movement. As that waned, however, they adjusted. A few remained true to the original values but most modernised to survive and to thrive, and as such, they continued to be an important and distinctive part of the Scottish holiday portfolio.

Notes

1 Walton, John K., *The English Seaside Resort: A Social History 1750–1914*, (Leicester, 1983), pp. 187–215.
2 Williams, Gareth, *A Monstrous Commotion: the Mysteries of Loch Ness*, (London, 2015).
3 *The Irish Tourist*, 1 (June 1894), p. 1.
4 *Chamber's Edinburgh Journal*, Vol. 17 (1852), p. 346 on 'Summer lodgings'.
5 Paterson, Alan J. S., *The Golden Years of the Clyde Steamers*, (Newton Abbot, 1969).

6 *The North British Review*, March 1865, 'The Rise and Progress of the Scottish Tourist', p. 2.

7 Berry, Simon and Whyte, Hamish, *Glasgow Observed*, (Edinburgh, 1987), p. 110; citing James Burns 1858.

8 Hawthorne, Nathaniel, *Our Old Home and English Notebooks*, Vol. II, (London 1883), p. 459.

9 Paterson, Alan J. S., *The Victorian Summer of the Clyde Steamers*, (Newton Abbot, 1972), pp. 206–7.

10 Paterson, *The Golden Years*, p. 69.

11 *The North British Review*, March 1865, 'The Rise and Progress of the Scottish Tourist', p. 35.

12 Deayton, A. and Quinn, I., *200 years of Clyde Paddle Steamers*, (Stroud, 2012).

13 Select Committee of the House of Lords on Intemperance Fourth Report, 5 August 1878. The Lord Provost drew attention, as did others, to the number of hotels which could not exist but for their Sunday traffic in alcohol, serving the bona fide traveller, whether bona fide or not.

14 Paterson, *Golden Years*, p. 26.

15 Walton, John K., *The English Seaside Resort. A Social History*, (Bath, 1983), Chapter 8, 'Styles of Holidaymaking', pp. 187–215.

16 Durie, *Travels in Scotland*, p. 181.

17 Mitchell, John, 'Protest at the Pier', *Scottish Local History*, Vol. 62 (2004), pp. 36–37.

18 *Blackwood's Edinburgh Magazine*, DLXIII, September 1862, 'Watering places', p. 265. The writer blamed amongst other things 'the vileness of cookery at the spa lodging houses, and the general lack of amusement; it would be a vain quest to repair to any of the northern watering places in search either of luxury or social amusement.'

19 See, for example, Manson, D., *On the Sulphur Springs of Strathpeffer in the Highlands of Ross-shire*, (London, 1877) and Fox, Fortescue, *Strathpeffer Spa, Its Climate and Waters*, (London, 1889).

20 This section draws on Durie, Alastair, *Water is Best*, (Edinburgh, 2006).

21 Durie, *Water is Best*, p. 9.

22 Muirhead, Andrew, *Reformation, Dissent and Diversity: The Story of Scotland's Churches 1560–1960*, (London, 2015), p. 101.

23 *The Baillie*, Vol. XLIII, (February 1894), p. 1.

24 Brown, Ivor, *Summer in Scotland*, (London, 1952), p. 179.

25 Durie, Alastair J., 'Sporting Tourism Flowers: The development of grouse and golf as visitor attractions in Scotland and Ireland', *Journal of Tourism History*, Vol. 5, No. 2 (August 2013), pp. 131–45.

26 *Hull Daily Mail*, 30 August 1894.

27 *Stirling Observer*, 1 September 1894.

28 Sinclair, Catherine, *Shetland and the Shetlanders: Or The Northern Circuit*, (Edinburgh, 1840), p. 259.

29 Cockburn, *Circuit Journeys*, p. 195.

30 Malcolm, George and Maxwell, Aymer, *Grouse and Grouse Moors*, (London, 1910), pp. 29–30.

31 Tindly, Annie, *The Sutherland Estate 1850–1920*, (Edinburgh, 2010), p. 111.

32 *Stirling Observer*, 10 June 1885.

33 Blackie, J. S., 'The Highlands, Men and Sheep', *The Edinburgh Review*, Vol. 106 (1857), p. 501.

34 Joynson, Peter, *Local Past*, (Aberfoyle, 1996). See also Durie, Alastair and Magee, Karl, '"Come North": Glassert game books and diaries', *Forth Naturalist and Historian*, Vol. 31 (2008), pp. 117–19.

35 Durie, Alastair, '"Unconscious Benefactors": grouse-shooting in Scotland, 1790–1914', *International Journal of the History of Sport*, Vol.15, No. 3 (December 1998), pp. 58–73.

36 *Glasgow Herald*, 26 April 1870.
37 Sargent, Harry R., *Thoughts upon Sport*, (London, 1895), p. 252.
38 Jacobs, Arthur D., *Arthur Sullivan. A Victorian Musician*, (Oxford, 1984), p. 71.
39 Lambert, Robert, *Contested Mountains*, (Cambridge, 2001), p. 36.
40 Brooker, W. D. (ed.), *A Century of Scottish Mountaineering*, (Berwick, 1998), p. 12.
41 Orr, Willie, *Deer Forests, Landlords and Crofters*, (Edinburgh, 1982), p. 42.
42 Gardiner, Juliet, *The Thirties: An Intimate History*, (London, 2010), p. 252.
43 Lambert, Robert A., *Contested Mountains*, (Cambridge, 2001), p. 67.
44 Carpenter, Edward, 'The Cost of Sport', in Salt, Henry S., *Killing for Sport*, with a preface by George Bernard Shaw, (London, 1915). This series of essays was issued for the Humanitarian League.
45 Gordon, Sir Robert., *A Genealogical History of the Earldom of Sutherland to the Year 1630*, (Edinburgh, 1813), p. 6. I owe this reference to Wade Cormack.
46 Geddes, Olive, *A Swing in Time*, (Edinburgh, 1998), p. 63.
47 Simpson, *Wish You Were Still Here*, pp. 97–8.
48 Jamieson, Bruce A., *North Berwick. Biarritz of the North*, (East Lothian, 1992), p. 53.
49 Baddeley, *Thorough Guide to Scotland*, (tenth Edition 1903), Pink special Golf Courses 1906.
50 Hamilton, David (ed.), *A Girl's Golf in 1894: A North Berwick Holiday Diary* (St Andrews, 2015), p. 7.

6   Growth and fluctuations

Tourism history has tended to focus, understandably, on the growth of the industry. The issues that have been highest on its agenda have been the rise of new destinations and individual resorts, the development and diversification into new forms of tourism, the role of public and public enterprise in its promotion. That tourism could be grown by publicity and the provision of amenities had been recognised already in the nineteenth century by resort authorities, railway and steamship companies. Travel agencies, of which Cook's is the best known, played their part, as did a profusion of literature. There were periodicals, such as the *Journal of Health Resorts*, comprehensive guides – Murray's, Black's, Baddeley and even Baedeker – and travelogues which advised on how to see Scotland. Event tourism made its appearance. The organisation of periodic fairs and exhibitions was pioneered in Britain with the Great Exhibition of 1851 which drew very large numbers – over six million – from around Britain. There is an argument for seeing the Exhibition as groundbreaking in that it drew visitors of all social strata who had never before travelled such distances for pleasure (as opposed to work). From Banffshire a party of fishing folk went to the Crystal Palace[1] and an engineer from Lasswade near Edinburgh took his family with him to see the Exhibition – a mere 24 hours on the train to a 'country of which I had seen nothing and knew almost as little'.[2] The success of the Crystal Palace led other cities in Europe and North America to follow suit: Vienna in 1873, Paris in 1878, and so on. But one city's success could be another destination's loss. The Columbian Exposition of 1893 at Chicago had a major impact on the flow of American tourism to Scotland, which collapsed. Hotels in Edinburgh found themselves in what should have been the high season with many rooms unlet.[3] Manchester and Edinburgh got in on the act, but it was Glasgow which took the top billing in Scotland. Its first Exhibition was held in 1888 and drew 5.75 million visitors, a figure doubled in 1901, and nearly maintained in 1911. What is more, all three of these pre-1914 events made a modest profit.[4] On a lesser scale, but no less important to the communities concerned, was the development from the 1850s of Highland Games, – sixteen up to 1902, of which Ballater (founded 1864) and Cowal (founded1871) were the most famous[5] and popular with tourists.

Tourism could be stimulated. But growth, and this is not a modern development, was never without check and dislocation. Tourism has always been vulnerable to external factors that have affected both the direction and volume of activity. There are the 'known unknowns' (such as the weather) and the 'unknown unknowns', random events of nature such as tsunamis or volcanoes, or man-made events, of which war[6] is the most serious. Other forms of shock include pandemics, which have inhibited travel and are indeed spread by travel: the swine flu epidemic in 2009–2010 is a recent example.[7] Economic conditions, which shape people's capacity to travel, and dictate their stay and their spending alike, are clearly always of importance. Recessions in tourism have seen resorts, travel firms, hotels and airlines feel the pinch, with some pushed into liquidation.[8] But, by way of adjustment, there has been the rise of 'staycationing', holidaying at home rather than abroad, which has cushioned the effect of the downturn for domestic tourism.

Of the known unknowns, high on the list of uncertainties was the weather. Nothing, most Scots would say, is more unpredictable than the Scottish summer.[9] Weather here is defined as short term fluctuation, as distinct from 'climate', which is long-term weather. It is quite clear that a resort's climatic reputation, as measured in annual hours of sun, temperature, ozone, dryness of air, was significant, especially to invalids and heath seekers planning ahead. Resorts competed with each other on those grounds. Rothesay boasted that it was the Madeira of Scotland. Nairn and towns elsewhere on the Moray Firth drew returned colonials because of their mild climate. But climate, in the sense of long-term weather patterns, was not random. It was a feature that could be documented, based on observations over many years, and was set out in books advising health seekers. Weather from day to day, week to week, or month to month was, on the other hand, far from being predictable. Short-term variations could affect tourist numbers. One sport which was very vulnerable to adverse weather was grouse-shooting, much more than deer-stalking. A wet spring, as in 1873 (or 2015) could mean a shortage of birds, which the counts in July would confirm, and shootings cancelled. As grouse were a wild stock, any shortfall in their numbers through the weather or disease could not be made good. The Douglas estate at Lanark saw a remarkable season in 1866 followed by an equally dismal one the next year when bags fell from 5,942 brace to only 208 because of a cold wet spring that killed the hatch of chicks.[10]

But what of holiday tourism, inland or at the seaside? It is a reasonable assumption that good weather attracts, bad weather discourages. Rain and wind could wreck shows and games. The abominable weather in the summer of 1938 – cold, wet and windy – kept attendance at the 1938 Glasgow Empire Exhibition well below the projected figures, and resulted in heavy losses.[11] It was why people might not choose to go. Yet in the nineteenth century bad weather may not have been as significant. By the 1870s, the habit of holiday-making was firmly established; and the question was not whether to go, or where (people were loyal) or when. There was little freedom (or desire) to decide not to go. For the working class with their trade weeks, fixed holidays as for the Glasgow Fair, that was their holiday opportunity, and they took it regardless of how poor the weather was. The middle classes going for a month had pre-booked their accommodation quarters well in advance. The more prosperous who owned a second home in a resort were committed to a spell there by that, as were the but and benners. There is some evidence of last-minute and impulse decision-making. But mostly people went whatever. The spring holiday at Easter of 1898 was very wet, but the local Stirling paper noted that despite 'the most unsatisfactory description, crowds of golfers, cyclists and other pleasure seekers still pursued their pastimes under torrents of rain.' Bad weather might affect how they spent their money. Wet days meant poor sales for the ice cream vendors, the donkey riders, the outdoor pools. If bad weather did mostly not deter, did exceptionally good weather boost numbers? This seems likely. An example of this comes from Dunbar, where phenomenally fine weather in early September 1898 both attracted large numbers of bathers and persuaded others who had taken lodgings for the summer to renew their let for another month.[12] What did help decision-making for the holidaymakers, particularly the day tripper, was the increasing availability of weather forecasts published in the papers, which gave a better idea of what the next day might hold. Thanks to the electric telegraph, the staff at the Meteorological Department in London could by the 1860s collate reports from every part of Britain, which went to the newspapers on a daily basis.[13] These could be married up with reports from the resorts carried in papers such as the *Glasgow Herald*. Cyclists, caravanners and campers were able to take advantage.

But if most people in the nineteenth century had just to cope with what the weather served up, in the longer term the unpredictability of the Scottish summer was what was greatly to work against Scotland. The motor car allowed better-off families in search of summer sun to foray south post the Second World War to Devon and Cornwall, long drive though that was, and when cheap air flights to the Mediterranean and to Florida became available in the 1960s, the flight to guaranteed sun was a flight away from uncertainty.

War was another unpredictable factor. Depending on its location, length and nature, it could be severely disruptive of existing patterns and flows in tourism if Britain was a participant or even if a neutral. The level of impact depended on where, for how long and how intense the conflict was. Colonial wars far away might have little significance, but war on the Continent or with Continental countries changed where British tourists went and which foreign visitors came from where. In the eighteenth and nineteenth centuries the main effect, as far as Scotland was concerned, lay in how it reshaped the direction and flow of tourism. War was a blessing to domestic tourism, as those who might have holidayed abroad turned their attention to home resorts. This was good for Scottish tourism, as during the Napoleonic wars, when the flow of British tourists to the Continent was suspended, and was occasionally experienced again during the nineteenth century. The Franco-Prussian war of 1870–71 led to boosted numbers of visitors to Scotland.[14] particularly in the Highlands, with one paper reporting that 'owing to the Continental war, tourists swarmed in the North'. But mostly the various European and colonial conflicts of the nineteenth century had little impact on Scottish tourism.

In the twentieth century the impact of war was much more wide-ranging, and severe, as was shown by the First World War. There is no dispute as to the impact of war on tourism between 1914 and 1918. It disrupted tourism throughout Europe, and some countries lost heavily, not just belligerents. Neutral Switzerland, that nation of hotelkeepers, was brought to its knees. Tourism within Europe, to Europe and from Europe withered. The Middle East became a war zone and Thomas Cook's profits plummeted. Pre-war profits of £596k annually between 1909 and 1913 turned into losses of on average £274k every year between 1914 and 1918. Few British tourists went to Europe, and even fewer came from Europe. Worst of all, there was a complete cessation of tourism from America. Once those 100,000 who had fled Europe in the summer and early autumn of 1914 got back home, they stayed safe on their side of the Atlantic; not until 1919 did any start to return. And Scotland felt their absence. Abbotsford, that useful barometer of American tourism, had welcomed 2,700 American and Canadian visitors in 1913, but during the war years only penny numbers called – a mere nine in 1917. Hotels felt the draught. Stronachlachar at the west end of Loch Katrine, a favourite calling point for Americans pre-war, saw its business so reduced that it shut its doors in 1917. But while there was loss of custom from overseas, the war did offer some opportunity for compensatory traffic from within Britain, a self-righting mechanism. Might not British tourists, frustrated of their normal overseas destinations, look instead to holiday at home? British spas were hopeful that those who had been habitués of Baden Baden or Aix would try Harrogate or Moffat, that they might perhaps turn from the Riviera to Rothesay, that tourers would tour Scotland instead of the Continent, as petrol was not rationed, though a certain level of social pressure was brought to bear on frivolous motoring.[15]

The tourist industry in Scotland faced a number of problems. The military put some areas, particularly in the Highlands, out of bounds to the public, and the navy did likewise with waters around its bases: all excursion sailings in the Forth around Rosyth were prohibited. Travel was more difficult. The railways, rather surprisingly, still managed, despite all the additional military traffic, to provide for a considerable number of holiday excursion specials. But the transport system was increasingly under-resourced and overstretched. Though the pre-war sporting traffic had disappeared, as grouse-shooting was largely suspended, military trains clogged up the Highland Railway and other lines; it is not coincidence that the worst railway disaster in Britain occurred at Quintinshill near Gretna in May 1915. Coastal steamers were taken over for duties as minesweepers, guard ships or transports, which meant long queues for visitors wanting to travel to places which were only reachable by sea like Millport and Rothesay. Some were lost. The famous Clyde steamer the *Duchess of Hamilton* was sunk in November 1915, and the *Edinburgh Castle*, a stalwart of Forth sailings, which was converted from a minesweeper into a hospital ship, was blown up in September 1919 in the far-distant waters of the White Sea, to avoid capture by the Bolsheviks.[16] Ironically the *Waverley*, pre-war stalwart of the Rothesay and Craigendoran runs, came through four years of Admiralty work in the First World War only to be sunk at Dunkirk in May 1940.

If getting there was a problem, tourists also faced a restricted choice of accommodation. Some hotels and hydros, as already noted, were taken over for military use. Edinburgh's Craiglockhart Hydro became the Craiglockhart Military Hospital, famous for pioneering work in the treatment of shell shock; Dunblane and Peebles became centres of treatment for convalescing naval patients. Two Scottish hydros benefited from attacks by the German navy on the English East Coast. St Felix's from Southwold went to Moffat, and the Queen Margaret School at Scarborough, whose buildings there were shelled on 16 December 1914, moved north in the following month to the Atholl Palace at Pitlochry for the duration of the war. This move was brought about by Sir Henry Lunn, who had a daughter at the school and who had just bought the Atholl with the intention of making it a high-class sporting hotel. The arrival of the school was a welcome bonus, as it provided trade during the off season, with the hydro able to reopen for visitors during the school's summer vacation. Some resorts tried to cash in on the threat of renewed German action. Callander Hydro advertised that as it was sixty miles inland it was 'Secure from War's alarms.' Stonehaven promised 'rest and quiet for the war weary.' The Glasgow & South-Western Railway's luxury hotel at Turnberry was converted in 1917 into a flying school and officers' mess for the Royal Flying Corps, with part of the golf course becoming an aerodrome. The Great North of Scotland Railway's flagship railway hotel at Cruden Bay, where profits had been on the slide for years, somehow achieved a healthy profit on its hotel operation (£628) in 1916, but suffered a heavy loss on the golf (-£327).[17] There were shortages of labour as German and French waiters vanished and other men were conscripted. Food and drink supplies were sometimes scarce. All hotels were faced with the problem of staff shortages, reduced transport and food rationing, but while some coped well, others did not, incurring growing losses. Places such as Melrose and Crieff, with Crieff maintaining its dividend level at 9 per cent, were able to tap into a continuing demand for short and longer breaks for relaxation or tonic amongst professional and retired people. Forres was not as successful: receipts from visitors fell from £7,376 in 1913 to £4,352 in 1917, and losses mounted. The business only survived by moving downmarket to become in effect a boarding house. Work on the grand Gleneagles Hotel was suspended for the duration.

But whatever the difficulties, holidaymaking did continue throughout the war. A stay in the country or at the coast offered better food, eggs or fish say, than was available in the towns. A census taken by the town council at North Berwick, for reasons which are not now known, taken over the weekend of the 10 and 11 August 1918 found 3,311 visitors staying in the town as against 2,505 residents, quite a healthy number which took no account, of course, of day trippers. Professional and retired people still took holidays during the war, and there were also those on leave or recuperating.

What of the working class? It appears that there was a surprisingly resilience in working class holiday taking. While many men were away on service, especially after conscription was introduced in 1916, for those at home the war meant full employment and accordingly disposable income, and the government recognised, even though under heavy pressure for munitions and materials, that a holiday period would benefit morale and productivity. The war put money into the pockets of munitions workers, male and female, from which resorts benefited. Working class girls in particular were to be found in increasing numbers at the seaside resorts; one estimate in 1916 was that in some places there were twenty women to every young man. Nor was their behaviour as decorous as was thought proper. Munitionettes wanted to enjoy their leisure. Holidays such as the Glasgow Fair regained their pre-war momentum, as employers and the government alike recognised the need for a break to re-energise the workforce. By 1918, or so the editor of the *Glasgow Herald* thought, Fair Saturday traffic actually exceeded per-war levels. And there were reports that some working-class travellers finding themselves on crowded trains were prepared to pay the difference to upgrade themselves to first class. But complaints of bad behaviour, notably over heavy drinking, abounded about the holiday influxes. This was no new phenomenon, but one which seems to have acquired an additional edge. There was real feeling that 'behaving in such a foolish way', as the *Helensburgh Gazette* put it, 'as if no war was going on' was not right, and that it was not fair that some could so safely enjoy themselves when others were enduring the misery of service at the front. The journalist observed that munition workers' families were able to pay higher prices for accommodation than the 'family of the tommy who is in the thick of it in the trenches could afford'.[18] While food supplies were a problem, a particular grievance was that, when supplies of drink were short, especially whisky, these visitors quite literally drank the town dry. A local complained that after these invasions 'decent folk could not get their thrapple wet'.[19] At Helensburgh in 1917, all but three of the pubs were shut to conserve supplies during the Glasgow Fair, which caused a near riot amongst a thirsty mob of munitions workers. But drink-fuelled rowdiness was the price paid by residents for the prosperity brought by the munition workers and other visitors during the summer. Shopkeepers found their takings up, and anybody who had a room to let could make big money. In many resorts beds were made to work a double shift. It was a bonanza time for some; lodging-house proprietors and landladies were in a strong position to set what prices they liked.

Throughout the war, Glasgow's Fair Week continued to be a time of mass exodus from Glasgow although there was a significant change in the direction of the flow. The Isle of Man, a favourite destination, was beyond safe reach, and with the shortages of Clyde steamers, fewer went doun the watter. This meant that a higher percentage of the flow stayed on the mainland, in Ayrshire and the Inner Firth: estuarial but inland resorts such as Lochgoilhead and Dunoon gained at Rothesay's expense. Some thought that traffic during the Glasgow Fair was actually higher than in pre-war years. The *Callander Observer* put the rush down to the extraordinary prosperity of the industrial workforce, and their willingness to spend freely. Fife and the east of Scotland felt the impact: the influx of Glasgow Fair visitors to Portobello reached record levels in 1917, and the resort was crowded out. Every room in the neighbourhood was taken, even at ransom prices, and hundreds had to sleep on the beach. Beer supplies were drunk dry. But the visitors were happy. The *Scotsman* reported that 'Money has evidently been no obstacle. Increased railway fares, enhanced terms for rooms, and dearer food have made no difference. Glasgow and the wife and wains have gone to the coast willy nilly'.[20] The report added that 'Men, women and children were wading with the enthusiasm that is familiar on Clydeside.' It was altogether a joyous, happy multitude. It is somewhat surprising that Portobello continued to be such a draw, as its attractions were much reduced with the loss of the Marine Garden, which had been a very popular pre-war amusement park. When opened in 1909 it had drawn 750,000 visitors in its first year. But it was requisitioned in August 1914, initially as barracks for the Territorial Army and latterly as quarters for the newly formed (1918) RAF; the associated funfair and cafes closed, although Cordona's funfair city further along the esplanade remained open.[21] A further blow to Portobello was that it also lost its pier. It had become increasingly rickety, and the refusal by the Ministry of Munitions to allow the purchase of repair materials led to its immediate demolition as unsafe in early 1918. Other resorts reported an exceptional influx of Glasgow folk, including Berwick-upon-Tweed. Its holiday visitors were normally drawn from the Borders woollen towns, but in 1917 and 1918 there were many Glaswegians there, their patois, as the local paper sniffed, rather grating on the locals' ears. 'English visitors have arrived in good numbers for August and one notes a pleasing change of accent compared with the awfu' Glasgae week'.[22] But their money was welcome.

Recent accounts of the Scottish economy during the First World War tend to have ignored tourism in favour of the munitions and war related industries,[23] leaving only a blank as to what happened to tourism, as if it came to a total halt in 1914, to restart only with peace in 1919. The fact is that tourism did not disappear, though it did mutate. There were many problems by way of legacy. There was no Scottish equivalent to a new form of tourism which developed after the war, that of visits to the battlefield and cemeteries, which brought coach parties in number to the war-ravaged areas of northern France. Shortage of demand was not an issue; in 1920 the volume of Glasgow Fair traffic was said to be enormous. The real difficulties lay in the condition of tourist amenities and attractions. Hotels and premises which had been requisitioned were handed back, but usually in very poor order and with a huge backlog of repairs, which compensation could not cover. Some managements struggled to find the necessary capital to modernise, and their businesses folded. Craiglockhart reopened briefly as a hydro but could not re-establish itself, and in 1920 it was sold for a Catholic educational college. The sisters faced a real struggle to clean the decayed hydro, infested as it was by rats and beetles. Moffat Hydro also briefly returned to civilian use but burnt down, some thought rather too conveniently, in June 1921. Elsewhere golf courses and sports grounds ploughed up for agricultural use had to be restored. The grouse moors likewise. A long-term demographic legacy was the shortage of young men; it was hard to find enough male partners for the tea dances.

While in no way downplaying the legacy of the war and the post-war challenge to renovate requisitioned properties and rebuild sporting tourism, the Scottish experience of the First World War illustrates the flexibility and resilience of tourism. It would seem that, once people had a taste for holidaymaking, they came to regard it almost as a birthright, to be experienced in some form or another, whatever the context.

The impact of the Second World War on tourism demands a full study. But there were parallels with what had happened in the First. Hotels and hydros were again requisitioned, as hospitals, military or naval establishments. The West of Scotland Convalescent Home at Dunoon was taken over for anti-submarine work and renamed HMS Osprey; Kyles of Bute Hydro (HMS Varbel) became a submarine base, and so on. Callander Hydro was used by the Poles, who sold off all the hydro cutlery and napkins for cigarettes. Transport was more difficult than in the First World War. Many steamers were requisitioned, petrol was tightly rationed and pleasure motoring almost completely out of the question unless fuelled by the black market. Bus services did operate, but sporting tourism was brought to a standstill; moors lay idle, golf courses converted for airfields or agriculture. Far more of the country was put out of bounds for military training, and of course, the beaches of the east coast of Scotland were covered with invasion defences – barbed wire, mines and concrete blocks. The last were at least to have a peacetime usefulness as shelter and changing cover – better than under a towel. And whereas the First World War had seen the horse-drawn bathing machine disappear, what was missing from many Scottish beaches by the end of the Second World War were the once ubiquitous beach huts: only seven of Gullane's 140 huts were left by 1946.[24]

The resilience of tourism is also borne out when we look at the impact of economic conditions. How much money – or how little – people had in their pockets seems bound to affect holidaymaking numbers when it came to travel and renting accommodation. There is corroboration of this. An example came in July 1879, when the numbers leaving Glasgow during the Fair exodus over Friday and Saturday were only about 120,000, whereas in the previous year, before the commercial crisis which had seen the City of Glasgow Bank collapse, the figure had been 180,000. This was a fall 'attributed to a want of money amongst the working classes'.[25] No depression should, therefore, have been worse for Scottish tourism than that of the early 1930s, the so-called Great Depression.[26] It was an international crisis which severely affected that key source of tourists, North America, and elsewhere. The number of visitors from North America to the UK fell by a half from *c.* 110,000 in the late 1920s to 54,000 in 1933, recovering only in the later 1930s.[27] This fall in the numbers of North American and other relatively well-heeled overseas visitors was a serious concern. Rightly so, as they were an important element in heritage tourism, on the trail of their roots, and as tenants of sporting estates, on which many of the sportsmen were English or American or Continental. There is some corroborative evidence to confirm the scarcity of American visitors in Scotland. Abbotsford in 1932, despite that year being the centenary of Scott's death, found itself with only 215 North American visitors instead of the two thousand or so annually in the 1920s. 'It is due, I suppose', wrote Sir General Maxwell-Scott in the house Visitors' Book, 'to the depressed times in which we live'. Castles, great houses and literary shrines suffered a drought, as did the hotels of Edinburgh.

But in Scotland it was the industrial working class that suffered worst and for longest from the slump. It was at its most severe in the leading sector of shipbuilding and in the associated heavy industries of coal and steel, worst regionally in west central Scotland, where between 1931 and 1935 near enough one-third of the workforce of the region as a whole was unemployed.[28] Unemployment was at its most acute in shipbuilding with 76 per cent of the workforce of nearly 30,000 in 1929 out of work two years later. Engineering was also hard hit, with 43 per cent unemployment in 1932. But it was not just shipbuilding, nor just the west of Scotland. The textile sector also suffered, with 70 per cent of the work force in jute at Dundee unemployed in 1931 and 1932. Other activities to suffer included fishing at Aberdeen, and even in agriculture, where there had been a collapse in prices, these were bleak times. The nadir came in January 1933 when nearly one-third of the insured working population of Scotland were out of work: over 400,000 people. Half of these were in the west of Scotland with no fewer than 136,331 registered in Glasgow alone. In the month of January there were 114,000 Glaswegians on poor relief.[29] The city was quiet, as the shipyards closed. One writer said that a steamer trip down the Clyde past '*an hour*' (his emphasis) of empty shipways gave an idea of how devastating the blight was.[30] Unemployment was severe and prolonged; there had been downturns before but what the 1930s brought was long term unemployment cases for years rather than months amongst the skilled working class, particularly those in the heavy industries, and money was very tight amongst those who had had disposable income, for whom a holiday had been part of their year. It would be reasonable to suppose that domestic tourism in Scotland should have taken a serious hit.

There were those who were relatively unscathed, which allows talk of 'two Scotlands.' For some, the 1930s were not hungry. For those who were in employment, money went further. The civil service, local government, finance and the professions were relatively unscathed, and it is not surprising that, whereas in 1933 unemployment in Glasgow – predominately a working class city – was at 33 per cent, in Edinburgh it was only 12 per cent. Edinburgh had a halo effect on the Lothians. Even in the worst years of the Depression, middle-class tourism and middle-class resorts alike seem to have done reasonably. The fading spa at Bridge of Allan was able to report in July 1932 that it was having a very successful season, with the early summer particularly busy, thanks to touring motorists and large numbers of American and South African tourists (plus a large medical conference). The continuing strength of middle-class demand was reflected in the robust financial health of the hydros, that peculiarly Scottish addiction. Peebles and Crieff, those flagship hydro hotels, saw a slight fall in their numbers, but not in their profits or dividends even though times were not easy. In August 1931 a leading hotel manager, John McDonald of the Waverley Hydro at Melrose wrote to his managing director that 'I am sorry to say that business is very indifferent... the Hotels in the district are also much below par: and I fear that the season generally will be unsatisfactory. It is distressing to hear that the Bank of England has had to receive assistance from France and the USA also that shipyards are being closed down permanently.'[31] What most concerned him and others in his sector was that the old pattern of respectable families coming for up to a month was breaking down. But it was not poverty but prosperity that allowed this, a new mobility particularly amongst the middle-class young, holidaying where they fancied rather than where their parents had gone (and continued to go). Some went youth hostelling or on holidays organised by the National Union of Students or some similar organisation.[32] One group of Edinburgh University students found free board at a south coast hotel in return for their turning out at the tea dances to partner the many unattached ladies. John McDonald did worry in 1931 that his clientele was getting older, and that there was undoubtedly 'a growing tendency for people to take shorter (and perhaps more frequent) holidays, and this of course applies especially to motorists... they are in a position to go further on with ease and comfort and speed.'[33] The *Daily Sketch* in an article of 15 August 1929[34] suggested that the 'whole process of holidaymaking is being revolutionised [with] the picnic habit amongst car owners, the growing popularity of camping, the end of family holidays, the desire of the young to see Europe etc.' Mobility did mean that some resorts and hotels did suffer. The Great North of Scotland's big golfing railway hotel at Cruden Bay closed (but the first-class golf course remained open). Some of the seaside resorts that had catered before the war for the well-off, where the pre-war pattern had been of the entire household decamping from the city, servants and all, for the summer to their property at the coast, had already noticed a change. Big seaside houses were subdivided or sold as boarding houses (as at North Berwick). Servants were fewer and more expensive, and there was some downsizing. But this was primarily a function of the war, rather than of the Depression.

There were certainly fears of recession at the working class resorts in particular, with so many either unemployed or on short-time working. The problem was not the time, of which the unemployed had all too much, but the money available. Even before the full onset of the slump there had been concerns, as reported in the *Daily Sketch*, 15 August 1929: 'Scotland is half empty this summer. Anxious hotel proprietors in all the holiday resorts are asking "where are all the people going?"' Some industrial communities were in dire straits, as was true of Dumbarton, where the shipyards were silent. Its local paper, the *Lennox Herald*, of 16 July 1932 commented that

> The fair holidays are here with us again but without their old expectancy. We are a town mostly existing on the dole and a great many of us have had too many holidays. But we cannot altogether ignore the Fair (although it is likely to be a 'stay at home' fair).

In the following year it spoke sadly of the 'many in town to whom the holidays will mean nothing.'[35] Another visitor to Glasgow commented sadly that

> You couldn't find a metropolis of over a million inhabitants anywhere in Europe that is less exciting than Britain's second city. Quick prosperity made it dull, and bitter adversity has made it pathetic, for Glasgow has been terribly hit and long held down by the great depression.[36]

But what the coverage in Scottish newspapers, which carried lengthy columns on travel and excursions, suggests is that the commitment of working-class people to their annual holiday outing was remarkably resilient in the 1930s, rather to the surprise of commentators at the time. If anything there was not a decline but an increase in the volume. 'With trade depressed and industry in a bad way, one would have thought that the holiday traffic would have dropped whereas it has increased.'[37] The writer added a significant comment: 'Glasgow people, especially the poorer classes would rather starve than go without their annual holiday.' Even two years later, when some had been out of work for the whole period, the Fair holiday still flourished. The *Glasgow Herald* observed in July 1932 that there was 'no evidence of the inevitable results of trade depression and those who have bemoaned the absence of money in the country must have wondered how it was managed.' Rail traffic was heavy, with the LMS having to arrange 103 additional trains to Morecambe, Southport, Blackpool, and Stranraer for Ireland. Said one railway official, or so the reporter sent to interview him recorded, 'as far as can be ascertained there is no falling off in the holiday traffic in any way'. Bus services were equally fully in demand as they had been in the previous summer, when amazing bus traffic from Glasgow to the east of Scotland had been seen (and suffered) in Stirling on the Fair Friday. At certain periods, the local paper reported, there were ten buses an hour passing through Stirling from Glasgow going towards the Fife Coast. On Saturday eighty buses passed through the town for Aberdeen. The following year 1933 saw huge queues in Glasgow for the steamers, as well as at the bus stations. It was estimated[38] that no fewer than 400,000 people had left the city on the Saturday by rail, road, sea and even a few by air. The *Evening Express* concluded that the 1933 'Fair had *scorned* [my emphasis] depression'. It was an annual challenge for the newspapers to produce a figure for the number of Glasgow Fair holiday makers, but 1933 was thought to have set a record at 500,000 travellers as against perhaps 250,000 in 1930. And this was from a city with a population in 1931 of 1.1 million. Depression did not deter. This is in line with what Walton has argued for Blackpool, that 'despite the advent of severe trade depression... visitors still poured in from the cotton towns, some allegedly returning to draw their dole'.[39]

It is clear how well Aberdeen did during the fair holidays of the early 1930s. It had been a resort on the up in the 1920s, aided by active railway company support in the form of attractive advertising and special excursion fares. The railway posters of Frank Henry Mason (London & North Eastern Railway (LNER) 1928) and of Alexander Mathewson (joint LMS & LNER 1935) of the 'silver city by the sea', which made much of the seafront and sand, are amongst the finest of the genre.[40] 'Aberdeen is becoming more popular every year', thought the *Stirling Observer* in July 1928, when the local trades holiday had seen 500 travel north by train for a weekend in the Granite City, their numbers swollen by 150 day trippers. There had been substantial investment by the town council in the 1920s, probably fortuitous rather than by foresight, in the beach area. This took the form of an improved and extended esplanade, with shelters and toilets, on which £108,000 was spent, a ballroom, and bathing station, tennis, putting, golf and other sporting facilities, with boating and fishing added in the 1930s. Private enterprise provided Cordona's carnival pleasure park, compete with scenic railway and 'automatic speedway', at which, the City's official Guide promised, 'the holiday maker could spend many a carefree afternoon and evening at.....infinitesimal cost'.[41] The city did well, and its beach was key to this, and much of the inflow seems to have been from Glasgow.[42] Twelve extra holiday trains had to be laid on from Glasgow to Aberdeen on the Saturday of the Fair holiday in 1930. Two years later the *Glasgow Herald* (Monday 18July 1932) reported that at the weekend over 20,000 holiday makers from Glasgow and the west of Scotland had arrived by rail and bus in Aberdeen. As the Glasgow Fair holiday coincided with the Aberdeen Trades Week, which generated as many going away from Aberdeen as were arriving, it is not surprising that there were 'animated scenes' at the main station as influx and exodus (plus their luggage) collided. The number from Glasgow was no less the following year, despite the heavy showers. If Aberdeen's experience was typical of Scottish resorts, it would be difficult to argue that there was any downturn in tourism. Or was it the more distant resorts that were at risk in straitened times? The Isle of Man saw its visitor numbers fall from 555,000 in 1929 to 451,000 in 1931.[43] Some of this may have been due to reduced numbers of Glaswegians, although numbers were still buoyant in 1930: 'the largest since the war', or so the *Glasgow Herald* thought.[44] But there is little evidence of the popular English resorts losing custom. Newspaper reports in 1932 spoke only of how well patronised that year were the Yorkshire and Northumberland resorts, as were those of the Clyde. The Glasgow Fair of 1932 saw record crowds of 20,000 in Largs on the

Saturday, and also on Arran. Rothesay reported that the crowds that weekend 'were fully as large as in former years'.[45] At Saltcoats bathing station on the Sunday of the Fair 16 July 1933 there was recorded a record number at the local swimming pool of 4,511 bathers in a single day, with 20,000 Glaswegian holiday makers in the town over the weekend. And with them came the usual petty crimes. Two enterprising youths were convicted on the Monday of stealing bathing costumes 'of a superior quality… to resell to newly arrived visitors', costumes which had been hung to dry in a back green.[46] Gang fights were not unknown and a much more unpleasant form of holiday crime.

What is clear is that in demanding times resorts had to invest in facilities, as Aberdeen did, and that some were making additional efforts, building new swimming and paddling pools, or at Rothesay floodlighting the esplanade, which allowed impromptu dancing and putting by artificial light. Councils begin to relax what could or could not be done on Sundays, long a moot point in Scotland. There was a general lifting of Sunday restrictions. At Gourock in 1932 for the first time the open-air swimming pool was opened on a Sunday afternoon as well as the morning. But what also mattered was the provision of entertainment and facilities. At Berwick-upon-Tweed, in 1933 a local councillor argued that it was time that Berwick was sitting up and taking notice.[47] He was very concerned that seaside resorts north and south were laying themselves out to provide better bathing, and cited the fact that Portobello was spending £50,000. If Berwick did not make an effort, there was a danger of 'disappointing visitors from Glasgow': the council had to spend to get a return. Eric Simpson has described[48] the politics involved in the construction of pools. Competition required these but economic conditions could work against a realisation. A proposal by the Town Council of Leven to build an open-air, seawater pool to replace the existing freshwater pond in Letham Glen was vetoed by ratepayers on the grounds of cost. The poll taken, as was required under 1892 legislation, on 4 February 1931 showed a clear majority against (739 to 619). But there were many successes, none more so than that at Portobello, where a large open-air pool, with lockers for 1,284 bathers, opened in 1936 at a cost of £90,000.[49] It had two very popular assets as well as the huge grandstand: wave-making machinery and heated water from the nearby power station. The previous year the Nardinis had opened in Largs their celebrated vast white art deco ice cream parlour, a restaurant which became synonymous with a day out for Clydesiders. To the need to upgrade it was councils and private enterprise that responded, not government. While a Treasury grant was made available to the Scottish Tourism Development Association in 1930, it was for a mere £345, (and subsequently reduced so that by 1939 it was down to £250).[50] Hoteliers and others in the tourism business wanted more significant assistance but nothing was forthcoming. The argument that 'if the govt [sic] has given subsidies to such wealthy concerns as Coal mines and the like, I cannot see any serious objection to their granting some assistance to an industry which employs large numbers of people'[51] fell on deaf ears.

If the volume of holidaymaking kept up, did its character and duration change? Given the scale of unemployment during the Depression, it would seem only inevitable that those Scottish coastal resorts which had catered for working-class custom would have suffered by people taking shorter holidays: the weekend or week-long holidays trimmed to a day trip, travelling nearer at hand, living more cheaply, or simply taking no holiday. The *Glasgow Herald* commented how a significant feature of the holiday traffic in July 1930 was the large volume of one-day excursionists. This was a recurring theme. The *Glasgow Evening Times*[52] in 1932 thought that the number of people who preferred to devote the Fair holidays to day trips 'had enormously increased'. The journalist referred to the popularity of railway runabout tickets, and bus tours: 'One bus company sent off 20 special coaches to London, and over 100 to elsewhere. Devon, South Coast, Highlands….and daily bookings remain very heavy.' Credit should be given to the transport companies for responding to hard times. What does emerge about the railways is that companies such as the Caledonian and the LNER were much more active in the face of growing bus competition than has been allowed. They were prepared to try new excursions and day trips to generate traffic. In July 1933 an evening excursion to Ayr during the local holidays was offered.[53] This left Stirling at 5.10 and arrived at Ayr at 7.20. Two hours only was allowed at Ayr and its beach before the return left. It would seem a lot of travel for a short blast of sea air, but the excursion sold out completely with 300 bookings and was repeated the next week. This is but one example of many ventures; evening trips to Portobello were another success. What also stands out is the degree of improvisation on the day, should the crowds outstrip the scheduled provision. The railways had an extraordinary (and unthinkable nowadays) reserve capacity in staff and coaches which gave them an ability to mount additional trains on the day. So busy was the Saturday of Glasgow Fair in 1933, despite cloudy weather, that even with the 600 specials already scheduled, including three overnight to London, both the LMS and the LNER had to – and were able to – organise additional trains as they found demand exceeded their timetabled provision. A third train, for example. was provided for the Oban West Highland route after the first two specials of the morning at 6 a.m. had left with about 1,000 people, and also others to Aberdeen and the North East; Monday services were provided for the 'stay at home' folk.[54] What helped was a pricing policy of cheap day and excursion tickets, and a new 'round about' ticket 'for many people of limited means these tickets will mean all the difference between a holiday at home and a holiday as it should be spent – seeing new places'.[55] The railways may have been forced by the buses to compete, but they played their part in allowing holidaymakers to travel.

This fondness for a day away, rather than committing to the same resort for the week, was a source of instability. 'Glasgow invasion of Berwick' was the headline of the *Berwick Journal* on 20 July 1933, more than for many years, prompted in part, it was speculated, by newspaper reports of how good the weather was. The first wave arrived on the Friday and at a late hour a number of visitors were going around in search of accommodation. It was a sign of the times of a new fluidity, of what could be called impulse holidaymakers, the old loyalty to place having broken down. The weather could and did affect whether a day trip was taken. That was serious for boarding houses and lodgings. Another problem for those who provided accommodation, and for whom the Fair had been the busiest time of the year, was the growing enthusiasm for tents and camping, holidaying on the cheap. The Glasgow correspondent of the *Stirling Observer*, 22 July 1930, noted that 'many people who cannot afford the cost of living in a boarding house now take tents with them and it is a common sight on the outskirts of any country or seaside resort to see a colony of tents gathered together like so many mushrooms'. In July 1932 there were tents 'dotted all over the outlying districts [of Arran], giving shelter to a cosmopolitan crowd of simple lifers', campers were 'numerous' on the outskirts of Dunoon, and near Troon at Barassie a holiday town had sprung up complete with temporary store and canvas church. Thus many tent dwellers have solved the problem of how to be happy though workless'.[56] It was not just folk from Glasgow that were doing this. In 1933 Berwick-upon-Tweed experienced an influx from the Borders, with lots of tents pitched near Spittal, some twenty above the beach and a further few on a farmer's ground at Sea View farm. 'Borderers like the rest of the nation are taking to the open air life more than has been evident for many years.'[57] It seems to have been a mixture of individual initiative in just finding a piece of vacant ground, or getting permission from a farmer, but there are signs of larger scale ventures as at Lunderston Bay. Camping was no new arrival. There was a long tradition of Volunteer and Territorial Army camps under canvas, and after the First World War, tents, marquees and camping equipment were readily available for scout and guide, Boys' Brigade, church and school camps, and for holidaying more cheaply in general. There were also, for the better-off, railway camping coaches. The membership of the Camping Club of Great Britain and Ireland grew from 820 in 1910 to 3,000 by 1927, 6,000 in 1933 and 8,000 in 1935, with some permanent sites. The idea of a tented holiday camp, cheap and cheerful, seems to have been pioneered on the Isle of Man, where Cunningham's Holiday Camp started in 1894.[58] Others followed suit, and Scotland's first cooperative summer camp was at Roseland farm near Rothesay in 1911, whose bell tents (later chalets) could accommodate 600.[59] But the Depression certainly accelerated enthusiasm for this form of holidaying: cheap, open air and healthy.

Another form of cheap holiday taking was simply staying with friends and relations. There was a long established pattern of families staying with relatives in the country or at the coast (the Broons landing on a cousin at South Queensferry). The problem is, of course, that the scale of this form of holidaymaking is largely submerged. Brunner estimated that in 1937 out of a total population in the UK of 46 million, perhaps 15 million took a holiday of one or more weeks. But she allowed that there are other forms of holidaymaking which 'are widespread but impossible to estimate...we can only guess how many go to stay with friends or relatives for their holiday, but it must be considerable. It is customary for children to be farmed out to relatives. [which] leaves little trace...their part as holiday makers may seem to be minimized in a study of holiday trades'.[60] Anecdotal evidence suggests, and it would be logical, that this was a way for people with very limited means to get away. It may not have been the whole family, but perhaps just the children.

An interesting observation was made in Dumbarton, that hard-hit shipbuilding town, that while everyone was surprised by the volume of holiday traffic, 'a local aspect was that there was not the old going-off of family parties. It was the young people who were able to spend the money on a trip to the holiday resorts.'[61] Some people in poverty had their holidays paid by others. In England there was the work of the Church Army, which took advertising in Ward Lock & Co's Guides to seek charitable giving: 'Sunshine in a £5 note. A mother and three children can be taken from over- crowded slums for a fortnight at the sea', as did the Shaftesbury Society. There was the Fresh Air Fortnight scheme of the YMCA. Of particular importance in the west of Scotland was Glasgow United Evangelistic Association, which had been in operation since before the First World War. The Glasgow Necessitous Children's Holiday Camp Fund, supervised by the Corporation's education department, sent on holiday between 1925 and 1937 some 67,984 children or an average of 5,000 children a year. Many more could have benefited, had the resources allowed.[62] A fundraising film, 'sadness and gladness', survives from 1928, showing tenement children enjoying a holiday at Gullane school in East Lothian.[63] Many children will have had at least an outing at some stage of the year, through a Sunday school picnic or the Band of Hope.

What was the effect on resorts of cheap holidaymaking? If people chose to camp, or not even to stay overnight, that hurt those whose living was from providing accommodation. But shopkeepers and others also suffered. There might be more day trippers, still coming but for shorter time and spending less. If the numbers of holidaymakers had not fallen, as has been argued above, there is some evidence that the average spend did fall. The week before the coming of the Fair customarily saw a rush by the few to get married (and thus use the Fair as a honeymoon). In July 1932, for example, civil marriages before a sheriff in Glasgow numbered no fewer than sixty-three on the Thursday before the Fair Holiday. It was also marked by a rush by many working-class people to withdraw holiday money from the Glasgow Savings Bank. The savings banks were where the working class put their small savings, whether for a rainy day or holiday spend. Confirmation of their importance comes from the intervention of the Provost of Greenock in a debate in August 1934 over the means test for benefits. Times were so hard, and unemployment had so sapped the savings of the decent ordinary working man, or so he said, that no fewer than 7,000 in Greenock had drawn out every penny of savings they had.[64] Withdrawals from the Glasgow Savings Bank in the month before the Fair Holidays fell by 30 per cent or so in the worst Depression years. While they were still over £700,000 in 1932 and 1933, the figure had fallen appreciably from their pre-Depression levels of about £875,000 in 1928 and 1929, and the astonishing figure of 'almost £1,000,000' in 1930.[65]

This was a significant fall and it hurt resort income. The spend may have mattered more to the resorts than the sheer volume of visitors; the impact of the Depression was not in terms of numbers but spend. It was the change in length of stay and expenditure that showed that times were hard and circumstances straitened for many of the working class. There were more day trippers, and fewer for the week, more camping or staying with relatives, and the fall in spend meant landladies and lodgings felt the impact (more than the hotels). Of course, economic downturns were not new. Stoppages in trade, lay-offs and unemployment, as well as the good times, had characterised the industrial economy for decades. Working-class individuals and families had in the past had to evolve strategies to cope. What was different about the Depression was that for many the downturn was so prolonged: months, even years, rather than weeks, and that the economy of taking the day trip or short weekend rather than the week away was the repeated experience of many rather than the few. What is also evident is that not all resorts suffered equally. And some resorts swam against the tide, notably Aberdeen, which managed to achieve growth. This mirrors the findings of Walton and Huggins about the seaside resorts of the north-east of England: 'What seems to be clear is that unemployment or short time work did not necessarily mean that people went without visits to the seaside... enjoyment of at least one visit to the seaside in the year, with its excitement and release seems to have been a spending priority.'[66] Holiday-making, of one kind or another, during the Depression seems to have held up as surprisingly well as the other two staple enthusiasms or addictions of the Scottish working class, football[67] and drinking.

The experience of the 1930s does underline how deeply tourism was now part of Scottish life. What had once been an experience only for the elite had become something enjoyed by all levels of society. The holiday was now part of the expected and desired pattern of life. No part of Scotland was untouched. Some areas, such as Bute, were destinations, others, as was true of Glasgow, only provided holidaymakers, and a third category were both suppliers and receivers. The extent of movement generated by holidaymaking had become extraordinary. Even a small industrial town like Stirling in the 1930s saw thousands of its own depart each summer, and as many thousands arrive as day trippers or summer visitors. There might be fluctuation, but tourism was by now embedded.

Notes

1   Fraser, David (ed.), *Christian Watt Papers*, (Edinburgh, 2012), p. 34.
2   Auerbach, Jeffrey, *The Great Exhibition*, (New Haven, CT, 1999) citing the unpublished diary of James Tod in the National Library of Scotland.
3   Durie, *Scotland for the Holidays*, pp. 147–48.
4   Kinchin, Perilla and Kinchin, Juliet, *Glasgow's Great Exhibitions*, (Bicester, c.1990).

5 Jarvie, Grant, *Highland Games: The Making of the Myth*, (Edinburgh, 1991), p. 72. There are currently (2015) around sixty.

6 See, for example, Page, Stephen J. and Durie, Alastair, 'Tourism in Wartime Britain 1914–1918: a case study in adaptation and innovation by Thomas Cook & Sons', in Ateljevic, Jovo and Page, Stephen J. (eds), *Tourism and Entrepreneurship*, (Oxford, 2009), pp. 60–88.

7 Devine, T. M. (ed.), *The Transformation of the Scottish Economy*, (Edinburgh, 2005); the chapter on the modernisation of agriculture by Euan Cameron states (p. 205) that an effect of foot-and-mouth disease was that tourism numbers fell by 7 per cent in 2001.

8 For example, the Scottish air travel firm, Globespan, in January 2010.

9 Dawson, Alastair, *So Foul and Fair a Day. A History of Scotland's Weather and Climate*, (Edinburgh, 2009), p. 189, argues that there was benign weather in the later 1920s, and that many of the summers of the 1930s were warm and good.

10 Malcolm, George and Maxwell, A., *Grouse and Grouse Moors*, (London, 1910), pp. 278–9.

11 Kinchin and Kinchin, p. 166.

12 *Haddingtonshire Courier*, 10 September 1898.

13 Moore, Peter, *The Weather Experiment*, (London, 2015), pp. 274–5.

14 Crieff Hydro Records, Directors' Minute Book 4 May 1871; 'that sad cause which led so many tourists to visit Scotland instead of going to the Continent'.

15 *The Times,* 23 December 1914. 'The most conspicuous difference which the war will make will be in travel to the Continent. This year the crowds of Germans will not be seen at Liverpool Street Station making their way to Cologne, Bremen, Hamburg, Berlin or elsewhere in the Fatherland, nor will there be flocks of tourists going to Paris and the Swiss resorts. The South-Eastern and Chatham Railway hope that the seaside towns will attract a considerable part of the traffic that has been wont to go to the Continental resorts.'

16 Brodie, Ian, *Steamers of the Forth*, (Newton Abbott, 1976), p. 79.

17 Sangster, Alan (ed.), *The Story and Tales of the Buchan Line*, (Oxford, 1983), p. 36.

18 *Helensburgh Gazette*, 24 May 1916.

19 *Helensburgh Gazette*, 30 July 1917.

20 Foley, Archie and Munro, Margaret, *Portobello and the Great War*, (Stroud, 2013), p. 42.

21 Foley and Munro, pp. 40–1.

22 *Haddingtonshire Courier*, 2 August 1918.

23 See, for example Lee, C. H., 'The Scottish Economy', in Macdonald, Catriona M. and Macfarlane, E. W. (eds), *Scotland and the Great War*, (East Linton, 1999).

24 Cox, Michael (ed.), *Two Villages at War*, Gullane and Dirleton History Society, (1995), p. 8.

25 *Glasgow Herald*, 25 July 1879.

26 This section summarises a much fuller examination to be found in Durie, Alastair, 'No Holiday this Year? The depression of the 1930s and tourism in Scotland', *Journal of Tourism History*, Vol. 2, No. 2 (August 2010), pp. 67–82.

27 Middleton, Victor C., *British Tourism. The Remarkable Story of Growth*, (Oxford, 2005), Appendix 5, p. 189. Though the fall is similar, these figures differ from those given by Norval, A. J., *The Tourist Industry, A National and International Survey*, (London, 1936), p. 73.

28 Harvie, Christopher, *No Gods and Precious Few Heroes*, p. 47. See also Gibb, Andrew, *Glasgow. The Making of a City*, (London, 1983).

29 Slaven, A., *The Development of the West of Scotland*, (London, 1975), p. 199.

30 Clark, *Scotland on £10*, p. 112.

31 National Archives of Scotland, Kemp papers GD 327/381 I August 1931.

32 Barton, Susan, *Working-class Organisations and Popular Tourism 1840–1970*, (Manchester, 2005), pp. 154–6.
33 NAS GD 327/212 Kemp MS: memorandum about the Progress of the Waverley Hydropathic Company, 1931.
34 *The Daily Sketch*, 15 August 1929.
35 *Lennox Herald*, 15 July 1933.
36 Clark, *Scotland on £10*, On Glasgow [chapter XIV].
37 Glasgow Correspondent of the *Stirling Observer*, 22 July 1930.
38 *Glasgow Herald*, Monday 17 July 1933.
39 Walton, John K., *Blackpool*, (Edinburgh, 1998), p. 120.
40 Furness, Richard, *Poster to Poster: Railway Journeys in Art. Volume 1. Scotland.* (Cleckheaton, 2009), pp. 69–71. Other resorts in the north-east that are featured include Cruden Bay and Fraserburgh.
41 Perren, Richard, 'Survival and Decline: The economy of Aberdeen 1918–1970', in Fraser, W. Hamish and Lee, Clive H. (eds), *Aberdeen. 1800–2000 A New History*, (East Linton, 2000), pp. 122–3.
42 An account of the pleasures of Aberdeen, its beach, trams and harbour for a Glasgow child on holiday is given by George Rountree, *A Govan Childhood*, (East Linton, 1993), pp. 62–5. His father, an engineer in employment, took his family north to Aberdeen in 1932, 1933 and again in 1935.
43 Beckerson, John, *Holiday Isle. The Golden Era of the Manx Boarding House*, (Douglas, 2008), p. 63.
44 *Glasgow Herald*, Monday 21 July 1930. 'Thirty thousand people were landed at Douglas over the weekend, the arrival of Glasgow holidaymakers being the largest since the war. A large number of Scots people are this year wearing the national dress which adds brightness to the animated scenes on the promenades and shores.'
45 *Glasgow Herald*, Monday 18 July 1932.
46 *Glasgow Evening Times*, 17 July 1933.
47 *Berwick Journal*, Town Council Affairs, 27 July 1933.
48 Simpson, Eric, 'East Fife's Open-Air Swimming Pools – safe places for dooking', *Scottish Local History*, Vol. 67 (Summer 2006), pp. 5–11.
49 Smith, Janet, *Liquid Assets: The Lidos and Open Air Swimming Pools of Britain*, (London, 2009), pp. 120–1.
50 Hay B., and Adams, G., *History and development of the Scottish Tourist Board*, STB Working paper, July 1994.
51 NAS, GD 327/219 Kemp Papers: Letter from McDonald to Kemp, 7 August 1930.
52 *Glasgow Evening Times*, 18 July 1932.
53 *Stirling Observer*, Tuesday 18 July 1933: 'a remarkably low-priced evening excursion fate of 2/3 which defies competition'.
54 *Glasgow Herald*, 15 July 1933.
55 *Stirling Observer*, 18 July 1933
56 *Glasgow Evening Times*, Monday 18 July 1932, 'What's doing at the Coast'.
57 *The Berwick Journal*, 16 July 1933, 'Spittal subjects'.
58 Beckerson, *Holiday Isle*, pp. 109–11.
59 Barton, *Working Class Organisations and Tourism*, p. 154.
60 Brunner, Elizabeth, *Holiday Making and the Holiday Trades*, (Oxford, 1945), pp. 7–8.
61 *Lennox Herald*, 22 July 1933.
62 In a House of Commons debate, one of the local MPs for Glasgow, David Kirkwood, (*Hansard*, 26 April 1934) said that there were 67,000 children in Glasgow whose parents were too poor to afford a holiday that year.
63 National Library of Scotland. Scottish Screen Archive. See also Scotland on Screen for a 1934 film, Tantallon Castle Canvas Camp.
64 Levitt, Ian, *Poverty and Welfare in Scotland*, (Edinburgh, 1988), p. 139.

65 *Glasgow Herald*, Saturday 19 July, 1930. Durie, *Scotland for the Holidays*, pp. 196–7; *Lennox Herald*, 15 July 1933.
66 Huggins, M. and Walton, J. K., *The Teeside Seaside between the Wars*, (North-East England History Institute, 2003), pp. 24–5.
67 Ross, David, *The Roar of the Crowd. Following Scottish Football down the Years*, (Argyll, 2005) talks of the hungry thirties, but 1930 saw a new phenomenon: the six-figure mid-week attendance.

7 The balance sheet in economic and cultural terms

This chapter considers what the impact of tourism was on Scotland. It will suggest that the value of tourism, in terms of employment and income, was already so significant by the end of the nineteenth century as to allow tourism to rank alongside the recognised staples of the Scottish economy: shipbuilding, coal, fishing and agriculture, for example. But there are no neat statistical runs for the value or volume of output or the level of employment as there are for industries such as coal. Tourism has been undervalued, in part because of government's almost total indifference to it in Victorian and Edwardian times, an indifference which the academic community shared. Not until the 1930s did things begin to change, notably with F. W. Ogilvie's path-breaking study *The Tourism Movement. An Economic Study*, which appeared in 1933. Ogilvie, then Professor of Political Economy at the University of Edinburgh, and later Director General of the BBC and Chairman of Imperial Airways, was the first British scholar to start to assemble the raw data on numbers of foreign visitors to Britain and British visitors aboard, and – which he recognised was a more delicate task – to ask what was the tourist spend in the UK, and the British tourist spend abroad. It was a beginning. But before then there had been no systematic analysis of the volume and value of tourism. And as happens, because there was no statistical corroboration, no nice solid figures to be cited, officialdom simply ignored the subject. Resorts made their own way, unhelped by central government, apart from – belatedly – some permissive legislation to allow revenue raising and expenditure for advertising.

But this chapter also asks what the cultural impact was. There is a substantial body of academic opinion that has seen and still sees tourism as a corrosive and degrading cultural factor, assuming that receiving cultures adapt and demean themselves to please the tourist gaze. Here we will be arguing that there is a case for saying that Scotland changed tourists more than tourists changed Scotland; there was a resilience to indigenous culture. The fundamental argument to be advanced is that tourism forced relatively little adjustment or accommodation by the Scots; indeed there was a considerable degree of acceptance of local culture by the visitors, and in some areas actual immersion in it for the season. When in Scotland they did as the Scots did; they went native. Many countries which receive tourists adjust their culture, cuisine and practice to ease the acceptance of the visiting clientele, or even import wholesale features of the sending culture – pubs and grub. Scotland did adapt, but the degree of adaptation and acceptance was greater by the tourists than by the locals. Scotland exported more than it imported. Visitors learnt to play Scotch, especially golf, dress Scotch, drink Scotch, dance Scotch reels, and even worship Scotch. And, of course, they used Scottish banknotes.

Modern statisticians are now able to pronounce on the value of tourism to the Scottish economy (though their estimates are rather less copper-bottomed than the figures imply): how many visitors there are, how many jobs are dependent on tourism, what the tourist spend is, and so on. The reality is that it has been hard and indeed impossible to quantify with any certainty until recently the value of tourism in terms of jobs, earnings, and spend. We do not even have any overall figures for the numbers of visitors to Scotland pre the 1960s. Or what the duration was of the average visit. And what the level of domestic tourism was – Scots holidaying in Scotland – can only be gauged very approximately. Any balance sheet has also to consider whether tourism brought more revenue into Scotland than Scots took out by holidaying away from Scotland.

If numbers are a problem, even more so uncertain is what the spend was by visitors in Scotland on travel and accommodation, subsistence, souvenirs, postcards and general amusement. Individual travellers did keep accounts – and of course there were the budget tours with Cook. There were tour guides which did offer estimates of expenditure, or plan travel for those with a fixed budget, as with the 1935 publication *Scotland on £10*,[1] which laid out a ten-day tour. But so many pieces of the jigsaw are missing that it is impossible to complete any sort of picture. We know nothing of the earnings of lodging-house keepers, of whom there were many, or of the camping sites, or the country inns, or indeed of beach entertainers, German bands or golf caddies, ice cream sellers and other casuals. There is the great unknown of what tips may have amounted to on top of formal wages. One can only wonder how a post boy at Dalmally, according to a local bank agent in 1867, had been able to save £1,400![2]

There are two parts to tourism where it is possible to find firmer economic ground. The first is sporting tourism, where there is (as we have seen) information about rental income, and for employment. The census data does show how many gamekeepers, ghillies and water bailiffs were employed. Not all worked only for sporting visitors, but many did, and were part of the tourism industry. The flow of income through field sports was a stream which contemporaries did attempt to put a figure on, revenue from rents and wages which had to be qualified by expenditure on lodges and roads. The presence of well-heeled visitors did have spin-off effects, underpinning the viability of inns in remote areas, such as the Crook Inn in Tweedsmuir. Golf and other sports benefited from visitor income, through green or court fees, teaching lessons, and the hire or sale of equipment.

The accommodation of tourists took many forms: hotels and inns, lodgings and apartments, tented and camping sites, caravan parks and holiday camps.

The nineteenth century saw the hotel sector expand to new levels with hundreds of hotels instead of handfuls. In the main cities not all their business was from tourism as there were other kinds of travellers. Glasgow and Edinburgh's hotels understandably catered for commercial travellers, trade reps and those in town for commercial or legal business. But in the rural and country districts much of this sector was tourist orientated. There was even a hotel built on top of Ben Nevis, open from June to September, which must have been the highest in Britain, and with reasonable service. One comment in the Visitors' Book for July 1910 was that it was 'really comfortable, food and attendance very good. Laundry was pretty efficient... coffee good.'[3]

One category was the railway hotel, to be found at or near stations throughout Scotland. While most were fairly modest and few were actually owned by the railway, railway companies in Scotland (as in England) came to want to have their own flagship hotel. The process was kicked off in Scotland in 1855 by the Inverness & Nairn Railway company with its Inverness Hotel in Station Square, and climaxed in the 1890s with the magnificent North British or Waverley Hotel at the east end of Princes Street, Edinburgh; at the other end was the rival Caledonian Hotel. The ten-storey North British had over three hundred bedrooms, fifty bathrooms and seventy lavatories, the last then quite a novelty, besides bars, writing rooms and hairdressing salons – and menus written only in French![4] It was prestige as much as profit that motivated such projects, and it was many years before the North British Station Hotel showed a profit. In 1913, however, £64,084 of business done yielded a net profit of £7,766, a 12 per cent margin, which was very respectable indeed. The railway companies also erected golf hotels, as noted elsewhere, and hotels in some inland resorts, as at Strathpeffer, making a total in 1913 of some twenty-five railway-owned hotels in Scotland.[5] But most investment in hotels came from private capital either through wealthy individuals or limited company investment. There were sporting hotels for fishing, shooting, golf or walking, as at Ballater and Grantown-on-Spey. There were temperance hotels, private hotels, and lodging establishments which mushroomed in all the key tourist localities such as Callander, Birnam and Pitlochry. The number of hotels in Oban rose from just three in 1841 to thirty-three in 1901, with corresponding increases in the number of lodging houses (two to forty) and of private accommodation, seventy-seven in 1871 and one hundred and forty-six in 1901. Oban was a town whose 'very existence depends on tourists', or so wrote a local resident in a letter to the editor of t*he Oban Times* on 18 November 1905. There was some fishing and island trade, but increasingly its economy was dominated by tourism. In 1871 an editorial in the *Oban Times* stated 'Oban is very dependent on its tourist visitors and on those who base themselves there during their tour of the west.'[6] Speaking at a meeting of the Lorn District Roads Board in 1881, local landowner Colonel MacDougall stated 'Oban exists simply by tourists.' His comments were backed by local businessman John Fraser Sim, who agreed, advising 'there is no industry whatever in Oban. We live on the tourists.'[7]

Sometimes the new hotels were redevelopments of earlier inns, as at Tarbet, but many were entirely *de novo*. In the Trossachs, the local landowner, Willoughby d'Eresby, prompted by his wife, financed the forty-room Trossachs Hotel with its remarkable candle-snuffer twin towers, which opened in 1852. A near neighbour, the Earl of Moray, not to be outdone, followed suit with the New Trossachs Hotel in 1851, where Millais and Ruskin were to stay; it, however, burnt down in November 1864.

What level of investment this represented in aggregate is difficult to gauge. It is possible to track what the costs were of construction of individual hotels; much harder to get any notion of what was then spent on extensions and renovations. Walker tells us that the Glasgow & South Western Hotel at Ayr (1886) cost £50,000, and that of the Highland Railway at Aviemore £25,000.[8] It was estimated in 1877 that over £500,000 was being invested in hydropathic hotels, a boom which was soon pricked. Some schemes were aborted as at Oban and Morningside in Edinburgh, and others became bankrupt. The Atholl Palace at Pitlochry, opened in 1880 at a cost of £80,000 was one such casualty, changing hands in 1886 for a mere £26,000. The shareholders there, and at Dunblane and Craiglockhart which suffered a similar experience, took heavy losses.[9] The sector did recover. Clunyhill Hydro at Forres, for example, was paying an astonishing annual dividend of 12.5 per cent at the end of the nineteenth century.[10] Nevertheless, failures were a reminder that hotels were not licences to print money. The hotel sector had always been prone to a high level of mortality and turnover. There were special circumstances during the hydro mania of simply too many curative institutions coming on stream at the one time and supply outstripping demand. But ventures could fail through bad service, bad management, or just bad luck, as with coaching inns whose trade was killed by the railways. Alexander MacDonald, proprietor for over twenty years of the refreshment rooms at Perth Station, acquired the Atholl Hydropathic in 1890. A venture into ownership of a hotel on the French Riviera was the undoing of this experienced hotelier, leading to his bankruptcy. Fire was another problem, an occupational hazard of premises with so many coal fires. Amongst the casualties, fortunately without any loss of life, were the hydros at Rothesay in 1891, Callander in1893, Peebles in 1905 and Kyles of Bute in 1909. They were all rebuilt, but Moffat's destruction in June 1921 finished what had become a failing business. There is always a degree of suspicion attached to fires in the hotel sector, that they may have been arranged with a view to an insurance claim, but Moffat's appears to have been pure accident, coming as it did during the height of its season.

A key problem for Highland hotels was the shortness of the season, which made the economics difficult. Nearly half of the annual takings at MacDonald's Atholl came from the single month of August. Many closed over the winter. A basic dilemma was to match supply and demand. A resort hotel might be too small in summer, when visitors were plentiful, and far too large in the winter when visitors were few. And if people arrived without having reserved accommodation in advance, there could be ugly scenes. Lord Cockburn saw

Figure 7.1 The burnt-out shell of Peebles Hydro the morning after its near total destruction by fire during the night of 7–8 July 1905. Note some of the rescued furniture scattered on the front lawn. (Author's collection)

this in the Trossachs at a small inn, with beds for no more than a dozen or two, when in the autumn of 1837 over a hundred visitors arrived. After what he described as 'horrid altercations, entreaties and efforts, about fifty or sixty were obliged to huddle together all night.'[11] Anthony Trollope's fictional Killancodlem Hotel could offer 120 beds, but on occasion at half as many more guests would sleep under the tables.[12] Killancodlem had its many Highland counterparts in real life, something that the post, telegram and phone helped to alleviate. Inevitably the shortness of the season led to complaints of high charges, a charge levelled against all Scottish hotels. One critic wrote that the hotels at Oban, Aberdeen and Inverness were 'excellent but terribly dear.'[13] Hotelkeepers were accused of profiteering,[14] but the defence made, by Thomas Cook and others, was perfectly reasonable: they had only the summer season to make their year's income. There was for some kinds of hotels, notably the hydros, during the later nineteenth century a lengthening of the season in some areas, thanks to the advent of Christmas as a holiday observed in Scotland.[15] It also helped that the promotion of hydros had shifted from the ill to the worried well: those who were brain fatigued, or ladies exhausted by the demands of running a household.

Hotel management was often a family business, passing down from generation to generation and in which family firms did well; there were dynasties such as the Calazels at Peebles and the Leckies at Crieff. Some started small, with an inn or modest hotel and scaled up, drawing on family personnel to assist, who in due time would succeed to management. Andrew Philp was a shrewd operator. Originally a tea merchant, his first venture into the hotel business was in Dunfermline, where in 1849 he rented the Railway Hotel, which he outfitted, or so the local paper reported, as a 'Teetotal Hotel and Lodging House'. The emphasis on temperance was to be a dominant characteristic of both Philp and his establishments, which was to underpin a life-long friendship with Thomas Cook, also a temperance man. When Philp acquired the newly built Cockburn Hotel in Edinburgh, next to Waverley Station, Cook made that his headquarters when in Scotland. The no-alcohol rule of the hydros drew Philp to put together in the 1880s and 1890s at bargain prices a portfolio of hydros from Craiglockhart and Dunblane in Scotland to Conishead Priory in England. His family were to profit on his death in 1902 from his shrewd investments. Another hotel dynasty were the Blairs, who had a cluster of inns and hotels in the Trossachs area, including the Rowardennan, Loch Achray, and the Bailie Nicol Jarvie.

Women played an appreciable part in the hotel business, sometimes taking over from a husband or father. When Alexander McGregor, proprietor of both the Dreadnought Hotel in Callander and the New Trossachs Hotel, died in 1864, his wife simply continued to run operations. Robert Angus, a long established hotelier in Oban, who had started in the 1850s with a small inn, had moved upmarket with his acquisition in 1869 of the twenty-nine-roomed Imperial Hotel, which he ran with his daughter Agnes along with another hotel in the same street, The Queen's. On his death in 1882, she inherited everything and ran the hotel business until her death in 1901. An able businesswoman, she was able to cope with the burning down of the Queen's in a major fire, reopening it in 1891 in a much grander style at the cost of £8,000 and further extending it in 1898 to provide 120 bedrooms, with shops on the ground floor. Women were omnipresent in the hospitality sector during the Victorian and Edwardian period: as cooks, servants, maids, bookkeepers, entertainers and indeed manageresses. After the First World War things were to change as service fell out of favour. In 1921 the census data showed that women made up nearly two-thirds of the workforce in Scotland's inns and hotels, but by 1931 their share at 40 per cent had fallen below that for men. There was no such matching change in the boarding house and lodgings category.[16]

It was a sector which provided opportunities for progression for a woman with ability which may not have been available in other professions. Nepotism helped: Andrew Philp employed his daughter as housekeeper at Dunblane Hydro. Angus was not the only woman in Oban to be a senior figure in the hotel business. Jean Ritchie from Dumfries worked her way up from being a barmaid and then bookkeeper to become the hotelkeeper with her husband George Campbell of the Great Western Hotel. After his death, she kept charge until her retirement in 1879, when the hotel was leased by David Sutherland, who had learnt the catering business as steward on David Hutcheson & Co.'s saloon steamer, the *Lord of the Isles*.[17] The Caledonian Hotel in Oban was also managed by a woman, Catherine Smith from Falkirk, who paid £400 rental per year for the 100-bedroomed hotel.[18] She came from a hotel background, as her parents had initially operated a hotel in Falkirk, which, following the death of her father, she had continued to run with her mother and sisters. Prior to her arrival in Oban she and her sisters had managed hotels in Greenock, Inverkip and at Arrochar.

Inns, with their lower running costs, were less vulnerable, though not immune, to bad times or self-inflicted misfortune. In 1822 Dorothy Wordsworth had stayed at what she called a villainous inn at Tarbet, going to decay. 'The father is lamed, the mother a whisky drinker. Everything is in disorder and children ill-managed.'[19] Some inns remained resolutely unmodernised, which may have been part of their charm, such as the fishing inn Tibbie Shiel's at St Mary's Loch near Selkirk, run by the remarkable widowed Mrs Richardson for nigh on forty years until her death at the age of ninety-six in July 1878. Tibbie's was no more than a but and ben initially, with garret, which could accommodate overnight a dozen guests or so but occasionally more; Tibbie did say that she had had thirty-five staying but that was only about 12 August when the shooters came. 'After a' the beds are filled they just lie on the floor or onygate.'[20] One wonders how she catered for such a large company. Another female innkeeper was 'Big' Kate Ferguson of Brig O'Turk, whose takings were kept in a leather pouch (including the two sovereigns given her by Queen Victoria). That, however, was the old order. New hotels and inns required new systems of management and of accounting. Hotel-keeping became a recognised occupation, moving towards a profession with a business structure, with hotel managers, answerable to a board of directors.

A whole range of rented provision was available to the summer visitor: houses, especially manses for the better-off, rooms in cottages, apartments or lodgings, often owned and run by landladies. Income from the provision of accommodation was appreciated at much less formal levels. In the resorts and country districts alike, there were many who let rooms, banking on the income from Glasgow Fair folk, for example. At peak times, the resorts were packed to excess. In August 1916 it was reported that every room in Helensburgh was let out at big prices, with some folks sleeping out and others sleeping by day and walking at night. Beds were working 'the double' shift'.[21] Some moved their own families out to backhouses, tin sheds or tents; others simply crammed up. Mrs Campbell of Mill Row, Campbeltown, despite having a family of eleven, managed to let the bedroom every year to a family of four from Glasgow. Her own tribe all lived, eat and slept in the kitchen: one of her sons recalled that he slept in the press (large cupboard) with his feet out the door.[22] Tens of thousands of working-class families holidayed this way cheaply, and thousands of crofters and working-class householders welcomed the income, little though it may have been. It made a difference, and some estates began to consider whether they ought not to put up the rents that they were charging tenants. Proceedings went to court. The Scottish Land Court in April 1914 heard an action raised by the Duke of Hamilton arguing (unsuccessfully) that summer letting on Arran by his tenants to visitors should be taken into account when fixing their fair rent. A similar case was raised later that year against crofters at Balquidder; cross examination extracted just how significant the summer income was at £5 or so a month against an annual rent of £20. These summer earnings went a good way to lessen the crofter's burden.

We rightly look at the big earners from tourism – the hotels, the railway companies, the sporting estates – but we should not overlook the importance in aggregate of the small sums earned by the many. There were those whose livelihood rested on tourism and many of them were seasonal workers only; they earned during the tourist season, and survived somehow in the off season: hoteliers in the Highlands, apartment and lodging house keepers in the spa towns, businesses in seaside and rural areas, including photographers and postcard manufacturers. Painters cashed in on the demand for Scottish scenes. While the most successful was the English artist Edward Landseer, there were Scots – McTaggart for one – whose scenes found a keen market. Photographers, as we have seen, did well from tourism. The Aberdeen firm of George Washington Wilson claimed that in 1880 alone it had sold more than 100,000 shilling albums.[23] Local printers turned out guides to their locality, and others firms diversified into the travel market. The *Contour Road Book of Scotland* and *Short Spins Round Edinburgh* were guides for cyclists produced in 1896–7 by the firm of Gall & Inglis, whose staples hitherto had been religious publications and ready reckoners. In Oddy's words, these were nice earners for the company, cashing in as they did on the cycling boom.[24] The provision of souvenirs was also a good earner. Take, for example, the enterprising custodian of Doune Castle who prepared a guide to the castle in 1882; a first print run of 1,500 copies soon sold out and a second edition was required only two years later. He had an additional fifty copies bound in ash from the gallows at the old castle, a prized souvenir for the wealthier visitor.[25] In 1864 Harriet Beecher Stowe bought some tubs made of plum tree wood from Dryburgh Abbey while staying in Melrose. Tourism created casual employment and earnings. Jobs such as selling ice creams, or hiring boats, or caddying for visitors, even though but for a short season, made a real difference to those on low incomes. There was a hidden many for whom the tips of the tourist were welcome, folk such as Janet Reid, 'poem Jenny', who in the 1840s sold her penny ballads to the visitors at the spa house in Bridge of Allan.[26] Or Alexander McGregor, nicknamed Ram Shackles, an old soldier who held a ladder for coach tourists to Callander to dismount at Lanrick Brae: their pennies and silver allowed him a monumental carouse at the end of the season.[27] The income, small though it may have been, was valued by such as him, and people like him did not prey on tourists, but lived off small but legitimate earnings from tourism. There was also begging, sometimes thinly disguised, as with the sale of pebbles and shells by children to visitors to Iona. Begging in general was a very great nuisance wherever you went in Britain or Europe, or so most visitors thought, and some saw tourism as a prime cause. The *Saturday Review* denounced the way that tourism resulted in demoralisation: 'there are villages which a generation back were inhabited by a really fine population, which are now in great part a mere nest of tourists' parasites, living partly on downright cheating and extortion, partly on more or less disguised begging, and spending a large proportion of their ill-gotten gains in drink'.[28] The very real poverty that visitors encountered in the Highlands and Islands did draw a response: Cook raised funds from his tourists to equip the islanders of Iona with fishing boats, one of which was called *The English Tourist*.[29] Elsewhere, visitors put money into the localities in which they were staying – assisting with bazaars, helping with church funds, and endowing sporting prizes.

All of these ways of parting tourists from their money were legitimate, but there was another avenue which was not, that of robbery and theft. There was the great jewel robbery at Moffat Hydro in September 1900, when jewels valued at £3,000 were stolen from the bedroom of an English lady, who had been in residence at the hydro for some time.[30] An American, who described himself as a professional betting man or bookmaker from the Midlands of England, was subsequently arrested. A further arrest followed of his accomplice, a German waiter at the Hydro. But theft was rare; indeed on balance tourists tended to be more light-fingered than the locals, and guides at historic monuments or great houses had to be on the lookout. The thirst for souvenirs led to some chipping off fragments from the tombs on Iona, which forced the Duke of Argyll to enclose them behind railings. An American was caught thieving from Abbotsford.[31]

There were other economic beneficiaries of tourism. Landowners benefited from the rental of sporting rights, but also indirectly through the expansion of villages, the feuing of land for summer residences, the leasing of ground for ground courses and other amenities. Their role could be positive or negative; sometimes they blocked development. The main line to Skye from Dingwall which should have been routed by way of the spa town of Strathpeffer was blocked by Sir William Mackenzie of Coul,[32] and instead had to pass to the north, to the lasting disadvantage of the railway's receipts and Strathpeffer's business. Builders are a constituency about whom we know little, but they found lots of work generated for them by tourism: summer villas, sporting lodges, hotels, restaurants, churches and other buildings. Transport companies, as we have seen, promoted tourism and prospered by it; the longer distance movement of people, their servants and pets and their luggage was in Acworth's words 'splendidly profitable'.[33] The only financial strand within the hospitality sector which has been investigated in some depth is that of hydro tourism. We know something about levels of investment in this sector, not all of it initially successful, and of the levels of dividends paid. With the crisis of the early 1880s behind them, most hydros settled down to years of steady profitability, thanks to their sober, staid and loyal clientele, paying annual dividends of 9–12 per cent.[34]

The question of the cultural impact of tourism has long been hotly contested territory. In the later nineteenth century some Irish nationalists were deeply concerned that tourism from England would erode the Irish language and culture alike. R. A. S. Macalister feared that mass tourism would destroy 'our melodious, expressive and poetical national language…. The Erin of the saints must not degenerate into a mere Cockney run.'[35] It remains today a deeply held belief of some writers that tourism has always been culturally destructive and exploitative, and that this holds true for Scotland as much as any other context. John Vidal (and others) have argued that what led to the collapse of the community on St Kilda was the arrival first of missionaries and then of tourist boats.[36]. Others see tourism as one of the mechanisms which hollowed out true Scottish identity to substitute instead images of a Celtic past as the insignia of Scotland, 'the kilt, the pipes, the haggis and the music hall Scot'.[37] It is an idée fixe[38] of this school that forms of tourism such as Balmoralism and tartanism, though economically beneficial, were poisoned fruits, warping Scottish identity and culture. There is however a counter argument that sees the process as less one-sided and more of an exchange; that some adjustments in local culture may have been promoted and welcomed by the locals rather than imposed, that tourists may have taken away ideas as well as bringing in new. The picture is more complex than simply that of the culture of the incoming flow of tourists overwhelming the indigenous. Not all receiving countries are monocultural, nor the incoming stream of tourists monochromatic. Countries varied by region, visitors by class, background and interest. The level of impact depends on the scale and nature of the incoming stream of tourism, and the resilience of indigenous culture.[39] There were and are, even or indeed especially within Scotland, receiving regional cultures rather than a single receptor, which produces a complex pattern of transmission and reception. The picture is not one of a tidal bore that rushes in to swamp indigenous custom and culture but rather a complex estuarial pattern with fresh, brackish and seawater admixing.

It must be agreed that those involved in Scottish tourism, as is true of all tourist destinations, were quite prepared to massage what was on offer so as to provide the Scotland that tourists expected to find. In marketing the dream and the image matter, truth trails in a distant third. Many tourists came with a set of expectations, shaped by what they had read or seen or heard. Chopin, visiting in the summer of 1848 enthused over Scotland, 'Walter Scott's beautiful country, amongst all the memories and reminders of Mary Stuart, of the Charleses etc'.[40] But to an actual point of connection were added many another, however tenuous, a task to which local antiquarians turned their attention with enthusiasm. What a place needed to get on the tourist map was some kind of literary or historical association to Wallace or Bruce, Burns or Bonnie Prince Charles or whomever. And what tourists wanted, they got. The American humourist J. M. Bailey commented after a tour in the Scottish Borders in 1879 that

> There are nearly five hundred old castles in this vicinity. Queen Mary was imprisoned in all of them. That unfortunate must have been in jail about four-fifths of the time. What I now want, what I really pant after, is a ruin that wasn't her prison, that Sir Walter Scott hasn't written about, and that Queen Victoria didn't visit in 1842. But I don't know where to look for it.[41]

Quite knowingly Scots were prepared to play to expectations. That Scotland was in visitors' eyes the Highlands, Lowlanders would acquiesce in with a shrug, knowing perfectly well that this was but a convenient and commercial fiction.

A number of issues are worth examining when trying to assess the impact of tourism on Scottish life and culture. Did tourist tastes affect food and diet? What of dress or music? Or indeed religion? Did tourism affect the popularity of Gaelic and indeed of Scottish dialect? The retreat of Gaelic was certainly noted by visitors. Mrs Thompson, a Methodist Lady from Hull, was ferried across Loch Lomond in June 1807 by a fine young Highland woman who said that, while her mother had good Gaelic, the Gaelic was very little in use amongst them now, especially among young people.[42] Few visitors bothered to learn any Gaelic, and guidebooks to Scotland provided only short glossaries, not sentences as would have been true of a handbook to France or Italy. It is seems true that the rise of tourism coincided with the decline of Gaelic, but whether there is a causal connection is hard to establish, and other factors, notably educational, were at work. That useful Scots verdict, not proven, might be usefully deployed here. Attention is usually focused on Gaelic, but it is worth noting that some dialects of Scottish-English such as Lallans or Doric may have been nearly as impenetrable to visitors and Scots from elsewhere. This results in Scots even to this day having two versions of conversational language – that which they use amongst themselves and another – less Scottish – for use with foreigners. Dialect was one aspect of regional identity; so also was humour. No stereotype was more widely known, and enjoyed, than that of the miserly Aberdonian. H. V. Morton[43] suggested that there was a great joke factory in Aberdeen in which 500,000 anecdotes a year were turned out to publicise the city's stinginess. Some Scots will not have thought that to be a fiction.

It can be hazarded that the effect of tourism on popular diet in Scotland, centred for example on potatoes, oatmeal and fish, was minimal. Stalls for the sale of lemonade did begin to appear at popular tourist locations, and of course there was the arrival of ice cream, which became an enthusiasm of holiday-makers of all classes. Thomas Adam found an ice cream seller in Aberdeen's market place in July 1857 serving a throng of customers, many of whom were evidently trying ice cream for the first time. 'Some', he reported, 'screwed up their mouths, but most were rather pleased'.[44] The manufacture and sale of ice cream became a near monopoly of the Italian community, with firms such as Nardini and Luca still prominent today. The number of ice cream shops in Glasgow rose from 89 in 1903 to 336 a mere two years later. The fish and chips business was also dominated by Italian families, with ice cream parlours and fish restaurants adjoining parts of the same enterprise. Hotels and restaurants in Scotland did start to provide for visitors a cuisine which was mainstream British and European, a process aided by an influx of Continental managers and chefs into the sector, and perhaps a visit to Scotland was in culinary terms only a bubble experience, with people eating as if they were in London.

Tourists may have taken away shortbread as a souvenir of their time in the North, but not a taste for haggis or craving for any other Scottish dishes. What they did come away with, however, was a love for Scottish whisky, which many imbibed freely while in the North. Mead and cider remained only regional English drinks, but Scotch travelled. It was no new product in Scotland, long part of the social fabric at weddings and wakes, but Highland and tourist images helped to promote and market it to a much wider constituency.

If a taste for whisky went hand in hand with travel and tourism, so also did an enthusiasm for tartan, and the kilt, once banned but now resumed, elaborated and extended. It became the souvenir that visitors carried back with them, or indeed ordered from a tartan emporium in Stirling or Inverness or London before travelling north so as to blend in with the locals, or so they thought. McDougall's Royal Tartan Warehouse in Inverness had subsidiary premises in London at Sackville Street off Piccadilly, and claimed to be manufacturers of Scotch goods (Highland Costume, Highland Cloaks, Tartans, Tweeds and Sporting fabrics) to the Royal family and the courts of France, Russia, Prussia and Spain. It was a standing joke in *Punch*, but one with some truth, that any person seen in full Highland regalia was bound to be English.[45] Highland dress, a regional emblem, was to break out from its northern fastness to become fashionable with Lowland and expatriate Scots, as well as with visitors, and of recent years has become de rigueur for men with no Scots connection whatsoever at weddings in the South. Tweed was another beneficiary; it became the fabric for outdoors – shooting, walking or fishing – and its success was linked to the place of Scotland as a sporting playground. Tourism was one of the mechanisms that made Scotland a very successful exporter of dress and clothing in a way that Wales was not; the steeple hat remained only a curiosity. The Southern sportsman may have come to Scotland clad in knickerbockers, but increasingly he went away in tartan and tweed.

In the field of religion so dear to Scottish society, there was a real potential for impact, particularly from English or European visitors, few of whom were Presbyterian. In general churches in the summer resorts benefited from higher attendance. The Episcopal chapel in Helensburgh found its numbers doubled during the summer, thanks to summer visitors.[46] Moneyed visitors from England who were Anglican helped through donations and support of bazaars to finance the erection of Episcopal chapels in the resorts, either tin tabernacles or more substantial buildings, as at Strathpeffer, where work on St Anne's started in 1891. Previously summer services for visiting Anglicans had been held in the Promenade Rooms or alternatively worshippers could have gone down the road to Dingwall. But while Episcopalianism was boosted by English visitors, and the English observance of Christmas and Easter began to creep into Scottish worship, along with the English organ, much to the disgust of Presbyterian traditionalists, Presbyterianism more than held its own. Many visitors went to the local kirk while in Scotland, none more so than Queen Victoria, who while at Balmoral attended the parish church at Crathie. She enjoyed the worship and sermons, notably those of her favourite preacher,

Dr Norman MacLeod, and in later life took communion there each autumn,[47] which caused some disquiet in court circles that she was too Presbyterian.

No aspect of Presbyterian Scotland grated more with visitors than the observance of the Sabbath, which some found very restrictive. It was not unique to Scotland – parts of Wales shared similar views – but it was very firmly held. There were no shops open, no amusements, no sport allowed, no newspapers or letters, travel was restricted, and so on. Golf courses remained shut, grouse moors were silent, and fishing rods stayed in their racks. Some visitors held a similar view of the sanctity of the Sunday and fell into line with local practice without any trouble. One party of Methodist young men from Lancashire found themselves in Dunkeld on 21 July 1871. They attended worship at the cathedral, of which they thought but little: 'it was a miserable affair, & poor food for hungry souls'. They would have then strolled through the Atholl grounds, but that was vetoed because a guide would be required, and to engage one would be to break the Sabbath; equally a walk was cut short because to go more than two miles would be to exceed what was permitted for a Sabbath day's journey.[48]

But others were less compliant. Arthur Sullivan, when in Glasgow in 1875, complained that 'A Scotch Sabbath is a ghastly thing. I tried to find a good Anglican church but they are all dull or else kirks. Cabs are double fares on Sunday, all locomotion and recreation are discouraged, and whisky drinking encouraged'.[49] He and many others wished for a more relaxed approach, as did tourism agencies and transport companies. There were voices raised on behalf of the working class; should they not be able to enjoy the day of rest by, if they wished, taking a steamer or rail or bicycle trip to the coast or countryside? Lay voices had been pressing for some time for freedom of travel – as one writer to the *Daily News* in September 1853 put it, 'a large body of working men in Scotland have been procuring for themselves and their families the benefit of fresh air and innocent recreations on Sundays. There are a good many people in Glasgow besides its wan weavers who need a Sunday airing because they can get it on no other day. The Clyde is a noble highway for this purpose... and there is no ascertained legal impediment to the running of vessels on Sundays.'[50]

The question of travel for pleasure on the Sunday, whether any could be acceptable, became especially contentious in Victorian Scotland, one of the issues on which Sabbatarian debate was focused, and which is a live issue yet in parts of the Western Isles. Some powerful lobbies within the churches held that any travel for pleasure was both wrong in principle and bad in practice. Sunday excursions were not improving, they said, but the opposite. 'Few spectacles are more riotous, more debased, more miserable than a Sunday excursion train when it comes back and empties upon a city its pleasure seekers and worshippers of nature.'[51] They denounced railway services, coach outings and steamer trips alike. The attempt in July 1836 of the Glasgow & Garnkirk to run Sunday trains so as to allow 'travellers to attend divine worship in Glasgow' was dismissed by them for what it was – a smokescreen for making profits. Resistance was headed by people such as Peter Drummond of Stirling, who exerted real pressure on railway companies not to run Sunday trains. He lobbied railway company boards and financed volleys of pamphlets and tracts. No. 341, The Sabbath Excursion train, was published in January 1854

> Be sure of where you are going and what you are going for
> You may see many places but get nothing for yourself
> The pleasure of this excursion is but one day
> At his right hand are pleasures for ever more
> The Directors invite you for their gain
> The Lord calls you for your own profit
> Directors provide for the Monday morning a weary body
> An empty purse and a guilty conscience
> The Lord secures you a body refreshed with rest, a soul satisfied...

Resistance was more than just in print and word. A trial Sunday cruise in August 1853 on the Clyde was made by the *Emperor* steamboat, which added to its bad reputation by the sale on board of liquor. It tried to call at Garelochead. But the local landowner had the pier barricaded against them, and a pitched battle ensued. Sunday access continued to be an issue, with some places holding out against Sunday landings, as at Dunoon. In 1897 the owners of the Clyde Steamer Company proposed a Sunday cruise from Glasgow to Rothesay via Dunoon. This aroused interest, with hundreds of tickets sold, but also a storm of opposition. The local ministers got up a petition to keep the pier gates locked, and the local paper published a poetical condemnation.

> Dunoon, Dunoon, Beware of the day
> When the Antis Sabaoths shall claim thee as prey
> And passenger steamers o' Sundays shall glide
> With wicked excursionists far down the Clyde.[52]

The departure point at the Broomielaw was picketed by the Salvation Army, and many would-be excursionists turned back. But those who set off were denied access to the pier and then by locked gates access to the town. The pier commissioners were denounced in the local paper as men who had 'succumbed in the most silly fashion to the united forces of teetotalism and of superstition in the name of Religion'. This rumbled on another five years until 1902, when it was decided that the pier commissioners had no legal right to prohibit landings.[53]

It was a long struggle but the campaign to keep the status quo, for a travel-free Sabbath, was gradually lost. The post office had insisted that mail trains run on Sundays, whether or not they carried passengers.[54] And there were embarrassments, as when in 1849 the Duchess of Sutherland was refused a seat on the Sunday mail train north to visit her dying father; the delay meant that he was dead by the time that she arrived on the Monday. Increasingly the strict could not control provision in the face of rising demand, and a growing number of figures argued that they should not try. More people had more money and more thirst for travel. There was for some the Saturday half-day, but for many or most, especially in the working class, Sunday was the only the big block of time they had free; was it right to deny them? When else were they to get away to the seaside or the hills, if not then? As one writer observed, Scotch Sabbatarianism, like faith, had moved mountains and placed them out of the reach of operative workmen. Even within the Scottish churches, there were those who were uneasy about strict Sabbatarianism. And some ministers agreed and were brave enough to say so. The Presbytery of Glasgow issued a pastoral letter in 1865 against the running of Sunday trains, which was to be read out from all pulpits. Dr Norman Macleod of the Barony Church complied but then told his congregation that he disagreed with it, and why. The minister of Rothesay, the Rev. Hutchison wrote in June 1897 that he had not a word to say against Sunday steamers, Sunday golf and so on. He knew 'many fine young people serving in grocers' shops in Glasgow all week behind the counter and until midnight on the Saturday, for whom the Sunday steamer must be a blessing and the golf too'.[55] It is worth observing however, that he qualified his stance by saying that once shop servants did get a weekly holiday, he would petition against Sunday steamers. What was further loosening Sunday strictness was bicycling; more and more people were taking to the country or coast whenever they could. In November 1889 the Glasgow Presbytery of the United Presbyterians denounced the deliberate violation of the Fourth Commandment by 'bands of young men. meeting on the Sabbath morning during the summer season with their bicycles, bent on an excursion for the day'.[56] The charabanc and the motor car were to accelerate the process, and sabbatarianism, along with its sister cause of temperance, were to fail. But it was a slow decline, mirroring the decreasing membership and influence of the churches in Scotland. Gradually, as we have seen, sporting and other amenities became available on Sundays, though in an interesting departure from the new norm, sporting estates still adhere even in the 2010s to the notion of Sunday as a day of rest. But no longer is the Scottish Sunday distinctive. It is one facet of an older Scottish culture that has gone, but although a disappearance much sought by tourist promoters and partakers, it is not the doing of tourism.

The balance sheet of tourism is much easier to calculate in economic than in cultural terms. It is clear that Scotland benefited, some parts more than others, from the inflow of tourists and tourist income. Some localities had become highly dependent on summer earnings, all sections of society from landowners to crofters, hoteliers to lodging-house keepers, ice cream vendors and beach donkeymen, photographers and artists, shared some part of the influx of money. The balance sheet is much harder to assess for culture, as, amongst other things, tourism was not the only factor at work in an evolving society. But it can be suggested that tourism was not as damaging to indigenous culture as some schools of thought might expect, that indigenous institutions such as the church, the law and the educational system buttressed a robustly separate Scottish identity. The periphery did not succumb to the centre, but instead there was more of an exchange or even an export of practice. And where there was change, it was not imposed but accepted, adjustments made by consent or shaped by perceived advantage.

Notes

1 Clark, Sydney A., *Scotland on £10*, (London, 1935).
2 Bank of Scotland, *Proposals for new branches*, agent at Aberfoyle, 4 October 1867.
3 Byrne, Lorna, 'Archives of the West Highland Museum, Fort William', *Scottish Archives*, 16 (2010), pp. 97–8. The Museum holds six volumes of Visitors' Books for the Ben Nevis Hotel, covering the years 1884–1904.
4 *Souvenir of the Opening of the Edinburgh Balmoral Hotel*, (Edinburgh, 1991), p. 95.
5 Simmons, Jack, *The Victorian Railway*, (New York, 1991), p. 41.
6 *Oban Times*, 19 August 1871.
7 This section draws on Fiona Morrison, 'The Development of Oban as a Tourist Resort', PhD, University of Bournemouth, May 2015, available at <http://eprints. bournemouth.ac.uk/22514>
8 Walker, David, 'Inns, Hotels and Related Building Types', in Steell, Geoffrey, Shaw John and Storrier, Susan, *Scotland's Buildings. Volume 3 of Scottish Life and Society. A Compendium of Scottish Ethnology*, (East Linton, 2003), pp. 127–89.
9 Durie, Alastair J., *Water is Best: The Hydros and Health Tourism in Scotland 1840–1940*, (Edinburgh, 2006), pp. 58–9.
10 Durie, *Water is Best*, p. 70
11 Cockburn, *Circuit Journeys*, p. 15 Tarbert, 11 September 1838.
12 Trollope, A., *The Duke's Children*, (London, 1880), p. 308.
13 Letter to *The Times*, 13 August, 1883. The writer Kenneth Bellais also complained strongly about the charges for posting, i.e. hiring a horse and trap from a hotel. Drink charges were exorbitant while the food at inns was generally detestable.
14 'The tourist season is the harvest time during which the natives levy blackmail upon their guests by a thousand ingenious devices', *Saturday Review*, 6 September 1873, p. 300.
15 Milligan C. and Mulhern, Mark A. (eds), *From Land to Rail: The Life and Times of Andrew Ramage*, (Edinburgh, 2014), p. 59. Ramage was a railway crossing keeper; who noted in his diary for Tuesday 25 December, 1888, 'By the way, Christmas is becoming more recognised as a holiday and day of rejoicing in Scotland than in former years.' His entry for the following day was that 'I received a great number of Christmas cards yesterday from friends near and far.'
16 Brunner, Elizabeth, *Holiday Making and the Holiday Trades*, (Oxford, 1945), p. 31. Her figures for Scotland show 21,943 employed in the hotel sector in 1921, of which 38.7 per cent were male, and 27,520 in 1931 (62 per cent male). The lodging and boarding houses sector employed 7,480 in 1921 (male 8.8 per cent) and 5,891 in 1931 (male 20 per cent).
17 Paterson, *Victorian Summer*, p. 231, has a tariff for the catering available from Sutherland on the Lord of the Isles: salmon, steaks, herring, ham and eggs etc. were offered for breakfast, cost 2/-.
18 *Glasgow Herald*, 26 January 1876.
19 De Selincourt, E., *Journals of Dorothy Wordsworth, Vol. 2, Journal of My Second Tour in Scotland*, (London, 1941), p. 357.
20 Robson, Michael, *Tibbie Shiel*, (Selkirk, 1986) citing the *Scotsman*.

21 *Helensburgh Gazette*, 30 August 1916. 'Every available room is occupied and in many instances it is said that visitors had to sleep in relays.'

22 Cronin, J., 'The Development of Tourism in Kintyre up to the First World War', University of Glasgow Undergraduate dissertation, 1993.

23 *Aberdeen Free Press*, 24 June 1893, 'Reminiscences of the late Mr G. W. Wilson'.

24 Oddy, Nicholas, 'Harry R. G. Inglis and the Contour Road Books', *Cycle History*, 9, (1998), pp. 79–92.

25 *Stirling Journal*, 5 June 1885.

26 Flint, David A., *'Poem Jenny': Janet Reid (1777–1854) of Carnock & Bridge of Allan, Scotland*, (Basingstoke, 2015). One such is entitled 'On Philp's Bonny Royal Hotel' (a recently extended hotel in Bridge of Allan): 'many a one comes there on their honeymoon jaunt / and good parlours and bedrooms they never will want.'

27 MacDonald, James, *Character Sketches of Old Callander*, (Callander, 1910, third edition 2006), p. 99.

28 *Saturday Review*, 6 September 1873, 'Tourists', p. 306.

29 Grenier, Katherine Haldane, '" Missions of Benevolence": tourism and charity on nineteenth-century Iona', in Colbert, Benjamin (ed.), *Travel Writing and Tourism in Britain and Ireland*, (London, 2012).

30 *Dundee Courier*, 6 September 1900.

31 Durie, *Scotland for the Holidays*, pp. 58–9.

32 Thomas, John and Turnock, David, *Regional History of the Railways of Great Britain. Volume 15. North of Scotland*, (Newton Abbott, 1989), p. 260.

33 Acworth, W. M., *The Railways of Scotland. Their Present Position*, (London, 1890), p. 63.

34 Durie, *Water is Best*, p. 70.

35 Macalister, R. A. S., 'The Debit Account of the Tourist Movement', *New Ireland Review*, VII (September 1899), p. 92.

36 Vidal, John, *Guardian*, 25 July 2009. It should be noted that the first tourist boats arrived in the 1830s but the island was not evacuated until August 1930.

37 Pittock, Murray, *The Invention of Scotland: The Stuart Myth and the Scottish Identity from 1638 to the Present*, (London, 1991).

38 McCrone, David, *Scotland the Brand: The Making of Scottish Heritage*, (Edinburgh, 1995).

39 This debate is analysed in more detail in Durie, Alastair J., 'The Periphery Fights Back: tourism and culture in Scotland to 1914', *The International Journal of Regional and Local Studies*, Vol. 5 (Autumn 2009), pp. 30–47.

40 Voynish, E. L., *The Letters of Frederick Chopin*, (London, 1931), p. 64.

41 Bailey, J. M., *England from a Back Window*, (Boston, 1879), p. 284.

42 Robinson, Arthur B., *Seeking the Scots: An English Woman's Journey in 1807*, (York, 2006), p. 62.

43 Morton, H. V., *In Search of Scotland*, (London, 1929), pp. 141–5.

44 Durie, *Travels in Scotland*, p. 145.

45 See *Mr Punch in The Highlands*, (London, 1910): Mrs Smith of Brixton to Mr Brown in full Highland Regalia: 'Lor, Mr Brown I hardly knoo yer. I suppose that's the costume you go salmon stalking in?'

46 Thatcher, Barbara, 'The Episcopal Church in Helensburgh in the Mid-Nineteenth Century', in Ward, J. T. and Butt, John (eds), *Scottish Themes* (Edinburgh, 1976), p. 103.

47 Duff, David, *Victoria in the Highlands*, (London, 1968), p. 258. George IV had attended Presbyterian worship at St Giles in Edinburgh during his visit in 1822, but had not taken communion.

48 Daniel Bates's Highland Tour, unpublished journal in family hands, which records a week-long tour in Scotland in July 1871. They start to walk to Rumbling Bridge, 'but when about a mile on the way we discovered that the bridge was some two

miles further away and & Willie thought that this exceeded a Sabbath day's journey.'
I am grateful to Mary Bates for permission to quote from this.

49 Jacobs, Arthur D., *Arthur Sullivan, A Victorian Musician*, (Oxford, 1984), p. 100.

50 Fair Play, 'Sunday Steamers in Scotland', *Daily News*, Wednesday 7 September 1853.

51 Thomson, Andrew, *The Sabbath*, (London, 1863), p. 15.

52 McRorie, Ian, *Dunoon Pier: A Celebration*, (Argyll, 1997), p. 54.

53 McRorie, pp. 51–9.

54 See Dr John McGregor, *Social History from Railway Sources*, Research in the Arts, Open University Conference, November 2009, p. 52.

55 *The Clyde Programme*, No. 1, June 1897.

56 *The Scottish Cyclist*, Wednesday 20 November 1889, 'Sunday Riding'. The editor responded that a man could cycle on a Sunday and not infringe any commandment. 'We consider that we have not transgressed the divine law one whit when after attending church in the forenoon, we doff our go-to-meeting garb for the unconventional freedom of cycling toggery.'

8   The past and the future

Tourism since 1945

Not even Nostradamus at his best could have foreseen how the topography of the Scottish economy would change after the Second World War. While some traditional staples have continued – fishing, the financial sector, whisky and agriculture – there has been the progressive and ultimately precipitous decline of the old sinews: steel, shipbuilding and coal, the last now virtually extinct, the others just hanging on. New industries have made their appearance – video games, computing and oil – but not all have stayed the course; remember Linwood and the Scottish car industry? Tourism has pushed its way up the economic ladder. It now generates employment on a large scale: 218,200 people in 2006 according to Visit Scotland.[1], an impressive figure which has to be qualified by the reality that many workers were part-time or seasonal, and indeed a significant proportion not Scottish. The hotel, guest house and catering sector has been a particular beneficiary. Employment in hotels and catering was static at less than 110,000 for most of the 1980s but rose thereafter to 180,400 in 2006. Lots of smaller businesses, specialising in hill walking or porpoise watching holidays, for example, flourish, and tourism's effect ripples out well beyond Edinburgh and the Lowlands to every part of mainland and island Scotland. Tourism is a national industry of prime importance to big businesses and small alike. This final chapter explores the more recent history of tourism in Scotland, and examines what relationship, if any, a study of the past holds to projections about the future. Can what has happened inform what will happen?

What has to be appreciated is just what a challenge there was in 1945 to rebuild tourism in post-war Scotland. Certainly there was pent-up domestic demand, assisted by the pre-war Holidays with Pay Act of 1938 kicking into effect post war. But Scotland's tourist industry, as elsewhere in Britain, faced a brutal legacy of the war years. Given Britain's financial position, government hoped for a speedy recovery, particularly in respect of attracting overseas visitors – and their dollars. A Board of Trade memorandum of August 1948[2] laid out an agenda for recovery, addressing problems such as petrol, food and clothing rationing, shortages of accommodation and hotel equipment, and the need for coordinated publicity. It concluded with a call to set aside what the authors called 'a deeply rooted tendency apparent at almost all levels of official circles to regard tourism not as a vital industry but as a slightly flippant luxury'.

But rebuilding tourism was not easy, keen though officialdom and people alike were to restore the holiday habit. Many of Scotland's beaches were still covered in anti-invasion defences; there were mines and barbed wire which were removed, pill boxes and concrete blocks which were not, which had the accidental benefit of subsequently providing generations of beachgoers with shelter from the wind and cover to change costumes. Golf courses had been ploughed up, or requisitioned, as at Crail, and had to be restored; sporting estates and moors had been run down through lack of care to the ground, the lack of gamekeepers and proliferation of vermin during the war; hotels and great houses had been converted to military or medical roles and had to be de-requisitioned. Some big houses were past retrieval. Compensation was paid, but mostly accommodation and transport facilities were (like Britain generally) in shabby condition, though unlike in England there were no actual losses through bombing to historic buildings or sites. There were even one or two bonuses. The entrepreneurial Billy Butlin converted HMS *Scotia*, a naval training base near Ayr built during the war, into the first of his holiday camps in Scotland, his sixth in Britain and served by a short rail line, which opened after renovation on Saturday 17 May 1947. There was some forward planning before the end of the war. In June 1944 on the initiative of the Hotels and Restaurants' Association it was proposed to establish a School of Hotel Management within the Glasgow and West of Scotland Commercial College, to which the first students were admitted later that autumn. This Scottish Hotel School moved to Ross Hall and was eventually absorbed into the University of Strathclyde.[3] Tourism as a discipline was beginning its long haul to attain academic standing, a process which advanced more readily in the new universities in the 1960s than in the old, where the study of leisure in any form – sport or tourism – was long regarded as not intellectually respectable.

Despite the difficulties, tourism did revive quickly after the war. According to returns made by hotel owners and boarding house proprietors, in 1951 there were 3.5 million visitors to Scotland, as against 2.7 million the previous year and 1.7 million in 1949. The minutes of the Tourist Association of Scotland report the results of a survey undertaken in 1954 by a Glasgow firm of chartered accountants, which found tourism to be valued at £44m and a later survey in 1957 of the Scottish Tourist Board through Gallup estimated £57 m. It was clearly an industry on the up, but it was still under-appreciated in political circles, left and right; undervalued when set against the old staples, shipbuilding or coal. A great problem was that the jobs being lost in the heavy industries were male and skilled; the jobs being gained were in service, seasonal and female. Tourism was looked down upon as not really a weighty industry in a political and economic world still wedded to the old industrial structures of steel, shipbuilding, engineering and coal; for example, this comment from a Labour party spokesman: 'if we are not careful, we may turn into a nation of hoteliers and trinket makers for tourists.'[4]

Progress was underpinned by a rise in disposable incomes from which all leisure activities benefited but especially holidaymaking, which in turn was persuaded and massaged by sophisticated marketing. Travel for pleasure was prompted by better transport, the motor car and especially cheap air flights, which, as we shall see, was a two-edged sword, increasing tourist flows away from, as well as into, Scotland. But also significant – quite how significant is open to question – was a much greater degree of involvement and support for tourism from national government. Previously the promotion of resorts and the provision of amenities had been largely in the hands of private enterprise (transport companies, travel agencies, hotel groups and groupings), and local authorities, many of whom issued guides to their burgh, with the town clerk in effect acting as chief tourism officer. There was the Tourist Association of Scotland, a board which had tried – on a shoestring as elsewhere in Britain – to stimulate and coordinate activities. It had a membership in June 1950 of just over 3,000, of which hotels were more than half. It liaised with shipping and travel companies, and issued a promotional magazine, much needed given the level of competition from other parts of the UK and Ireland. Nothing shows more the enhanced sophistication of publicity and promotion, when one compares the publicity material of the 1950s with that of half a century later. So much now is done online, not by way of paper, as consumers hunt their way through the Internet and websites such as TripAdvisor. The Scottish Tourist Board's magazine *Take Note!* looks now so utterly dated, in both content and presentation, with its list of transatlantic sailings scheduled from North America to Greenock. Yet the Board was making headway, and played its part in inducing government to take a much more proactive role. Government in the 1950s was not prepared to put much money into tourism, partly because heavy industry was seen as having a higher priority when resources were so limited. But changes in political thinking, and increasing recognition of the value of tourism events were to force a reappraisal, and tourism became big business, with major improvements in the quality of accommodation. In the early post-war years tourism had differed little, as Peden has suggested, from that of Victorian period, being largely geared to British visitors, with seaside resorts, hydro hotels, fishing and golf being the principal attractions.[5] But change came, and indeed was forced. The advent of cheap package air tours to resorts abroad where sunshine could be relied upon was a severe challenge that led in 1969 to the creation of the government-funded Scottish Tourist Board (Visit Scotland's predecessor). The 1969 Development of Tourism Act[6] created tourist boards for each component of the UK including, of course, Scotland. The Board's key objective was to market Scotland as a tourist destination, to draw in visitors from abroad. And to assist its work, it was given a budget of £26 million in 1990, most of which came from government. £10 million went on promotion, the rest on capital projects. Its work was complemented by the creation in 1991 of Historic Scotland, which was to project and promote the enjoyment of Scotland's built heritage, a portfolio then of over 300 properties, from standing stones to Border abbeys.[7]

But what added urgency was a tectonic shift in tourism thanks to the arrival of cheap air travel. All British resorts, but particularly those at the seaside, began to haemorrhage their traditional support as more and more Britons sought Mediterranean sun. Powering this was cheap air travel, thanks to the jet as opposed to the propeller engine, and the inclusive tour. It was a far cry from the first post-war flights from Prestwick to Portugal by an airline called Scottish Aviation using a converted Liberator at the high cost of £120. As aviation expanded, so costs of travel fell. Between 1967 and 1971 the cost of flights to Palma was reduced by nearly 30 per cent in real terms. By 1970 about 5.7 million Britons, six times the level of one million in 1955, were taking an overseas holiday, one-third to Spain. In the early 1950s 40 per cent of British tourists aboard had gone to France and another quarter to Ireland but within twenty years, it was Spain that took one-third (of a much higher volume) and Ireland only 5 per cent. New destinations became mass, rather than select, as was the case with Spain and Greece. New airlines pushed overseas travel, and fortunes were made and lost by entrepreneurs such as Freddie Laker, or firms such as Clarksons.[8] The loss of home holidaymakers to foreign parts made it more imperative to attract visitors from abroad, but they would not be drawn to those resorts which were in decline. The Scottish seaside, other than the golf resorts, held (and holds) little appeal for the European or American visitor. It was a dilemma that was not to be resolved.

The writing had been on the wall for some time. Summer traffic in terms of the number of passengers carried between May and September on the Clyde steamers had reached a high point in 1959 (3.6 million) but thereafter started to fall and by 1962 was down to 2.8 million[9]; and the picture was similar for passengers (all of whom were holidaymakers or tourists) on Loch Lomond, 120,000 to 103,000. Pier head arrivals at the Clyde resorts mirrored the change: falling gently at first, but with gathering momentum. There were 60,000 fewer at Rothesay in 1962 as against the previous year; 80,000 fewer at Dunoon. And things only worsened; by the late 1960s steamer cruising on the Clyde, Simpson concludes, had collapsed.[10] All seaside resorts in Britain suffered, but none more than the mass destinations, as those of all classes that could afford to seek the Mediterranean sun did so. The lust for guaranteed sunshine is deep-rooted in Scottish culture – witness the human lobsters to be seen in any Glasgow park during a hot spell. The lowered cost brought the Mediterranean resorts within range of middle- and working-class holidaymakers. Hotels in Scotland (and elsewhere in Britain) began to lose bookings, apartments went unlet, traditional boarding houses gave way to self-catering or caravanning. Beach cafes felt the draught, donkeys went to pasture permanently, boat hirers lost their trade, and in some places, a vicious downwards spiral set in: lack of investment in new or upgraded facilities further weakening resort appeal, except to the ageing traditionalists or lowest income groups. Businesses folded. In Dunbar, once a very popular east coast resort, three of the large hotels shut, and had it not been for the construction of Torness power station, and the accommodation required for construction workers, the B & Bs of the area would have seen hungry times. Across the water in Fife, according to Simpson,[11] in the select seaside and golf centre of Lundin Links, the last big boarding house closed in 1980.

The story was much the same elsewhere, though some smaller resorts bucked the trend. These tended to be middle-class and professional ghettoes, with many of the properties second homes, used on and off during the summer but largely empty thereafter. A third of all the dwellings in Elie, a small seaside resort in Fife with a population of 942 in 2001, were either second homes or holiday lets. Arran, Millport and the East Neuk of Fife were where professional Scotland was to be found from June onwards, and these localities held their own. By contrast, once popular places like Portobello, Aberdeen and Rothesay were, as Simpson says, 'Meccas no more'. Aberdeen at least had the oil boom to mop up surplus accommodation capacity, but there was no such relief for Rothesay. Ceasing to be a mass market destination, the town's fortunes fell into sharp decline, compounded by a fall in population from 10,141 in 1951 to half that in 2001. As the town's economic base shrank, so amusements such as cinemas and dance halls shut and there was less for the fewer summer visitors. The situation was not just meekly accepted. There was real debate as how to best rebuild the island's appeal; the opening of Bute's Gothic gem, Mount Stuart House, did help, as did the refurbishment of the pier head toilets. Other options were explored elsewhere. After the liberalisation of Britain's gaming laws in 2002, there was a lobby that argued that casinos and gambling could rejuvenate decaying seaside resorts. But the proposition that a place like North Berwick, once happy with the title 'the Biarritz of the North', could reinvent itself as the Atlantic City of Scotland sank almost as soon as it was floated. No form was immune: Billy Butlin's Heads of Ayr camp began to feel the pinch. In 1967 it had welcomed 72,000 campers, of whom about one in eight had arrived by train as against half in the 1950s, but that was more than 10 per cent down on the previous year's figure of 81,000 in 1966[12] and the camp eventually passed into the ownership of Bourne Leisure Limited.[13] As the traditional clientele of working- and middle-class Scots sought the sun abroad and found a more relaxed culture, with excess leading one resort to be dubbed Shagaluf, there was a serious loss of domestic tourism.

But not all was gloom in Scotland. Some forms of tourism continued to do well, and grew, and new or re-invented forms filled out Scotland's portfolio. The story of tourism in the 1960s, and since, indeed has been one of upwards development, not entirely without some checks and challenges, but with an onwards momentum which other Scottish industries can only envy. There have been recessions, but no equivalent for the industry of the financial crisis of 2008–9, when Scottish banks such as HBOS nearly went to the wall, or the collapses in oil prices as in 1995 and 2015. Tourism however, well planned, is always subject to the unpredictable: terrorism,[14] tsunamis, Chernobyl or foot and mouth disease. But the industry in Scotland has ridden these out.. Why has tourism done so well? Clearly what has underpinned it, and other leisure activities, has been the rise in disposable incomes across western and indeed more recently Asian, particularly Chinese, society. Demography is also a factor: an ageing population is more inclined to travel and more interested in heritage. For whatever cause, there has come to be simply more holiday taking, both of the longer and short break kind. The capacity to consume is qualified of course by wealth and time. A recent survey found that highest fliers take[15] eight holidays a year, whereas one in four of the population take none at all, the latter a figure up from one in ten four years ago, because of lower-income people feeling the pinch. The biggest factor is how much people earn: affluence has pushed the average up to 3.2 breaks per person as against 3.0 in 2014, with 81 per cent of the higher social grades participating as against of 49 per cent of the less advantaged groups: unemployed people, pensioners, low earners. It would be a challenge for any forecaster to work out which forms of tourism benefit most from shifts in the distribution of leisure income within different social groupings; is the greater impact in volume or value derived from the few holidaying a lot, the middle holidaying some, or the least well-off managing some form of break?

As before in history, in shaping growth promotion and publicity have played a key role, some elements of which have been pure serendipity, luck and happenstance. The accelerants are now not so much books or prose, but film, video and social media. Films such as *Braveheart* (historical hokum, but with immense appeal), *The Wicker Man* and now the *Outlander* series, with the books and spinoffs, have brought a surge of visitors from the USA. These are random stimuli which have in the case of *Outlander*[16] put up visitor numbers at Doune Castle by 30 per cent , a location previously a beneficiary of the *Monty Python and the Holy Grail* film of 1975 as Castle Anthrax. The Harry Potter films have spun off the Hogwarts Express.

A lot of promotional ventures have been tried, some of which have succeeded spectacularly, as with Glasgow in 1983 when John Struther's 'Glasgow's Miles Better' slogan comprehensively outgunned Edinburgh's riposte 'Count me in'. It was an unparalleled successful exercise in rebranding, cemented by the National Garden Festival in 1988 and the awarding in 1990 of the title European City of Culture. It was said that some street buskers deserted Edinburgh for Glasgow. Industrial Glasgow had been a place that visitors came to only to pass through to other destinations but now it had become a tourist destination in its own right. According to a recent newspaper report,[17] thanks to the Commonwealth Games of 2013 Glasgow appears actually to have overtaken Edinburgh in terms of visitors staying overnight. But not all marketing campaigns achieve success. Some have bombed, such as the Year of Clan Homecoming in 2009, which was yet another scheme designed to tap into the clan market so strong in North America, with its many well-attended Highland Games and Scottish societies. Devised by Event Scotland and Visit Scotland, part-financed by European monies, it failed to attract the numbers hoped for, and several suppliers were left unpaid. A debacle, as it was rightly termed. Another example was Bannockburn 2014, planned to mark the 700th anniversary of the battle in 1314; ticket sales were poor and the programme had to be scaled back.

Some of the traditional forms of tourism are still highly significant. Castles, abbeys and battlefields, older sites and new, attract ever larger numbers of visitors such as Culloden, Bannockburn, New Lanark, Stirling and Edinburgh castles, the last of which had 1.4 million visitors in 2013 (as against 443,000 in 1962 and 375,000 in 1957). The poster image of Scotland – tartan, bagpipes, whisky and Highland cows – seems to have an enduring appeal, and can be marketed. What powers tourism is a mixture, but heritage underpins a lot of appeal in Scotland, whether battlefields, genealogical research or graveyards. There is the role of Festivals, notably the Edinburgh Festival but there are many others: local and regional – Celtic Connections, book, music and food festivals. In a sense all this is a remake of a model that started with the Great Exhibition of 1851. Recognition has been fanned by the award of World Heritage status to six sites in Scotland, to which the Forth Rail Bridge is the latest addition with the creation of a visitor centre planned. Edinburgh's appeal is buttressed by its UNESCO status, which makes any development or redevelopment in the central very sensitive. One proposed new hotel scheme in the revamped St James' Centre has been labelled by its critics as a 'Golden Turd'.

Sporting tourism is still much in vogue: grouse-shooting, deer-stalking and salmon fishing for example, with big prices paid. The Scottish beach is reviving, thanks to the wetsuit, and there is surfing at Thurso and Tiree and other places. Hill walking is popular, as is cycling, with the creation of longer distance trails such as the West Highland Way.[18] Winter sports, a long-awaited answer to the question of the offseason, are now firmly established: skiing but also snowboarding and other activities makes centres like that at Ben Nevis commercially viable. But while there is a remarkable level of continuity, there have emerged new forms of tourism. Within scenery, there has emerged an enthusiasm for dark sky – places where the night sky can been seen to best advantage unpolluted by street and other artificial light. Part of the Galloway Forest Park has been designated a Dark Sky park and nearby Moffat has just been recognised (February 2016) as the first dark sky town in Europe. There is the rise of wildlife tourism, watching rather than killing – red kites at Argaty, dolphins off Chanonry Point in Cromarty, sea (white-tailed) eagles on Mull. There is food tourism, given a boost by an STB initiative in the mid-1990s under the title, 'The National Cooking of Scotland', intended to give Scotland more of a culinary identity. At the launch in London, the Secretary of State for Scotland said that Scotland 'needed to make more use of its own original cuisine in order to stamp its own unique identity on visitors to our shores.'[19] Nineteenth-century Scotland had a culinary reputation only as the land o' [oat] cakes, but now its seafood restaurants have an international standing, a reputation perhaps to be qualified by the pioneering at Stonehaven of the deep fried Mars bar. Standards of accommodation for the visitor are creeping up at campsites, B & Bs and caravan sites: the old landlady regime is no longer quite as acceptable.

Heritage railways are a new form of tourist attraction, to which older men are particularly susceptible. Operational centres include Bo'ness, the home base of the Railway Preservation Society, the Strathspey railway between Grantown and Aviemore, and the Caledonian at Brechin. There are steam or diesel specials hauled on the the main lines – for example the Jacobite between Fort William and Mallaig, but there is no narrow-gauge network to match that in Wales. The railway preservation movement in Britain is a tribute to the keenness and commitment of enthusiasts, not to government planning, and Scots were part of this. The first was John Cameron's Lochty railway in Fife. It must be in retrospect a matter of regret in East Lothian that, when in the early 1970s the Scottish Railway Preservation Society tried to buy the recently closed Haddington line as a centre for their steam-hauled operations, local worthies blocked the proposal on the grounds of pollution, noise and risk.[20] It is a reality that not all development is welcome, and interests clashed. In East Lothian, for example, moves to 'vulgarise North Berwick' by amusement arcades and souvenir shops were stymied by local opposition; and indeed Ballater turned down a swimming pool which went instead to Aboyne through the same sort of snobbishness. Hoteliers disliked caravan parks because they lowered the tone.

But not all the sporting scene is rosy. Golf may be in decline amongst Scots, if not amongst overseas visitors to whom golfing packages are being marketed with gusto. But there is the problem for many clubs in Scotland that, because of the new (2014) drink-driving legislation, which has lowered the limit, the nineteenth hole (which generated a lot of clubhouse income) is no longer anything like as popular, with some places reporting bar takings down by 40 per cent or more. This loss of income, an unintended consequence of the legislation, has had serious implications for country pubs, hotels and other licenced bodies. Competition from Spain and Dubai has also drawn Scottish golfers from home fairways. There has been the revival of older forms of tourism, not perhaps taking the spa waters but in the form of hydrotherapeutic treatments, which are now much in vogue at upper-end hotels, and Moffat has reinvented itself as a centre for wellness. While the fleet of paddle steamers has but one active survivor, the *Waverley*, cruising in the form of calls by large passenger cruise ships has become big business for ports such as Greenock, Leith and Lerwick when several of these mega liners arrive together. Greenock Cruise Terminal welcomed fifty-six ships with 109,000 passengers in 2015, 14 per cent up from 2014. There is the unkind quip that their clientele are the newly wed, the overfed, and the nearly dead. Even that most venerable form of travel, pilgrimage, has re-emerged: Scotland now has several pilgrim ways, of which St Cuthbert's, between Melrose and Lindisfarne, was the first to be delineated in 1999. However, there is nothing equivalent in Scotland, as yet, to Lourdes or Ireland's Croagh Patrick.

Old forms continue and mutate; new forms emerge. Tourism is amazingly resilient and flexible. There are new flows which have emerged. Who could have foreseen the recent influx of Asian visitors? Some of this is a spinoff (friends and family) of those studying in Scotland. But tourism in Scotland does face challenges and issues. There is continuing conflict over land use. Who should get access to the countryside and on what terms is a long running sore. We have already see how there was conflict in the nineteenth century over access to the hills, in particular to the ground of sporting estates, as with the 6th Duke of Atholl at Glen Tilt in 1847. Mountaineers and ramblers have long been free spirits.[21] The right to roam, when not exercised responsibly, raises hackles amongst landowners and farmers alike. Litter in high places or lochsides, or indeed anywhere, causes offence to lovers of the countryside. There have been clashes over wild camping at Loch Lomond. Field sports, particularly grouse-shooting and deer-stalking, are under pressure from hill walkers and animal rights campaigners, as well as enthusiasts for rewilding, the re-introduction of species such as the lynx. Wind farms divide opinion: blot on the landscape or necessary on environmental terms? Big golf schemes, especially that of Donald Trump in Aberdeenshire, were and remain hugely controversial, pitting tourism and jobs against the preservation of a natural links environment. There are real uncertainties of context. In 1989 Scotland achieved substantial devolution with its parliament at Holyrood, but that proved only to be a staging post in a movement gathering momentum towards independence. The referendum in 2014 seemed to have settled that question for at least a generation, but the 2016 Brexit vote may well have reopened the door for what is being called indyref2. It remains open as to what independence, if achieved, would mean for Scottish tourism. But given the precipitous decline in oil revenues, tourism will be needed. The changed power structure in Scotland, into Nationalist hands, has had one visible effect. Gaelic signs have spread even into the Lowlands, where they are regarded with utter indifference by most there who consider the revival (or imposition depending on perspective) of Gaelic for place names as more a function of ideology than of need.

Other questions include the effects of global warming, about which one can only speculate. It will change weather and the environment alike. It may not, however, convert Scotland's islands into the Bahamas. The wider world context for tourism is also important. Now that tourism and tourists are targets for terrorism, as seen sadly recently in Egypt, Tunisia, and elsewhere, it may well be that Scotland's reputation as a safe destination will play as important a part in its attractiveness as do scenery, sport and heritage. Fortunately the troubles in Northern Ireland never spilled over, as they might have done, into Scotland, nor, apart from one small-scale attack on Glasgow airport in 1997 has terrorism from other sources been a factor in the Scottish scene. There was however the 1984 PanAm flight blown up over Scotland, marked by the cemetery and memorial at Lockerbie.

The study of the past has its own value and interest. But what lessons, if any, are there for the continuing development of tourism in Scotland? There is no kind of formula, a da Vinci code, to be uncovered which will guarantee future success; past performance is not necessarily a guide to future returns.

Tourism, as a global industry, is fiercely competitive: pitting resort against resort, region against region, country against country. Yet there are some pointers from the past. Clearly the political stability and safety have played an important part and will continue to do so; tourism flows to where tourists are safer. The range of attractions in Scotland is clearly an asset, with scenery, culture and sport, as is the ability to adapt, renew and add new forms. But what the past does caution is that tourism is an industry which is subject to random shocks, either stimuli or handicaps. What is sure is that this activity, once the province of the few, is now an industry whose importance to Scotland is going to be a major factor for the future. Post-industrial Scotland is an increasing prospect; post-tourism Scotland is not.[22] Writing in the late nineteenth century the editor of *Murray's Handbook for Scotland*, Scott Moncrieff Penney could look back on all the changes in transport and facilities and conclude that there had been a *perfect* revolution effected in Scotland in favour of the tourist. It can be agreed that there has been revolution, but it is one which is far from complete. Tourism since 1945 continues to change and advance, never finished or final. And innovation continues to be a feature – witness the impact of the web site Airbnb. It is an industry of the past, for the present and for the future.

Notes

1 Peden, George, 'A New Scotland? The economy', in Devine, T. M., and Wormald, Jenny (eds), *The Oxford Handbook of Modern Scottish History*, (Oxford, 2012), p. 665.
2 Public Records Office CAB 134/167 5819.
3 Gee, D. A. C., 'The Scottish Hotel School – the first fifty years', in Seaton, A. V., *et al.* (eds), *Tourism: The State of the Art*, (Chichester, 1994).
4 Cited by Ednyfed Hudson-Davies, 'British Tourism at the Crossroads', paper given to the Tourism Society, 12 March 1979.
5 Peden, 'A New Scotland', p. 665.
6 The process is well described in Middleton, Victor T. C., *British Tourism: The remarkable story of growth*, (Oxford, 2005), Chapter 7.
7 McCrone, *Scotland the Brand*, Chapter 4: 'Manufacturing Scotland's Heritage'.
8 See Bray, Roger and Riatz, Vladimir, *The Flight to the Sun. The Story of the Holiday Revolution*, (London, 2001). Also Segreto, Luciano, *Europe at the Seaside: The Economic History of Mass Tourism in the Mediterranean*, (New York, 2009).
9 Scottish Tourist Board Annual Report March 1973, Table 8.
10 Simpson, Eric, *Wish You Were Still Here: The Scottish Seaside Holiday*, (Stroud, 2013), p. 135.
11 Simpson, *Wish You Were Still Here*, p. 105.
12 McConnell, David and Rankin, Stuart, *Rails To Turnberry and Heads of Ayr*, (Oxford, 2010), pp. 193ff.
13 McConnell and Rankin, pp. 261–3.
14 For an analysis of the impact of terrorism see Page, S. J. and Connell, Joanne, *Tourism: A Modern Synthesis*, (third edition, Andover, 2009), pp. 587–96.
15 *The Times*, Wednesday 14 October 2015.
16 *Stirling Observer*, 8 April 2015.
17 *The Times*, 2 November 2015.

18 In March 2015 it was announced that a network of some thirty long-distance trails for cycling or walking are to be upgraded or created: a Great Trossachs path between Inversnaid and Callander; a Pilgrim's Way between St Andrews and Iona.

19 Fenton, Alexander (ed.), *A Compendium of Scottish Ethnology. Volume 5. The Food of the Scots*, (Edinburgh, 2007), p. 412.

20 Hajducki, Andrew M., *The Haddington, MacMerry and Gifford Branch Lines*, (Oxford, 1994), pp. 172–3.

21 Aitken, Robert, 'Stravagers and marauders', in Brooker, W. D. (ed.), *A Century of Scottish Mountaineering*, pp. 15–21..

22 Postma, Albert, Yeoman, Ian and Oskam, Jeroen, *The Future of European Tourism*, (Leeuwarden, 2013).

Bibliography

Primary Material

1 Archival, manuscript and other material

Bank of Scotland Archives, Proposals for new branches
Cook's Excursionist and Tourist Advertiser
Crieff Hydro Records, Directors' Minute Book 4 May 1871
Daniel Bates's Highland tour, 1871: unpublished journal in family hands
Glasgow City Archives TD 1/913: Babbington lettersJack family papers and photographs, personal collection of J. M., E. M. and J. C. M. Young
Journal of Mary Paterson, *Travels in France and Italy, 1848–49*. Original in private hands.
Land Valuation Acts
National Archives of Scotland (NAS) GD 327 Kemp Papers
National Library of Scotland, Scottish Screen Archive, 0705; Sadness and Gladness (1928); 0893 Sunny days (1931) and 0253 Tommy Trauchle's Troubles (1934)
New Statistical Account of Scotland, (Edinburgh, 1845) [NSA]
Oban Visitors' Register
Public Record Office CAB 134/167 5819
National Trust of Scotland. *The Hermitage* (2013)
Perth Public library. Parish of Logie, decennial census books
Royal College of Physicians of Edinburgh. The Cullen Project. The Consultation Letters of Dr William Cullen. www.cullenproject.ac.uk
Royal Commission on Motor Traffic, November 1905
Scottish Tourist Board. Annual Accounts and working papers
Select Committee of the House of Lords on Intemperance Fourth Report, 5 August 1878
Sinclair, Sir John (ed.), *The Statistical Account of Scotland*, (Edinburgh 1791–1799) [OSA]
Smith, Robert J., Precis of Evidence given on behalf of the RAC to the Royal Commission on Motor Traffic, November 1905
Stirling Archives, PD 16/4/2 Diary of Dr Lucas
Stirling University Archives: *Wheel Wanderings, the John O'Groats Grind, 1893*
Thomas Cook Archives, Testimonial to Thomas Cook, 30 October 1865
Vale of Leven website. Poem by an Edinburgh publican Willison Glass, cited by A. Graham Lappin, *The Loch Lomond Steamers*

2 Newspapers and periodicals

Aberdeen Free Press
Aberdeen Journal
The Baillie
The Berwick Journal
Blackwood's Edinburgh Magazine
Callander Advertiser
Campbeltown Courier
Chamber's Edinburgh Journal
The Clyde Programme
The Daily News
The Daily Sketch
The Dundee Courier
The Edinburgh Review
Glasgow Evening Times
The Glasgow Herald
The Haddingtonshire Courier
The Helensburgh Gazette
The Irish Tourist
The Inverness Courier
The Lennox Herald
The New Ireland Review
The North British Review
The Oban Times
The Peeblesshire Advertiser
The Saturday Review
The Scotsman
The Scottish Cyclist
Stirling Observer
The Times

Dissertations and Theses

Cameron, Anne, 'The Development of Tourism in Dunkeld & Birnam', Under-
    graduate Dissertation, University of Glasgow, Department of Economic History,
    1997
Cronin, J., 'The Development of Tourism in Kintyre up to the First World War',
    Undergraduate dissertation, University of Glasgow, 1993
Duncan, John, 'The Peebles Railway', PhD, Open University, 2004
Morrison, Fiona, 'The Development of Oban as a Tourist Resort', PhD, University of
    Bournemouth, 2015

Secondary literature

A'Beckett, Arthur and Sambourne, Edward, *Our Holiday in the Scottish Highlands*,
    (London, 1875)
Acworth, W. M., *The Railways of Scotland: Their Present Position*, (London, 1890)
Aitken, Robert, 'Stravagers and Marauders', in Brooker, W. D. (ed.), *A Century of
    Scottish Mountaineering*, (Berwick, 1998), pp. 15–21

Allan, J. Malcolm, 'Who was Charles Rogers?', *Forth Naturalist and Historian*, Vol. 13 (1990), pp. 97–106

Andrews, Malcolm, *The Search for the Picturesque: Landscape, Aesthetics and Tourism in Britain, 1760–1800*, (Stanford, 1989)

Auerbach, Jeffrey, *The Great Exhibition*, (New Haven, CT, 1999)

Baddeley, M. J. B., *Thorough Guide to Scotland*, (tenth edition, London, 1903)

Bailey, J. M., *England from a Back Window*, (Boston, 1879)

Barclay, J. B. (ed.), 'John Gulland's Diary 1846–49: a transcript and commentary', *Book of the Old Edinburgh Club*, Vol. 2 (1992), pp. 35–115

Barrett, John R., *Mr James Allan: The Journey of a Lifetime*, (Forres, 2004)

Barton, Susan, *Working-class Organisations and Popular Tourism 1840–1970*, (Manchester, 2005)

Barton, Susan, *Healthy Living in the Alps: The Origins of Winter Tourism in Switzerland, 1860–1914*, (Manchester, 2008)

Beckerson, John, *Holiday Isle: The Golden Era of the Manx Boarding House*, (Douglas, 2008)

Bede, Cuthbert, *A Tour in Tartanland*, (London, 1863)

Berghoff, Hartmut and Korte, Barbara (eds), *The Making of Modern Tourism*, (London, 2002)

Berry, Simon and Whyte, Hamish, *Glasgow Observed*, (Edinburgh, 1987)

Black, Jeremy, *The British and the Grand Tour*, (London, 1985)

Blackie, J. S., 'The Highlands, Men and Sheep', *The Edinburgh Review*, Vol. 106 (1857)

Bohls, E. A. and Duncan, Ian (eds), *The Oxford Anthology of Travel Writing*, (Oxford, 2005)

Brander, Michael, *A Hunt Around the Highlands*, (Bath, 1973)

Bray, Roger and Riatz, Vladimir, *The Flight to the Sun: The Story of the Holiday Revolution*, (London, 2001)

Brendon, Piers, *Thomas Cook: 150 years of Popular Tourism*, (London, 1991)

Brodie, A., 'Scarborough in the 1730s – spa, sea and sex', *Journal of Tourism History*, Vol. 4, No. 2 (August 2012), pp. 125–53

Brodie, Ian, *Steamers of the Forth*, (Newton Abbott, 1976)

Brooker, W. D. (ed.), *A Century of Scottish Mountaineering*, (Berwick, 1998)

Brown, A. S., *Guide to Madeira and the Azores*, (London, 1903)

Brown, Ian (ed.) *Literary Tourism: The Trossachs and Sir Walter Scott*, (Glasgow, 2012)

Brown, Ian G., 'Grand Tourists in General and Particular', *Scottish Archives*, Vol. 19 (2013)

Brown, Ivor, *Summer in Scotland*, (London, 1952)

Brunner, Elizabeth, *Holiday Making and the Holiday Trades*, (Oxford, 1945)

Buchan, Dr William, *Domestic Medicine*, (Glasgow, 1819)

Burnett, John, 'Some Perspectives on Railways and Railway life', in Veitch, K. (ed.), *Scottish Life and Society, Volume 8: Transport and Communications*, (Edinburgh, 2009)

Byrne, Lorna, 'Archives of the West Highland Museum, Fort William', *Scottish Archives*, Vol. 16 (2010)

Cadell, Patrick, '1822 and all that', *Scottish Archives*, Vol. 16 (2010)

Carpenter, Edward, 'The Cost of Sport', in Salt, Henry S. (ed.), *Killing for Sport*, with a preface by George Bernard Shaw, (London, 1915)

Caw, James, *Reminiscences of Forty Years on the Staff of a Hydro*, (Crieff, 1914)

Clark, Sydney A., *Scotland on £10*, (London, 1935)

Clyde, Robert, *From Rebel to Hero. The Image of the Highlander*, (East Linton, 1995)

Cockburn, Lord, *Circuit Journeys*, (Hawick, 1983)

Cook, Thomas, *Twenty Years on the Rails*, (Leicester, 1861)

Cook, Thomas, *Travelling Experiences, Leisure Hour*, (London, 1878)

Cormack, A. A., *Two Aberdeenshire Spas*, (Aberdeen, 1962)

Cox, Michael (ed.), *Two Villages at War*, (Gullane and Dirleton History Society, 1995)

Dawson, Alastair, *So Foul and Fair a Day. A History of Scotland's Weather and Climate*, (Edinburgh, 2009)

Deayton, A. and Quinn, I., *200 years of Clyde Paddle Steamers*, (Stroud, 2012)

Dendy, W. C., *The Wild Hebrides*, (London, 1859)

De Selincourt, E. (ed.), *Journals of Dorothy Wordsworth*, (London, 1933)

Devine, T. M. (ed.), *The Transformation of the Scottish Economy*, (Edinburgh, 2005)

Duff, David, *Victoria in the Highlands*, (London, 1968)

Durie, A. J., 'Tourism and Photography in Victorian Scotland: the contribution of G. W. Wilson', in Pringle, R. V., *George Washington Wilson Centennial Studies*, (Aberdeen, 1997)

Durie, A. J. (ed.), *The British Linen Company Papers, 1745–1775*, (Edinburgh, 1996)

Durie, Alastair, 'Tourism in Victorian Scotland: the case of Abbotsford', *Scottish Economic and Social History*, Vol. 12 (1992)

Durie, Alastair, '"Unconscious Benefactors": grouse-shooting in Scotland, 1790–1914', *International Journal of the History of Sport*, Vol. 15, No. 3 (December 1998)

Durie, Alastair, 'Medicine, Health and Economic Development: promoting spas and seaside resorts in Scotland *c.* 1750–1830', *Medical History*, Vol. 47 (2003)

Durie, Alastair, 'No Holiday this Year? The depression of the 1930s and tourism in Scotland', *Journal of Tourism History*, Vol. 2 (August 2010)

Durie, Alastair, 'Movement, Transport and Travel', in Foyster, Elizabeth and Whatley, Christopher (eds), *A History of Everyday Life in Scotland 1600–1800*, (Edinburgh, 2010)

Durie, Alastair, 'Tracking Tourism: Visitors' Books and their Value, *Scottish Archives*, Vol. 17 (2011)

Durie, Alastair J., *Scotland for the Holidays*, (East Linton, 2003)

Durie, Alastair J., 'Tourism and the Railways in Scotland: the Victorian and Edwardian experience', in Evans, A. K. B. and Gough, J. V. (eds), *The Impact of the Railway on Society in Britain: Essays in Honour of Jack Simmons*, (Aldershot, 2003)

Durie, Alastair J., *Water is Best, the Hydros and Health Tourism in Scotland 1840–1940*, (Edinburgh, 2006)

Durie, Alastair J., 'The Periphery Fights Back: tourism and culture in Scotland to 1914', *The International Journal of Regional and Local Studies*, Vol. 5 (Autumn 2009)

Durie, Alastair J., *Travels in Scotland, 1788–1881: A Selection from Contemporary Tourist Journals*, (Suffolk, 2012)

Durie, Alastair J., 'Sporting Tourism Flowers – the development of grouse and golf as visitor attractions in Scotland and Ireland', *Journal of Tourism History*, Vol. 5, No. 2 (August 2013)

Durie, Kate and Durie, Alastair, 'Earthly Paradise? The literature of the hydros', *Scottish Local History*, (Spring 2003), pp. 38–43

Durie, Alastair and Magee, Karl '"Come North": Glassert game books and diaries', *Forth Naturalist and Historian*, Vol. 31 (2008)

Fairfoul's *Guide to Moffat* (second edition, Moffat, 1879)

Fenton, Alexander (ed.), *A Compendium of Scottish Ethnology. Volume 5. The Food of the Scots*, (Edinburgh, 2007)

Fergie, John, *North Berwick: Wish You Were Here*, (Dirleton, 2013)

Flint, David A., *Poem Jenny: Janet Reid (1777–1854) of Carnock & Bridge of Allan, Scotland*, (Basingstoke, 2015)

Foley, Archie and Munro, Margaret, *Portobello and the Great War*, (Stroud, 2013)

Fontane, Theodore, *Across the Tweed: Notes on Travel in Scotland 1858*, (London, 1965)

Fox, Fortescue, *Strathpeffer Spa, Its Climate and Waters*, (London, 1889)

Fraser, David (ed.), *Christian Watt Papers*, (Edinburgh, 2012)

Freeman, John George, *Three Men and a Bradshaw*, (London, 2015)

Furness, Richard, *Poster to Poster: Railway Journeys in Art. Volume 1. Scotland*, (Gloucester, 2009)

Furniss, Tom, 'A Place Much Celebrated in England: Loch Katrine and the Trossachs before the Lady of the Lake', in Brown, Ian (ed.), *Literary Tourism: The Trossachs and Sir Walter Scott*, (Glasgow, 2012)

Gardiner, Juliet, *The Thirties: An Intimate History*, (London, 2010)

Geddes, Olive, *A Swing in Time*, (Edinburgh, 1998)

Geddes, Olive, 'Stephen Place's Journal: A footman's visit to Scotland in 1832', *Scottish Archives*, Vol. 19 (2013)

Gee, D. A. C., 'The Scottish Hotel School – the first fifty years', in Seaton, A. V. *et al.* (eds), *Tourism: The State of the Art*, (Chichester, 1994)

Gibb, Andrew, *Glasgow: The Making of a City*, (London, 1983)

Gold, J. and Gold, M., *Imagining Scotland: Tradition, Representation and Promotion in Scottish Tourism since 1750*, (Aldershot, 1995)

Gordon, Sir Robert, *A Genealogical History of the Earldom of Sutherland to the Year 1630*, (Edinburgh, 1813)

Grant, J. P (ed.), *Memoir and Correspondence of Mrs Grant of Laggan*, (London, 1844)

Grenier, Katherine Haldane, *Tourism and Identity in Scotland, 1770–1914: Creating Caledonia*, (Aldershot, 2005)

Grenier, Katherine Haldane, '"Missions of Benevolence": Tourism and charity on nineteenth-century Iona', in Colbert, Benjamin (ed.) *Travel Writing and Tourism in Britain and Ireland*, (London, 2012)

Grierson, Reverend Thomas, *Autumn Rambles Amongst the Scottish Mountains*, (Edinburgh, 1850)

Grierson, H. J. C., *Letters of Sir Walter Scott, 1808–1811*, (Oxford, 1932)

Grieves, Robert, *Scotland's Motoring Century*, (Paisley, 1999)

Griffin, Brian, *Cycling in Victorian Ireland*, (Dublin, 2006)

Groundwater, Anna, 'Ben Jonson's Performance of Union. A walk to Scotland, 1618', Lecture given to the Royal Society of Edinburgh, 8 December, 2014

Guide to the Trossachs and Loch Lomond (including the story of the Lady of the Lake), (Stirling, 1915)

Hajducki, Andrew M., *The North Berwick and Gullane Branch Lines*, (Oxford, 1992)

Hajducki, Andrew M., *The Haddington, MacMerry and Gifford Branch Lines*, (Oxford, 1994)

Hamilton, David (ed.), *A Girl's Golf in 1894: A North Berwick Holiday Diary*, (St Andrews, 2015)

Harrison, John, *The Steam Boat Traveller's Remembrancer*, (Glasgow, 1824)

Harvie, Christopher, *No Gods and Precious Few Heroes*, (Edinburgh, 1981)

Hay, B. and Adams, G., *History and development of the Scottish Tourist Board*, STB Working paper, July 1994

Hawthorne, Nathaniel, *Our Old Home and English Notebooks*, (London, 1883)

Heron, Robert, *Observations Made in a Journey through the Western Counties of Scotland in the Autumn of MDCCXCII* [1792], (Perth, 1793)

Hudson-Davies, Ednyfed, 'British Tourism at the Crossroads', paper given to the Tourism Society, 12 March 1979

Huggins M. and Walton, J. K., *The Teeside Seaside between the Wars*, (North-East England History Institute, 2003)

Hughes, Thomas, *Tom Brown's Schooldays*, (1857) (Penguin popular edition, 1994)

Irving, Washington, *Abbotsford and Newstead Abbey*, (London, 1835)

Jacobs, Arthur D., A*rthur Sullivan: A Victorian Musician*, (Oxford, 1984)

Jamieson, Bruce A., *North Berwick: Biarritz of the North*, (East Lothian, 1992)

Jarvie, Grant, *Highland Games: The Making of the Myth*, (Edinburgh, 1991)

[J. D. A], *Curiosities in Cures being the Experiences of a lady in Search of Health*, (London, 1895)

Jones, David S. D., *Gamekeeping: An Illustrated History*, (Shrewsbury, 2014)

Joynson, Peter, *Local Past*, (Aberfoyle, 1996)

Kelly, S., *Scott-Land: The Man Who Invented a Nation*, (Edinburgh, 2010)

Kinchin, Perilla and Kinchin, Juliet, *Glasgow's Great Exhibitions*, (Bicester, *c.* 1990)

Kramer, Lotten von, *Among Scottish Mountains and Lakes* (Stockholm, 1870)

Laing, William, *An Account of Peterhead: Its Mineral Well, Air and Neighbourhood*, (London, 1793)

Laing, William, *An Account of the New Cold and Warm Sea Baths at Peterhead*, (Aberdeen, 1804)

Lambert, Robert A., *Contested Mountains*, (Cambridge, 2001)

Lee, C. H., 'The Scottish Economy', in Macdonald, Catriona M. and Macfarlane, E. W. (eds), *Scotland and the Great War*, (East Linton, 1999)

Levitt, Ian, *Poverty and Welfare in Scotland*, (Edinburgh, 1988)

Littlewood, Ian, *Sultry Climates: Travel and Sex since the Grand Tour*, (London, 2001)

Lockhart, D. G., *Memoirs of Sir Walter Scott,* (London, 1900)

Lockwood, Allison, *Passionate Pilgrims. The American Traveler in Britain, 1800–1914*, (London, 1981)

Lumsden, James and Son, *Steam Boat Companion; and Stranger's Guide to the Western Islands and Highlands of Scotland*, (Glasgow, 1828)

MacDonald, James, *Character Sketches of Old Callander*, (Callander, 1910, third edition 2006)

McGregor, Dr John, 'Social History from Railway Sources', Open University Conference, November 2009

Mackaman, Douglas P., *Leisure Settings: Bourgeois Culture, Medicine and the Spa in Modern France*, (Chicago, 1998)

Macpherson, John, *The Baths and Wells of Europe: Their Action and Uses with Notices of Climatic Resorts and Diet Cures*, (London, 1873)

McRorie, Ian, *Dunoon Pier: A Celebration*, (Argyll, 1997)

Madden, Thomas More, *The Principal Health Resorts of Europe and Africa for the Treatment of Chronic Diseases*, (London, 1876)

Malcolm, George and Maxwell, Aymer, *Grouse and Grouse Moors*, (London, 1910)

Manson, D., *On the Sulphur Springs of Strathpeffer in the Highlands of Ross-shire*, (London, 1877)

Marshall, Peter, *Peebles Railways*, (Oxford, 2005)

Middleton, Victor C., *British Tourism: The Remarkable Story of Growth*, (Oxford, 2005)

Milligan C. and Mulhern, Mark A. (eds), *From Land to Rail: The Life and Times of Andrew Ramage*, (Edinburgh, 2014)

Mitchell, John, 'Protest at the Pier', *Scottish Local History*, Vol. 62 (2004), pp. 36–7

Moore, Peter, *The Weather Experiment*, (London, 2015)

Morton, H. V., *In Search of Scotland*, (London, 1929)

Mr Punch in The Highlands, (London, 1910)

Muirhead, Andrew, *Reformation, Dissent and Diversity: The Story of Scotland's Churches 1560–1960*, (London, 2015)

Mullay, Alexander J., *Scottish Region: A History 1948–1973*, (Chalford, 2006)

Mullen, Richard and Munson, James, *The Smell of the Continent: The British Discover Europe*, (London, 2009)

Murray, Sarah, *A Companion and Useful Guide to the Beauties of Scotland*, (Hawick, 1982)

Nelson, Michael, *Queen Victoria and the Discovery of the Riviera*, (London, 2001)

Norval, A. J., *The Tourist Industry, A National and International Survey*, (London, 1936) .

Oddy, Nicholas, 'Harry R. G. Inglis and the Contour Road Books', *Cycle History*, 9 (1998)

Oldham Field Club, *A Botanical Excursion to the Grampian Mountains*, (Manchester, 1876)

Orr, Willie, *Deer Forests, Landlords and Crofters*, (Edinburgh, 1982)

Page, S. J. and Connell, Joanne, *Tourism: A Modern Synthesis*, (third edition, Andover, 2009)

Page, Stephen and Durie Alastair, 'Tourism in Wartime Britain 1914–1918: a case study in adaptation and innovation by Thomas Cook & Sons', in Ateljevic, Jovo and Page, Stephen J. (eds), *Tourism and Entrepreneurship*, (Oxford, 2009)

Paterson, Alan J. S., *The Golden Years of the Clyde Steamers*, (Newton Abbot, 1969)

Paterson, Alan J. S., *The Victorian Summer of the Clyde Steamers*, (Newton Abbot, 1972)

Peden, George, 'A New Scotland? The Economy', in Devine, T. M. and Wormald, Jenny (eds), *The Oxford Handbook of Modern Scottish History*, (Oxford, 2012)

Perren, Richard, 'Survival and Decline: the economy of Aberdeen 1918–1970', in Fraser, W. Hamish and Lee, Clive H. (eds), *Aberdeen: 1800–2000 A New History*, (East Linton, 2000)

Pittock, Murray, *The Invention of Scotland: The Stuart Myth and the Scottish Identity*, (London, 1991)

Plowden, William, *The Motor Car and Politics, 1896–1970*, (London, 1971)

Postma, Albert, Yeoman, Ian and Oskam, Jeroen, *The Future of European Tourism*, (Leeuwarden, 2013)

Prebble, John, *The King's Jaunt: George IV in Scotland, August 1822*, (London, 1988)

Ranger's Impartial List of Ladies of Pleasure in Edinburgh, (Edinburgh, 1978 [1775])

Robbins, Nick S. and Meek, Donald, *The Kingdom of MacBrayne*, (Edinburgh, 2006)

Robinson, Arthur B., *Seeking the Scots: An English Woman's Journey in 1807*, (York, 2006)

Robson, Michael, *Tibbie Shiel*, (Selkirk, 1986)

Rolfe, W. J., *A Satchel Guide to Europe* (first edition, Boston, 1872)

Ross, David, *The Roar of the Crowd: Following Scottish Football down the Years*, (Argyll, 2005)

Rountree, George, *A Govan Childhood*, (East Linton, 1993)

Sangster, Alan (ed.), *The Story and Tales of the Buchan Line*, (Oxford, 1983)

Sargent, Harry, R., *Thoughts upon Sport*, (London, 1895)

Scarfe, Norman, *To the Highlands in 1786: The Inquisitive Journey of a Young French Aristocrat*, (Suffolk, 2001)

Scott, Ronnie, *Death by Design: The True Story of the Glasgow Necropolis*, (Edinburgh, 2005)

Seaton, A. V. *et al.* (eds), *Tourism. The State of the Art*, (Chichester, 1994)

Segreto, Luciano, *Europe at the Seaside: The Economic History of Mass Tourism in the Mediterranean*, (New York, 2009)

Senex, *Glasgow Past and Present*, (Glasgow, 1851)

Seward, Jill, 'How and Where to Go: the role of travel journalism in Britain and the evolution of foreign tourism, 1840–1914', in Walton, J. K. (ed.), *Histories of Tourism*, (Clevedon, 2005)

Shearer's Guide to the Trossachs, (Stirling, 1915)

Simmons, Jack, *The Victorian Railway*, (New York, 1991)

Simpson, Eric, 'East Fife's Open-Air Swimming Pools – safe places for dooking', *Scottish Local History*, Vol. 67 (Summer 2006)

Simpson, Eric, *Wish You Were Still Here: The Scottish Seaside Holiday*, (Stroud, 2013)

Sinclair, Catherine, *Shetland and the Shetlanders. Or The Northern Circuit*, (Edinburgh, 1840)

Slaven, A., *The Development of the West of Scotland*, (London, 1975)

Smith, Janet, *Liquid Assets: The Lidos and Open Air Swimming Pools of Britain*, (London, 2009)

Smith, Walter A., *Hill Paths in Scotland*, (Edinburgh, 1926)

Souvenir of the Opening of the Edinburgh Balmoral Hotel, (Edinburgh, 1991)

Stowe, H. B., *Sunny Memories of Foreign Lands*, (Boston, 1854)

Taylor, J., *A Medical Treatise on the Virtues of St Bernard's Well Illustrated with Selected Cases*, (Edinburgh, 1790)

Thatcher, Barbara, 'The Episcopal Church in Helensburgh in the Mid-Nineteenth Century', in Ward, J. T. and Butt, John (eds), *Scottish Themes*, (Edinburgh, 1976)

Thomas, John and Turnock, David, *Regional History of the Railways of Great Britain. 15. North of Scotland*, (Newton Abbott, 1989)

Thompson, Thomas, 'On the Mineral Waters of Scotland', *Glasgow Medical Journal*, Vol. 1 (1828), pp. 130–1

Thomson, Andrew, *The Sabbath*, (London, 1863)

Tindly, Annie, *The Sutherland Estate 1850–1920*, (Edinburgh, 2010)

Trollope, A., *The Duke's Children*, (London, 1880)

Voynish, E. L., *The Letters of Frederick Chopin*, (London, 1931)

Walker, Carol Kyros, *Walking North with Keats*, (New Haven, CT, 1992)

Walker, David, 'Inns, Hotels and Related Building Types', in Steell, Geoffrey, Shaw, John and Storrier, Susan (eds), *Scotland's Buildings. Volume 3 of Scottish Life and Society. A Compendium of Scottish Ethnology*, (East Linton, 2003)

Walton, John K., *The English Seaside Resort: A Social History*, (Leicester, 1983)

Walton, John K., *Blackpool*, (Edinburgh, 1998)

White, Alexander, *A Summer in Skye*, (Edinburgh, 1912)

Williams, Gareth, *A Monstrous Commotion: The Mysteries of Loch Ness*, (London, 2015)

Williams, William H. A., *Creating Irish Tourism: The First Century*, (London, 2010)

Wilson, Ben, *Decency and Disorder: The Age of Cant 1789–1837*, (London, 2007)

Withey, Lynne, *Grand Tours and Cook's Tours*, (New York, 1997)

Wordsworth, Dorothy, *Recollections of a Tour made in Scotland, 1803*, (Introduction by Carol Kyros Walker), (New Haven, CT, 1997)

Index

 Taylor & Francis eBooks

Helping you to choose the right eBooks for your Library

Add Routledge titles to your library's digital collection today. Taylor and Francis ebooks contains over 50,000 titles in the Humanities, Social Sciences, Behavioural Sciences, Built Environment and Law.

Choose from a range of subject packages or create your own!

Benefits for you

- » Free MARC records
- » COUNTER-compliant usage statistics
- » Flexible purchase and pricing options
- » All titles DRM-free.

 REQUESTYOUR FREE INSTITUTIONAL TRIAL TODAY

Free Trials Available
We offer free trials to qualifying academic, corporate and government customers.

Benefits for your user

- » Off-site, anytime access via Athens or referring URL
- » Print or copy pages or chapters
- » Full content search
- » Bookmark, highlight and annotate text
- » Access to thousands of pages of quality research at the click of a button.

eCollections – Choose from over 30 subject eCollections, including:

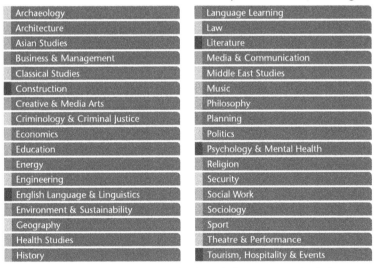

Archaeology	Language Learning
Architecture	Law
Asian Studies	Literature
Business & Management	Media & Communication
Classical Studies	Middle East Studies
Construction	Music
Creative & Media Arts	Philosophy
Criminology & Criminal Justice	Planning
Economics	Politics
Education	Psychology & Mental Health
Energy	Religion
Engineering	Security
English Language & Linguistics	Social Work
Environment & Sustainability	Sociology
Geography	Sport
Health Studies	Theatre & Performance
History	Tourism, Hospitality & Events

For more information, pricing enquiries or to order a free trial, please contact your local sales team:
www.tandfebooks.com/page/sales

 Routledge
Taylor & Francis Group

The home of
Routledge books

www.tandfebooks.com

For Product Safety Concerns and Information please contact our EU
representative GPSR@taylorandfrancis.com
Taylor & Francis Verlag GmbH, Kaufingerstraße 24, 80331 München, Germany

www.ingramcontent.com/pod-product-compliance
Ingram Content Group UK Ltd.
Pitfield, Milton Keynes, MK11 3LW, UK
UKHW020946180425
457613UK00019B/549